The Stock

MW01227471

Everything You Need To Know To Win In The Stock Market

Disclaimer

No content published in this book constitutes a recommendation that any particular security, portfolio of securities, transaction or investment strategy is suitable for any specific person. You further understand that neither the author nor their affiliates are advising you personally concerning the nature, potential, value or suitability of any particular security, portfolio of securities, transaction, investment strategy or other matter. To the extent that any of the content published in this book may be deemed to be investment advice or recommendations in connection with a particular security, such information is impersonal and not tailored to the investment needs of any specific person. You understand that an investment in any security is subject to a number of risks, and that discussions of any security published in this book will not contain a list or description of relevant risk factors.

This book is not intended to provide tax, legal, insurance or investment advice, and nothing in the book should be construed as an offer to sell, a solicitation of an offer to buy, or a recommendation for any security by *The Sick Economist* or any third party. You alone are solely responsible for determining whether any investment, security or strategy, or any other product or service, is appropriate or suitable for you based on your investment objectives and personal and financial situation. You should consult an attorney or tax professional regarding your specific legal or tax situation.

Contents

Foreword

When people ask me if I'm rich, my first question is, "rich in what?" I'm a firm believer that there are different kinds of rich. You could be from a warm and loving family; then you are rich in family. You could have a great college education and read three books a week; then you're rich in knowledge. Or you could have enough money invested in cash flowing assets that you don't need to work every day. Then you are rich in money.

Often, one kind of wealth leads to other kinds of wealth. People from supportive families often have the confidence and emotional support that they need to take business risks, resulting in financial wealth. Most people who own substantial businesses learned a lot along the way; so they're wealthy in knowledge and money.

I have assembled some of my best-selling work into this anthology so that I can help you become rich in knowledge. I believe with all of my heart that everything you need to be wildly successful in the stock market is contained in this anthology. There is nothing I can do about your family life, but there is a lot I can do about your knowledge of equity ownership and how American business really works. If you study the following pages carefully, and commit the lessons to heart, you are very likely to wind up rich in both knowledge and financial wealth. I know I did.

I spent more than twenty years getting my butt kicked in business so that you don't have to. Not all knowledge comes from the classroom. A lot comes from painful trial and error, and a lot comes from that infamous "school of hard knocks." I took the blows over the years (as we all do), but I learned a lot and I wrote it all down. I promise that I am not any smarter than you (in fact, I'm pretty bad at math... ask anyone who knows me). I just went through the grinder enough times that I learned my lessons, and those lessons paid off for me. They can pay off for you too.

Lastly, I hope that you gain a feeling of fulfilment from the knowledge in these pages. As important as money is, none of it really matters if you aren't having any fun. I have taken immense pleasure not just in watching my stock market wealth grow, but also in growing to better understand a lot of the forces that shape our society and our daily lives. If "money makes the world go 'round," then you will be in for a better ride when you understand money.

My sincere hope is that you get as much enjoyment from reading these books as I got from writing them. This is truly my life's work. If my life's work can make your life a little better, then I have succeeded.

No MBA? No Problem.

An Essay

ere are two shocking numbers for you: $200,000 and 1.07%. Of course, these two numbers alone don't mean anything, but when viewed in context, they are devastating. According to TopMBA.com, $200,000 is now the average "soup to nuts" cost for a two-year MBA from a nationally known program. The high price must be well worth it; everybody knows that education pays, right?

Wrong. In a bombshell study recently published in *The Journal of Labor Economics (2021, Volume 39, number 2, University of Chicago),* Professors Joseph G Atloni of Yale and Ling Zhong of Cheung Kong Graduate School of Business find that the average MBA only confers a 1.07% annual pay premium. 1.07%!

That means that if you made $100,000 before your MBA program, you only made $101,070 afterwards, on average. This 1.07% did compound after time, but this would mean that the average MBA graduate only made about $110,000 ten years after her MBA (if she had made $100,000 before her MBA). In other words, it would take decades to pay back the cost of the MBA, if ever. Many graduates would remain underwater for the rest of their lives.

Just for context, here is a chart that illustrates the ROI of an average MBA versus other common investments:

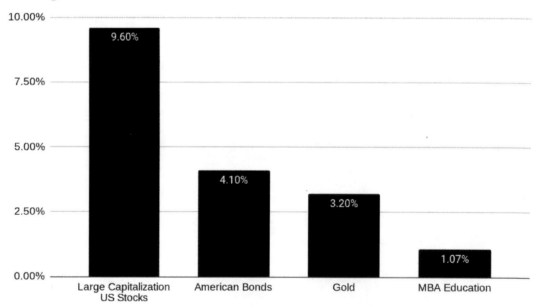

(Source: Visualcapitalist.com)

There is some evidence that graduates from elite MBA programs fare better. However, for your average MBA graduate, Drs. Altoniji and Zhong have exposed an uncomfortable truth… the MBA is a lousy investment.

Some might say that comparing the investment in an MBA to stocks, bonds, or other assets is unfair. Afterall, most MBA students don't have $200,000 to invest. So, it's not as if they have a $200,000 nest egg, and are choosing to invest in an MBA as opposed to investing in stocks. Rather, they are *borrowing* the $200,000 and investing in themselves to increase their earning potential over the long term. Since the MBA student started with nothing, some would say that they are turning nothing into something by taking the standard "MBA student loan" route.

Unfortunately, the analysis published in *The Journal of Labor Economics* takes all of this into account. Factoring in the cost of invested money for the average student loan borrower, the outcome is that abysmal 1.07% annual return. In that scenario, the average MBA graduate would be facing monthly student loan payments of about $1,200 (assuming a 20 year repayment schedule at 4% interest). What if that student had never gotten the MBA, but somehow scrimped and saved to be able to invest $1,200 a month in the stock market, instead? If our young investor had only average skill, discipline, and luck, here is what that would look like:

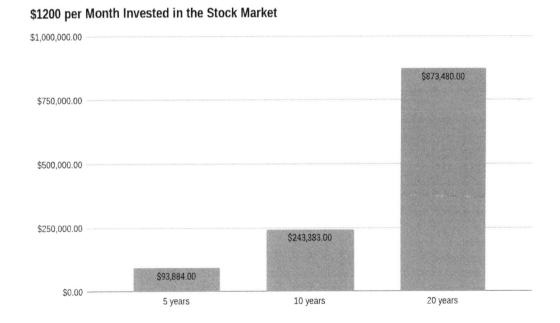

(Assumes 9.6% annual return, the stock market average over the last hundred years.)

So, if our young investor chose to invest $1,200 a month rather than to borrow for an expensive MBA program, she would be sitting on roughly $870,000 of assets as opposed to earning an annual salary premium of just 1.07%. Finding $1,200 a month to invest—come hell or high water—is no easy feat, but neither is gaining admission to a competitive academic program, borrowing a huge amount of money, and praying that your subsequent job pans out.

These latest academic findings probably come as a bitter pill to the 200,000 Americans who earn an MBA degree every year (as per poetsandquants.com).

Afterall, isn't knowledge always supposed to pay? Didn't our revered founding father, Benjamin Franklin, once say, "Investment in knowledge pays the best interest"? Aren't we supposedly living in the "information age" where people get paid for brains over brawn? How could an investment in brains produce such a poor return on investment?

There are two main reasons why MBAs often don't pay off.

"There is Always Room at the Top." Nope, not really!

The first reason why most MBA graduates wind up with disappointing earnings is because corporate America, by and large, just doesn't pay that well. Most MBAs wind up working for others, typically in large, publicly-traded corporations, and those careers tend to plateau at a certain level. Afterall, Microsoft currently employs 181,000 people, but just one is CEO.

Of course, not just the CEO makes good money. According to comparably.com, the average executive at Microsoft makes $227,000. Not a bad pay day at all. But if you ask anyone with experience in corporate America, they will tell you that 99% of corporate employees rise in their 20s and 30s, then hit a certain rung on the corporate ladder and stay there the rest of their lives. Afterall, corporate America is built in a pyramid structure; only the people at the very tippy top of the pyramid make the huge paydays that are the stuff of legend. When you graduate with an MBA and embark on a career in corporate America, there is a 99% chance that your earnings will be limited.

Now think of the example above with the $1,200 per month invested. You may have noticed that the total capital grows dramatically between 5 years and 20 years. What happens after 20 years of stock market investing? Then, due to the math of compounding, your assets grow exponentially, with no work on your part. Not only are stock market investments uncapped, they are actually *very likely to keep growing indefinitely.* No matter how educated you

6

are as a corporate executive, the odds are greatly against outsized income growth over time. When you are an investor, the odds favor almost unlimited, exponential growth of your capital as you age.

There is nothing at all wrong with having a job, and working as hard as possible to advance your income and prospects in that job. But if you succeed in building wealth this way, it will likely be because *you are also an investor.* You may use the knowledge you acquired during your MBA to grow both your salaried career and your investment portfolio.

So once again, we are forced to wonder if knowledge is a good thing, and MBA knowledge can be used both to advance in a career and to invest in stocks at the same time, why shouldn't I invest in that MBA? If knowledge is so valuable, why did Ivy League researchers find little numerical indication of that value?

"You don't make money when you sell, you make money when you buy."

The saying above encapsulates the reason why most MBA graduates only earn 1% annually on the money they invest into their education. It's not that the education is faulty, it's that the education is overpriced!

If we consider the MBA degree to be an investment, then we should take into consideration the cardinal rule of investing: your long-term return on investment is inexorably linked to your original purchase price of the investment. If you buy something of high value, at a low price, then you have a big winner. If you buy something of high value at a high price, then you have lackluster (or worse) returns.

Let's go back to the Microsoft example. If you bought shares of Microsoft in 1999 at $37 per share, at the very height of the infamous dot-com stock boom, then you earned about a 10.19% annual return over the next two decades. Not bad... just about in line with the market average. However, if you bought those same shares in 2002 for $15.55, after the tech bubble had burst, then you averaged an eye-popping 16.91% annual return over the subsequent decades. Same company, same management, different price. The different (lower) purchase price made all the difference in the return on investment.

Same thing for education! Dare I be so bold as to correct the great Benjamin Franklin? Well, I won't correct him, but I will add an important corollary. "Investment in knowledge pays the best interest (if you get a good deal on the knowledge)."

Universities purport to sell knowledge in the form of an MBA. Is it a good deal? Take a look at these two charts, and decide for yourself.

At What Price, Knowledge? (Part 1)

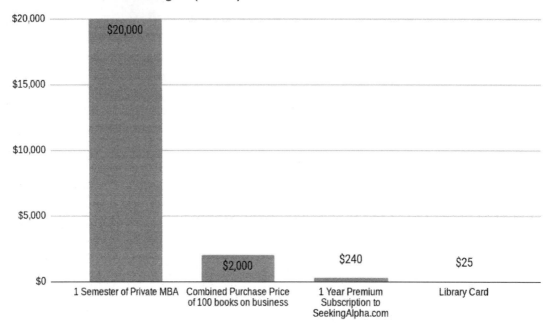

At What Price, Knowledge? (Part 2)

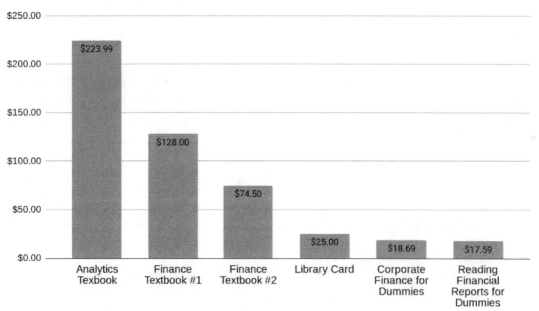

(Comparing the cost of one semester of MBA coursework to other educational options: the total purchase price of 100 different books on business, one year premium level subscription to the investment analysis website Seeking Alpha, and Library Card. The first three books are textbooks required by Ivy League MBA programs, the last three books are options for self education.)

They say a picture is worth a thousand words, but let's just digest the two charts above for a moment. The first chart compares the cost of *just one semester* at an MBA program offered by a private university to other educational options.

If I introduced you to a friend, and somewhere I casually mentioned that my friend had read one hundred different books on business, would you consider that person learned? To put that in perspective, he would have to have read one book per week, every week, for two straight years. Most would consider that person to be fairly well versed in the literature of business. If that avid reader had purchased every book for his future reference, that *still* would have cost him only $2,000, or 10% the price of a semester at Boston College.

Even cheaper than that would be an annual premium subscription to Seeking Alpha. Seeking Alpha is the premier gathering place for stock analysts and investors from around the globe. Every single day an avid learner can find hundreds of different posts there, always focused on some aspect of investing and business. Just by purchasing an annual membership to this website, the avid learner could actually run circles around the business book guy at a fraction of the price. If you signed up for an MBA at University of Miami, you would have a two-year learning period. For a tiny percentage of University of Miami tuition, you could read thousands of different authors on finance, from now until whenever the internet ceases to exist.

If you were too cheap, or too poor, for that annual subscription, you could always roll old school and hit the library. It's a vast repository of free information in the form of books, magazines, newspapers, and now even an ample digital offering. Amazingly, even with the competition from so many digital 21st century information sources, your local library is still a thing. And it's free. Accounting and financial terms are always the same, whether taught in the hallowed halls of Harvard, or pulled from a dusty book in Sheboygan, Wisconsin. $200,000 to study accounting and stocks, or $20. The choice is yours.

The second chart compares book prices between texts blessed by Ivy League brahmins and the more prosaic "how to" books you might find at Barnes & Noble. Inc. Magazine recently published a story entitled, "The Ten Most Assigned Books at Ivy League Business Schools" (By Jessica Stillman, January, 18th, 2021). One of the books on the list is *Business Intelligence and Analytics, Systems for Decision Support* by Ramesh Sharda, Dursun Delen, and

Efraim Turban. Should you decide to purchase this tome on Amazon, it will set you back a shocking $223.99. *Corporate Finance for Dummies*, on the other hand, costs $18.99. If you pay $223.99 for a fancy version of the same material you could have bought for $18.99, who is the dummy?

Other Ivy League books are somewhat more reasonable, although still charging an awfully stiff price for basic business math. *Corporate Finance, 10th Edition,* by Stephen Ross, Randolph W. Westerfield, and Jeffery Jaffe can cost as much as $128 on Amazon, almost seven times as much as *Corporate Finance for Dummies.* Now, Ross, Westerfield, and Jaffe may be respected instructors with Ivy League credentials. But are they really *seven times* better than the dummies? Does math change that much depending on the pedigree of who's teaching it?

If you think of education as an investment, and you realize that the initial price of the investment is a huge factor, you will start to understand why most MBA graduates wind up getting screwed. The education they got was just fine. They just paid too much for it. Way too much.

"Knowledge is Self Determination" (Black Star, 90s rap superstars)

If you have picked up this book, it's very likely that you have a burning desire to learn about finance and the stock market. I passionately believe that everything you need to know to win big in the stock market is contained in these pages. Maybe you didn't sign up for a traditional MBA because you didn't have the time, you didn't have the money, or maybe you guessed (correctly) that it just isn't necessary. What is necessary is *self-education.* You won't be alone; this text will be your partner in financial empowerment. But you alone have decided to take this journey of knowledge. You have already cut through the hype and myths surrounding the stock market, and you're ready to acquire the knowledge that will allow you to invest your money wisely for decades to come. You won't be needing any Harvard instructor on this knowledge path. On the knowledge path of self-determination, the most important instructor is… yourself.

Money Mind

Psychological Strategies
To Dominate Stock Market Investing

Introduction: Why I Wrote This Book, and How This Book Can Help You

I had to write this book because the same thing happens every time. It happens. Every. Time. It could be because the Stock Market has had a big swing up or a big swing down; some kind of major political or even historical event may have occurred that seems as if it will affect stock prices. Or it could be that a friend of mine just experienced a major life event, like the birth of a child or the death of a parent. Or it could simply be because it's 3:00 PM on a Tuesday, someone felt anxious or bored on that day.

My phone rings. My friend speaks first. The conversation typically goes like this:

"Man, can you believe that market today! Down 3% ! What should I do? Should I be selling?"

I would almost always reply like this. "Do you have a well balanced portfolio of different stocks, say at least ten different stocks?"

"Yes."

"Do you need the money right away for some kind of emergency?"

"No."

"Ok, then, just do nothing. Study after study demonstrates that 'buy and hold' is the way to go. Relax, go play golf or something. The market goes up and down ... it's no big deal."

"Yes, yes, I know ... but I should be doing something, shouldn't I? Maybe I should just sell half my stocks."

"No, really, just go play golf."

"Maybe I'll just sell 10% and then, when the market goes down, I will buy more."

"You could, but really, just go play golf."

"If the market is going down for X or Y reason, maybe I should be shorting stocks?"

"No, probably not necessary. Trust me, the market does quite well over time ..."

"You're right. You're right. So I should be buying? Maybe I should borrow money and buy even more?"

"Please don't. Just buy a little here and there and spend the rest of the time on your boat."

"All together, I heard the real money is in options. Maybe I should be using stock options to protect my gains and stop losses. I heard that's what the pros do."

"You're not a pro, and, believe me, even the pros often get it wrong. Just go to the beach today, it's nice outside."

"Go to the beach? There is money to be made in this market! My friend's cousin told him that this hot tech stock, xyz inc. is set to triple. He said it's a lock. Shouldn't I be buying that?"

"Please. Go. To. The Beach. Leave your computer at home."

"God, this stock game is so complicated. No wonder the pros make all the money. What would you do?"

"I would do nothing. Stick with the stocks I have. Occasionally buy more if I can. Then go enjoy my life. Any chance you will follow this advice?"

"Yeah, sure, I know you must be right. Just buy and hold. Ok, good. Thanks for talking."

End of the conversation, but never the end of the ordeal. Almost always the same guy calls me up a month later, a year later, or even ten years later, and announces that he lost too much money in the market. It's too complicated, he tried everything, and from now on, he's just going to invest in other things. This is how high-income professionals and entrepreneurs, people who make well into the six figures or beyond, make so much but keep so little. This is how high-performance professionals, people who have excelled and dominated in executive roles, wind up just scraping by in old age. They made a lot but kept very little.

I used to think that only poor people made dumb moves in the stock market. Afterall, the data show, again and again, that the US Stock Market has been an unparalleled profit-generating machine, year after year, decade after decade, for centuries. How could an educated professional, someone with above-average education and above-average income, somehow miss financial layups with alarming regularity?

Even a cursory glance at stock market research demonstrates that the phone call above is not unusual; in fact, it's the norm. According to a study published by the research organization, Dalbar, as of 2017, the S&P 500, a broad basket of America's largest companies, returned 7.68% per year over the previous two decades. However, the average investor gained only 4.79%. To put that in real terms, an investor who invested $10,000 initially and then $500 a month every month for twenty years would have wound up with $308,954 after twenty years, if he bought the S&P 500 and never did anything. If the same investor, described in my phone conversation above, achieved the average returns described in the research literature, he would only have $219,540. So, what's the reward for the eternally vigilant and active investor? $100,000 less than if he had just played golf for twenty years. And, remember, these are just averages. That means that a lot of smart, educated, and generally successful people chronically lag the averages by more than 3% points. It could be anyone you know and respect. You might even recognize yourself in this group.

So, it's been mathematically proven, again and again, that buying and holding is the way to go for most investors. Very simple. So why does almost no one do this? As Warren Buffett, one of the world's most successful investors, is fond of saying, making big money in the stock market is "simple, but not easy."

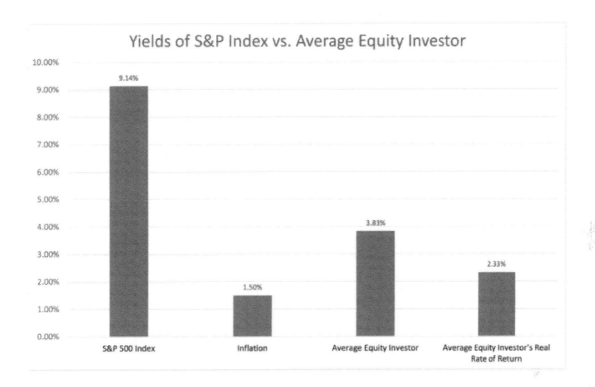

The barriers to stock market riches are not intellectual. The barriers are not educational or even financial. The barriers to sustained long-term investment success are emotional. I know people with dazzling intellect and superior executive skills who are constantly losing their shirts in the market. They don't have the emotional toolkit to succeed.

That's what this book is all about. The goal of this book is to help you gain the emotional tools to ride out any storm in the Stock Market.

Some people are just born more patient and calmer than others, just like some people are born with a better genetic propensity to be muscular and buff. Your thoughts and feelings come from your brain, and your brain is a muscle that can be trained, just like any other muscle in your body. If you doubt that this approach can work for you, try the following exercise:

Think of your favorite movie star. Go on the internet and type in "before he was famous."

You'd be amazed how many were just average schlubs before they "went Hollywood." Hollywood is famous for taking average-looking leading men (or women), putting them on a strict training routine, and turning them into lean, mean, Instagram photo op machines. The goal of this book is to do the same with your mind. The following chapters are filled with thought exercises that will make your self-control and patience just as buff as the Rock's legendary pecs and abs.

When you choose to invest in stocks, the successful investor learns to accept that there are many factors that she can't control. But she can control her mental attitude regarding her money, which will in turn control her actions and her outcomes.

The traditional saying is, "Mind over matter." I will teach you that when it comes to investing success, the saying should be "mind over money."

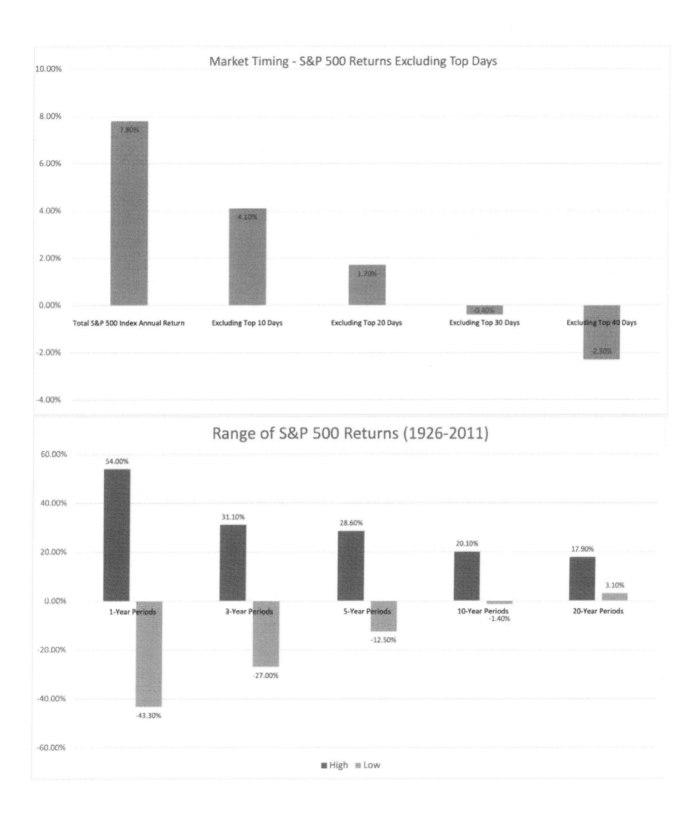

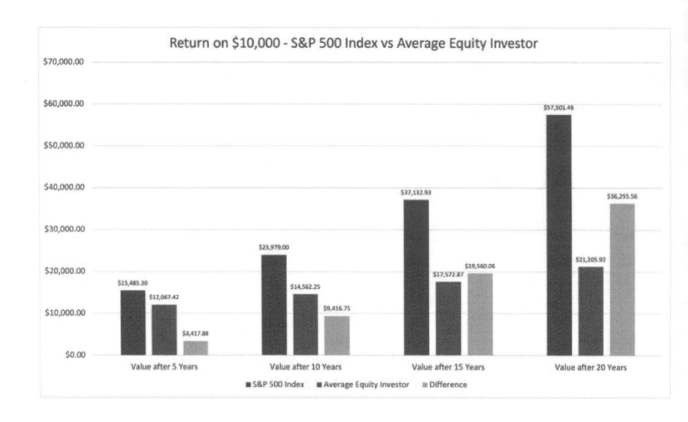

Return on $10,000 - S&P 500 Index vs Average Equity Investor

	Value after 5 Years	Value after 10 Years	Value after 15 Years	Value after 20 Years
S&P 500 Index	$15,485.30	$23,979.00	$37,132.93	$57,501.48
Average Equity Investor	$12,067.42	$14,562.25	$17,572.87	$21,205.92
Difference	$3,417.88	$9,416.75	$19,560.06	$36,295.56

Chapter 1: Better Off Dead

Top executives that run Fidelity Investments, one of the largest wealth management firms in the world, ordered a private internal review of investors' accounts to see which kinds of investors do the best over time. If you have ever opened a brokerage account, you know that they ask all kinds of seemingly asinine questions when you fill out the initial paperwork. The reason they do that is so that they can track and measure data and 'get to know their customers'.

Based on the data that Fidelity had religiously collected over decades, and their very intimate knowledge of clients' investment outcomes, the wisemen running Fidelity decided to figure out who did best. Was it retired executives? Young punks who trade a lot? Stay-at-home moms who manage the family's finances?

None of those, actually. It turned out that the best accounts with the juiciest long-term returns were owned by dead people. That's right; your dead grandma outperformed a retired CFO or a kid with a Harvard MBA.

Sounds both terrible and great at the same time, doesn't it? How could all of those seasoned pros, with decades of business experience, be left in the dust by someone currently six feet under? On the other hand, if a corpse can do well, couldn't you also do well?

However, if you take the time to really research the authenticity of this story, it's tough to find hard evidence that this study ever really happened. Fidelity certainly doesn't admit to it. But then again, why would they? They make money every time an investor trades, and they make money off active management and vigorous investment advice. "Buy and hold until you die" won't make money for Fidelity. So it's hard to prove that this story is 100% true. But it's child's play to prove that it's 100% true in terms of results and findings.

The Cold Hard Facts

It's debatable whether Fidelity ever conducted the above study, but many other credible institutions have. According to The Journal of Finance (Volume LV, #2), a team of Professors from the Haas School of Business at Berkeley, found that investors who traded the most, lost the most. This was a study involving 66,000 households. The households that were constantly buying and selling lagged the overall market indices by a whopping 6.5%. You will remember from the Dalbar study in the Introduction, a difference of just 3% in annual performance equated to huge differences over time. Losing out by 6.5% is catastrophic.

The investigators at the Haas school of Business weren't the only ones to find this kind of data. In a study published in The Financial Analysts Journal, professors Douglas J. Jordan and J. David Dilitz utilized two different methods to analyze the profitability of a sample of 'day traders'. Day traders are a type of financial speculator who trade constantly in and out of stock positions, often relying on technical metrics and borrowed money. The authors found that, even when analyzed two different ways, 80% of the traders lost money consistently. Of the 20% who made money, the authors found substantial evidence that they only made money because the overall market was going up during the study period. In other words, the 20% that made money by trading heavily just got lucky.

These studies are only the tip of the iceberg. Research after research has found that more trading does not equal more profit. In fact, it's almost always an inverse relationship. He who trades most, loses most.

But what about our hypothetical dead man? Well, let's imagine a financial Rumpelstiltskin. He's not so much dead, but simply 'asleep'. The well-known financial advisory firm, Raymond James, investigated this idea. Let's say you had invested $1 in a broad basket of large stocks in 1926. By 2010, that measly $1 would be worth $2,982. You could have been collecting stamps, exploring the Amazon, or just napping for 74 years. But you would have earned a 2900% return on your money while paying no attention at all. If you had chosen to invest the same $1 in a broad basket of smaller, lesser known stocks, your $1 would have multiplied to an astonishing $16,055! Not bad, considering you spent the last 74 years knitting blankets, flying kites, or studying interpretive dance.

The numbers are unequivocal and crystal clear; less is more when it comes to stock market investing.

Simple, But Not Easy

If study after study has employed simple arithmetic to demonstrate that 'buy and hold' is the best strategy, why do I keep getting phone calls like the one described in the Introduction? Why do rational, well-educated people turn into stark raving lunatics when it comes to stock market investing?

There are a few reasons for this; none of which have to do with pure math or rational self interest. Almost all have to do with feelings.

First of all, everything about American culture relates to action: taking action to make things happen. Think about the basic history lessons you were taught in grade school. Almost always, great men and women are introduced as what they did. George Washington led the

Continental Army and founded America. Abraham Lincoln led the Union to victory in the Civil War and freed the slaves. Harriet Tubman escaped slavery and formed the Underground Railroad. We are, fundamentally, a nation of doers.

The same ethos expands to our pop culture references related to business, especially Wall Street and Big Business. Anyone between the age of forty and seventy remembers the character of Gordon Gekko from the movie "Wall Street." Slicked-back hair, suspenders, and a hell raising devil may care attitude. That was a man who made things happen. A doer.

Another reason why people feel they must do something to their stock portfolio on a regular basis is due to American ideals about work. It may seem like our Puritan founders are long-gone, buried, and forgotten, but their ethos remains embedded deeply in the psyche of many Americans. Our Puritan founders were obsessed with work and even associated work with ethical goodness and godliness. Even in today's more cynical and frustrated times, the majority of Americans would associate the phrase 'hard work' with 'The American Dream; In America, 'good' people work hard.

Outsized financial returns with minimal or no work flies in the face of our most core American teachings. Therefore, many otherwise rational people feel compelled to make work when there is none. To most Americans, it just seems impossible to believe that they could invest $1, do absolutely nothing, and come back 74 years later to find that it had increased to $2,982. Someone must have done hard work to make that happen. Well, it turns out, someone did. But not the investor. The investor had everyone else working for him. We will go over this much more in depth in a later chapter.

Fear is also a big factor. Because most American investors also work in other capacities, they know the value of a dollar in an emotional sense. They work hard to achieve a decent (or better than decent) income and they put those hard-earned dollars to work in the stock market. When the market goes through one of its violent swoons, which it always will from time to time, it's just too much for those fearful investors. They worked so hard for that money! But it goes up, it goes down, it goes sideways … it's nauseating.

If you were in a speeding car that suddenly started swerving all over the place, would you grab the wheel and try to regain control? Or would you just chill out as the car careened from side to side, serenely relaxing as the car almost spins off the road at 70 MPH? The impulse of many fearful people is to grab control and do something. That may well be the right thing to do in a car, but with stocks, it's the dead wrong move.

So, we have a toxic stew of an action-oriented culture, a work-obsessed culture, and fear that isn't based on fact. Then, of course, we have the most fundamental of American ingredients; Capitalism.

Raymond James' study demonstrated that you could earn a 2900% return by just doing nothing. This was terrible news for Raymond James. Financial Advisory firms really only make money by rousing people to action. If you buy and hold, the only person who makes money is you. If you are constantly trading, everyone else makes more money. So which course of action do you think you will be guided towards?

It's true that there has been an evolution in the business of financial advice and that the industry has generally evolved to be less exploitative. However, most companies in the business of financial advice have something to sell, and doing nothing doesn't help your advisor buy a ski lodge in Montana.

For many years, the only way to buy and sell stocks was through a broker. This is an old-fashioned relationship. To buy shares in a company, one would call up the broker, who earned a commission for selling shares. Although generations of well-to-do individuals built up trusting working relationships with these brokers, the core incentives were still all wrong. Brokers made money by selling you stuff. More trading meant more commission for them. The results for the investor were barely relevant.

As we entered the '90s, the discount electronic brokerage was born. This was similar to the original concept of buying stocks through a broker, except instead of calling a broker, having an in-depth conversation, and paying a big commission on stock, one could pay a small commission and do the work themselves online. This may have reduced conflicts, but an online discount brokerage was still a brokerage; brokers still got commission based on the trades of their investors. More trading remained good for them and bad for the investor.

Lately, the online brokerage business has experienced new competitive pressure as young upstart brokerages have joined the fray. Trading commissions have actually fallen to $0. When it became 'free' to trade, trading went through the roof. Despite 10 different Harvard studies, no one seemed to care. With no obvious incentive not to trade, legions of wannabe Gordon Gekkos are currently furiously busy losing money or getting ready to lose money.

You may notice how I wrote 'free': Does anyone ever really do anything for free? Of course not. Online brokerages still make money when you trade, because there is a tiny markup on the securities you are buying from them. They're only making on average one penny per share (more or less), but with over tens or hundreds of millions of trades per day, it adds up. So what's the bottom line? Even with no obvious fees to the investor, the brokerages still want them to trade as much as possible. They make money that way.

I am not the only person who has noticed the obvious conflicts that arise from giving advice on a commission-based compensation plan. Over the last 20 years or so, we have seen the rise of fee-based advisors. These could be advisors that are paid by the hour (the way you would a lawyer) or, more commonly, paid with a fixed percentage of your assets (typically 0.5%–1.5%). This arrangement reduces the incentive for an investor to churn their account. The advisor gets paid the same whether the investor trades once a year or once a day and if the investor's account value shrinks, the advisor's fee is less.

This incentive system is better, but still not great for the investor. If they are not trading much, then what kind of advice are they paying for?

I recently had a wealthy friend that came to me and said, "I am paying 0.75% of my assets every year to just sit there. This fee adds up to over $10,000 a year. What am I paying for?"

In my friend's case, his very scrupulous advisor was actually dispensing wise counsel. However, many professional money managers fear exactly the conversation that I described, so they wind up feeling pressured to advise clients to take some kind of action. Studies from Berkeley or not, everybody has bills to pay, including your financial advisor.

The reasons for trading discussed here are just the tip of the iceberg. I have heard every bizarre reason why stocks just must be bought and sold, financing must be arranged, and options and complicated derivatives must be part of a portfolio. Not one of them holds up to math. But feelings are far more important than math any day of the week.

Be the Marshmallow Man

Every study utilizing a range of different techniques, completed by a wide range of different investigators, indicates that 'patience pays'. So be patient and make big money.

End of book, right?

No. Not even close. Anyone will tell you that patience pays. But they never seem to tell you how to be patient.

Super investor Warren Buffett is famous for aphorisms, such as, "If you can't own a stock for ten years, then you shouldn't own it for ten minutes." He has said dozens of these kinds of quotations. But notice that he never tells you how to be patient. Most people assume that a person either is patient and calm or isn't, just like a person is tall or isn't. But, once again, we have a wealth of studies and data that indicate just the opposite.

One of the most famous of these studies is the Stanford Marshmallow experiment. This study was first conducted in 1972 by the famous psychologist, Dr. Walter Mischel. The study was very simple. A kindergarten-aged child was offered a treat (typically a marshmallow) and given a choice: They were told that they could either eat the marshmallow on the spot and enjoy it or they could wait fifteen minutes and they would get two marshmallows. The researcher would leave the room, with the marshmallow sitting on a plate in front of the child, and allow the child to decide for themselves.

Most of the children gobbled up the marshmallow immediately. However, a significant minority of the children waited for the researcher to return. They wanted those two marshmallows and were willing to do what they needed to get them. The progress of those children was then followed through adulthood. Guess which group had much more successful lives? (As measured by SAT scores, educational attainment, body weight, and other common measurements). Of course, the more patient children did much better over time. Mini Warren Buffetts, each of them.

But the results were not the most relevant findings, but rather that each child employed different techniques to delay gratification.

When describing the behavior of the children, the researchers explained that "They made up quiet songs … hid their heads in their arms, pounded the floor with their feet, fiddled playfully and teasingly with the signal bell, verbalized the contingency, prayed to the ceiling, and so on. In one dramatically effective self-distraction technique, after obviously experiencing much agitation, a little girl rested her head, sat limply, relaxed herself, and proceeded to fall sound asleep."

It wasn't easy to resist the temptation of that sweet marshmallow, but some of the tykes pulled it off. They used tools and tactics to remain patient. Their successful patience didn't just come naturally.

So, if Warren Buffett can praise the virtues of patience when it comes to investing, why doesn't he explain how he does it? "The stock market is a device for transferring money from the impatient to the patient." Thanks, Uncle Warren; how about some tips on how to achieve your Zen-like level of financial composure?

There are two reasons why people like Buffett tell you to be patient but don't give any more instructions than that. First, Buffett's aphorisms are meant to be a great way of telling you something without really telling you anything. If the stock market is indeed a device for transferring money from the impatient to the patient, then Buffett has been on the good end of that deal for decades. You don't become the richest man in the world by giving away your true trade secrets.

But there is probably a more fundamental reason why champion long-term investors like Buffett would never bother to write this book. They have been in this game so long, as in the case of Buffett, almost seven decades, that their mental processes and techniques are now automatic. They have such a fundamental, core way of thinking about things that it rarely occurs to them that there are other ways to think. They have practiced patience for so long that they hardly even have to think about it anymore.

As we discussed before, your mind comes from your brain and your brain is part of your body. And bodies can be trained.

One person who trained both his body and mind to a state of near perfection was Michael Jordan. What Warren Buffett is to investing, Jordan is to basketball. Of course, Jordan was born with a freakish amount of raw talent. But so are most NBA players. What really set Michael Jordan apart was his maniacal training regime.

'To his teammates and coaches, he was notorious for his diligent work ethic. Jordan's longtime coach, Phil Jackson, once wrote that Michael "takes nothing about his game for granted." He spent so much time preparing for competition that when it was game-time, he didn't have to think about what to do next'. (November 30, 2016, Willa Rubin)

If you had asked Jordan, very specifically, how to win an NBA game, you might have been given some general tidbits of advice. But mostly, he had practiced his moves so many times that it all just happened. Think of the emotion and psychological shock of playing in front of tens of thousands of screaming fans and knowing that millions more are watching you at home! Jordan practiced and practiced until there was no emotion or shock that could throw him off his game. He internalized his game until he became one of the greatest athletes of all time.

I would like to turn you into the Michael Jordan of investing. But that would be a big promise. What I can promise you is that the rest of this book will focus on the mental tools and tactics that will help you keep your calm, even when the markets are not going the way you would like. Just like the Marshmallow Children or Michael Jordan, you will have a list of specific exercises that will keep you from losing your cool and making unnecessary and unwise moves in the market. Jordan would surely tell you that champions are not born; champions are made. I intend to teach you how to bring your 'A' game to the market for the rest of your life.

Chapter 2: Don't Buy Stocks, Buy Businesses

Perhaps the most fundamental, easy way for you to change your behavior around your stock market investments is simply to re-define what a stock is. Actually, I wouldn't say 'redefine' is an accurate description. What you are trying to do is simply define accurately something that becomes distorted in a lot of people's minds.

At its most basic level, one share in a publicly-traded business means that you own a percentage of that business. This would be no different at all than if you owned one third of a family dry cleaning business. The only real difference is that in a publicly traded company, the ownership units are more easily bought and sold to strangers without permission from the other partners. This is what we call liquidity: the ability to easily buy and sell. So, the only real difference between owning one third of a family dry cleaning business and 0.003% of General Electric (GE) is that the ownership of General Electric is easier to buy and sell (it is more liquid). This liquidity should be a really good thing as it just makes life easier for the company's owners. However, too many people turn what should be an asset into a liability. Just because you can buy and sell your GE stock with ease, that doesn't mean you should!

This mental separation between direct ownership of a small business and indirect ownership of a large business is where people get lost. In fact, there is a whole industry built around mentally divorcing those two things. People who treat stock shares as units of ownership in a business are called investors. People who treat stock shares as widgets to be bought, sold, borrowed, or optioned are traders.

As we discussed earlier, traders rarely make money in the long haul. There are all kinds of psychological reasons why people get sucked into trading instead of investing.

There are three kinds of traders, and you should be none of these. The first kind of trader operates in a realm where stock shares and share prices have been completely divorced from the underlying fundamentals for the individual company or even the broader economy. They have developed a deep voodoo science, where they divine, by signs and portents, the direction of share prices by the day, by the hour, or even by the minute! They have all kinds of mystical techniques that have to do with numerical patterns, the way a pattern looks on a chart, or even mumbo jumbo that is spit out by software. They have their own specialized vocabulary that has nothing to do with the fundamental long-term earnings of the companies that they own.

The second kind of trader doesn't necessarily want to be a trader, they just feel like they know better than anyone else. They follow every news break about a company, they scour every report, they follow all of the commentators on the internet. They 'know' when things are headed in the right or wrong direction and they act accordingly. They are a firm and confident hand behind the wheel and they know best. In these cases, these traders are typically over-confident, less well informed than they think, and poorly employing their precious time.

The third and last kind of trader is actually the opposite of the character we just discussed. Rather than over-confident, they are under-confident. They also follow every news break, scour every report, and all of the commentators on the internet. But, in their case, their constant buying and selling of stocks is based on fear. They are constantly worried about their shares losing value, they don't view any dips as temporary, and they feel they need constant vigilance to avoid disaster in an inherently risky market.

Trading Debunked, Again

I won't even bother to spend a lot of time disparaging the first kind of trader. This is the day trader; the 'technical analyst; the person who has three screens on their desk and believes in things like 'levels of support', 'candle patterns', and 'breakouts'. As discussed earlier, every study in the world demonstrates that few people make money this way consistently over time. At any rate, the world of the technical trader is a totally different realm and not actually the most common form of trading.

The second two types of trader, the overconfident trader and the underconfident trader, are much more common because they are driven by two things: uncontrolled emotion and poor fundamental understanding of how Corporate America works.

The overconfident trader essentially takes an inherently passive investment and tries to turn it into an active investment. This makes no sense if you understand how truly wealthy people operate.

It may seem cruel, unfair, or just plain mean, but the reality is that truly wealthy people don't work much. In fact, everyone else works for them. A great example of this is Michael Bloomberg, the erstwhile presidential candidate, three term mayor of New York City, and legendary entrepreneur.

Bloomberg is one of the richest men in the world. His mind-boggling fortune is larger than the total net worth of many sovereign nations. How on earth did he achieve this? Bloomberg invented a machine called the "Bloomberg Terminal", which is used by security investors and analysts all over the world. Almost every stock broker in almost every country has at least one of these very expensive machines.

To this very day, Bloomberg owns 85% of Bloomberg, LP. The firm is classified as 'private', meaning that the people who own the other 15% can't just willy nilly sell shares on the open market.

You would think that owning such a huge company with billions of dollars in revenue and products all over the world would be a lot of hard work. It is, for someone. Just not the owner, Michael Bloomberg. He hasn't run his own company for 20 years.

While owning 85% of his eponymous business, he also ran the largest city in America for 12 years. Do you think the Mayor of New York City has a lot of time for other side gigs? At some point, Bloomberg hired staff to run Bloomberg LP and the beast of a company proceeded to run itself. This left Bloomberg ample time to run New York City and attempt to run for president, or anything else he might choose to do. But what he doesn't spend time on is running the company that he owns.

What is the point of all this? The point is, the real money is never in working. The real money is in owning. Whether you own 85% of a private company or 0.085% of a public company, the long-term financial gains are merely in the ownership. Other people run the company for you so that you don't have to. The overconfident investor thinks he is adding value by constantly second-guessing the management team that he employs.

Is the overconfident investor likely to add value by reading up on the company's every gyration and then making his own moves?

The answer is 'no', for two reasons. First, empirically, we have already gone over the wealth of data that shows that the more investors trade, the more they lose in the long run. The overconfident investor is also likely to destroy value for several intrinsic, logical reasons.

All kinds of media coverage is constantly devoted to the large, often mind-boggling, pay packages that top executives can earn in Corporate America. Whether or not these pay packages are excessive is always a matter of debate. However, there is one thing that I can assure you. $20,0000,000 or more in annual compensation often hires you one hell of a good manager.

I say 'often' and not 'always' because anyone who has been investing long enough can identify one or two stories of abusive or incompetent CEOs who slithered their way into the boardroom of some major American Corporation. But, generally, you get what you pay for. C-Suite executives in Corporate America have typically beaten thousands of other candidates for that top job and they generally work much harder than you and know a lot more about that specific business. They also tend to be absolutely ruthless.

I once had a friend who graduated from the Ivy League and promptly landed a job at one of the top law firms in the world. He began to specialize in corporate law. In addition to the massive paydays and cutthroat culture of his own law firm, he also wound up with an unusual window into the C-Suites of some of America's largest publicly traded companies.

Sounds like a great gig, right? Not really. In fact, it was a nightmare. It was as close to modern slavery as is still legal. He worked 12 hours a day for six (and sometimes seven) days a week. He was expected to work holidays and nights and often, literally, slept in the office. Do you know why he was expected to work so hard at his law firm?

Because his corporate clients were working those very same hours. Week after week, month after month, year after year. His insight? The big pay package isn't just to motivate the CEO at the top of the corporate pyramid, it's to motivate the hundreds of underlings who dream of one day bringing home The Big Paycheck. Every one of these corporate slaves works grueling hours without compromise to make the share price rise. The very same shares that you own. In short, when you own shares in Corporate America, you have thousands of people doing the work so that you don't have to.

Leaving aside the inhuman hours that top corporate executives put in on your behalf, there is also the simple question of expertise. I would never advise anyone to own less than 10 stocks. I would always advise an investor to be somewhat knowledgeable about the companies that they own. But no one is an expert in all things. In a 10-stock portfolio, one might own shares in a computer company, a car company, and pharmaceutical firm. The overconfident investor somehow imagines that they are an expert in all of these different fields. Unlikely. Each company is paying big money to hire the best and brightest in each specialized field. They have toiled years in a specific field to gain specific knowledge that you just aren't going to acquire by staring at your computer screen for hours on end.

Lastly, those very well-paid experts that you employ as corporate shareholders are often ruthless when it comes to creating shareholder value. It is well documented that these corporate managers will do almost anything (and sometimes, anything) to make that share price go up. Of course, this is a double-edged sword. Sometimes, aggressive and assertive can become criminal. As a shareholder, you wouldn't want criminality. But there are plenty of other perfectly legal but terribly unpleasant things your executives do on your behalf so you don't have to. While you are out playing golf or going to the beach, they are busy firing underperforming employees or outsourcing jobs to Myanmar. Not fun, but profitable. You are already paying someone else to do the dirty work for you. Why make more work for yourself by constantly trading?

In short, the overconfident trader believes they are adding value when they're not. They are trying to take something that is inherently passive, and trying to turn it into a job. If you're bored, get a new hobby. It's likely to cost you a lot less than constantly trading stocks.

What about the under-confident investor? They suffer from a lot of the same delusions as the overconfident investor. The under-confident investors think that they know better than the highly-paid experts that they have already hired to run their company. In this case, they're not driven by arrogance or boredom, but by fear. Stocks go down as well as up, and if they're not watched carefully, the under-confident investor fears that they could lose everything.

Of course, it's unlikely that, if you have already hired expert race car drivers, your car is going to crash. But it's also simply not factual on a mathematical basis.

Simply put, large, profitable publicly-traded companies have a strong tendency to stay large and profitable for long periods of time. Once a company is listed on the S&P 500 (the largest 500 companies in the United States), it tends to stay on that list for at least 20 years (see innosight.com). If you had bought a simple index fund of those same large stocks, you would have averaged a 10.5% annual return over the last century (see investopedia.com). There would have been a few scary years along the way, but all in all, that broad index has only declined more than 10% four times since 1960. Remember our Rumpelstiltskin example and his $1 that compounded over time? That example factored in those occasional very bad years. The fearful investor has nothing to fear as long as they are diversified and long-term.

Gas Station or Exxon Mobil, whatever...

Perhaps you recognize yourself as one of the over-eager traders described above? That's ok, everybody is human. The mental tactics that I am about to discuss will immediately help you improve your performance and claw back your precious free time.

If you suspect that you may be the over-confident trader, just remember: You are already paying big bucks to highly experienced and skilled management to manage your investment for you. Most extra management would be a waste of your time.

Let's go back to the family business analogy. This time, let's say it's a gas station instead of dry cleaners. You own one third of a highly-profitable station, along with your other siblings. Your family has hired someone else to manage the station for you. Why? Because it's a grind and because the management may not even matter that much. If it's a good location with a nice looking store, you will sell a lot of gas. You just need someone reliable to show up every day, turn on the lights, and manage the day-to-day details. You don't want to do it yourself because you have better things to do with your life and reasonably competent management can be hired at a price that makes sense. This is how most successful businesses run.

Owning shares in a gas company like Exxon Mobil is no different. You own a smaller share in the company, but the actual dynamic is no different. If the world needs gas and there are only so many super major companies that can produce oil, you are going to sell a lot of oil and make a lot of money. If the world experiences an oil crash, then you are going to make less money. Skilled management can make a difference on the margins. But really, it's no different than the small gas station. Running that business day-to-day is one hell of a grind, so just pay someone else to do it and go to the beach.

I find it helpful to research the background of the management team I hire. Of course, the best time to do this is before you purchase shares. Since we are talking about public companies, the information about them is all over the web. You can find the biographies of the top few executives (the 'C-Suite') directly on a company's website, on LinkedIn, or through interviews in the Media. Chances are, you will be impressed by a laundry list of world-class executive positions that they have held and a strong track record of success. If you add up the industry experience of the top three or four executives in the company, they often have more than a century of experience in the kind of business that they are managing. Do they really need another manager? (You?) Are you really going to add value as the computer cowboy? Obsessing over details found through your personal computer doesn't rationally hold a candle to your management team's decade of hard-earned experience.

The next time you get an itchy computer finger while going through your online brokerage, just envision that gas station. Would you really want to spend your time managing something dirty and dull? Why would you waste your time when you've already hired someone to do that boring work? Turn off your computer and go to the pool. Enjoy. Your investment performance is someone else's responsibility. If they don't meet some pretty high standards over time, you can bet they will be fired. You have better things to spend your time on.

But perhaps you are not the overconfident investor? Perhaps you are constantly making portfolio changes due to fear? Yes, you have hired good people to run the corporations you own, but if they screw up, it's your hard-earned wealth that gets hurt.

If you find yourself trading through fear, I would urge you to review the data from earlier in this book. Think of our financial Rumpelstiltskin! His $1 turned into $2900 while he was asleep for 75 years. He would have turned $100,0000 into $2,900,000 while never selling a single stock. Are you really going to do better than that through your constant buying and selling? Just like the overconfident investor, you have better things to do with your life. Turn off the computer. Go to the beach. Forget you even own the stocks.

There is one other trick I will share with you that will greatly boost your confidence. One of the cruelest facts about business is that "the rich get richer, while the poor get poorer.

This is sad, but 100% true. Why is this? Simply put, it's because the Rich don't need the money, so they can ride out tough periods, and they don't get all that concerned by temporary portfolio dips. Why would they? If your assets greatly exceed your liabilities, it's not going to make a practical difference if your portfolio has a bad year, or even a couple of bad years. This feeling of security helps rich investors stay calm, cool, and collected. Not only do they not sell in down markets, they may actually buy.

What if I told you that you don't even have to be rich to use the same tactics? In the next chapter, I will teach you how to banish fear-based trading through proper asset allocation. It's easier than you think.

Chapter 3: Building A Solid Base

Imagine that you are going to custom-build your dream home. You have spent hours on end with architects and contractors planning all of the parts of the house that will give you pleasure over the coming decades. Your living room has been arranged and rearranged until you know it's just right. Your kitchen will have all of the finest appliances and be ready to host many joyful family meals. Your master bedroom will be a sanctuary for you and your significant other, and you are dreaming of lounging in there for many satisfied years.

What you probably aren't spending a lot of time fantasizing about is your foundation. You know, the solid base that nobody sees, but keeps the house safe and intact. The unglamorous concrete blocks that help your home resist storms, earthquakes, and the simple passage of time.

We never snap on HD TV and see a couple touring their potential dream home and marveling at the solid foundation that the house is built on. We should. Without that solid foundation, all the marble, crystal, and teak wood could wash away in the blink of an eye.

When we are talking about your financial home, a strong cash supply is your base. Strong access to cash in a pinch is the foundation that you will eventually build your stock holdings on. Without ample access to emergency cash, you are just building a house of cards that can blow down the next time the wind blows.

Before you buy a single share of stock, you should have at least 6 months of reserved cash stashed away in case of emergency. Your cash and credit together should equal at least 1 year of living expenses, if not more. This way, the stock market can soar, crash, and soar again without you ever needing to sell 1 share. Staying power is the number one super power for stock investors. If you want staying power, you've got to build a strong financial foundation first.

The Facts of Life

Of course, it has been very well reported over the last decade that the Rich are getting richer and the poor are getting poorer. I don't dispute that finding; I am just going to help you be in the richer group instead of the poorer group.

Why do the rich get richer while the poor get poorer? There are a lot of reasons for this and thousands of books have been written on the topic. But the most relevant reason for this chapter is the following: rich people have better staying power and thus can turn crisis into opportunity. They rarely have to sell assets at depressed prices. In fact, when assets are depressed, the rich are typically buying. It's not fair. It's not nice. But it's the way our world works. If you play the game right, you can have staying power as well.

Obviously, I am a big fan of stock market investing. That's why I wrote this book. But I am not going to tell you that stocks only go up. In fact, I have survived at least three massive stock market crashes myself. Stocks sometimes go down. Temporarily.

So what's my key to survival? Whether smart or just lucky, I never needed to sell my stocks during a recession. When the market crashed, which it did, I didn't enjoy it, but I remained calm. Why? I didn't need the money. I knew I would need the money eventually, but not any time soon. That is what my emergency fund is for.

I am only human. I sometimes faced difficult decisions during moments of financial crisis, but I never needed to sell the gift that keeps on giving, which was my stock portfolio. I dipped into my emergency cash fund, I even took out some modest loans, but I left the stocks alone. I knew that if I kept them, they would eventually rebound. But if I sold, I would be cooking the goose that lays the golden egg.

Over the years, I went to some pretty extreme lengths to build up that cash reserve and avoid selling my stock shares. But it worked. I survived crash after crash because I made sure that I didn't need the money. It's cruel. It's not nice. It's downright sadistic. But it's the way the world works. Rich people make more money because they don't need money. When everyone else is selling, they are buying cheaply. They remain calm when the world is falling apart because they have enough cash reserves to ride out the crisis. You should strive to do the same if you want to successfully build wealth in the stock market over time.

How Much is Enough?

There is no one size fits all 'magic number' that represents an adequate reserve fund. But the number should equal about six months of your monthly expenses. So, let's say you spend about $5000 per month on rent, food, transport, etc. You should have about $30,000 sitting in a savings account before you buy one share of stock. If you spent about $3000 a month, you would need $18,000 in a savings account before you can really start investing.

Does that seem like a lot of money to you? If so, then do whatever you need to do to bring down your monthly expenses and up your saving rate. It is hard for most people; that is why most Americans will remain wage slaves their whole lives if they are even lucky enough to be employed their whole lives. Move in with your parents, share a house with another family, ride the bus instead of a car. Yes, all of these options suck. But living in constant fear because your bank account is anemic also sucks. More cash on hand and lower expenses means less fear. Less fear will eventually lead to more wealth. Much more wealth.

I actually don't think that 6 months of cash on hand is enough, especially if you are an entrepreneur or white-collar executive. Why? If you were to lose your job or your business (which happens, often through no fault of your own), it would take some time to replace that good job or good business; maybe a lot of time if you got laid off during a recession. You want to be able to take your time looking for new income. Again, that cash in the bank gives you power. Power to not sell your assets during a recession, power to not accept a bad job at low pay.

If you wanted greater security you could keep up to a year's worth of cash on hand. Unfortunately, with today's super low interest rates, our current economy punishes savers. Your cash savings are likely to earn very little or no interest, which actually means you'd lose money over time. So try this instead.

A Word About Credit Cards

Any financial advisor would tell you to stay away from credit cards. They charge absurd interest rates and screw you over with egregious fees that are often disguised in tricky ways. This rule of thumb is generally true. Credit card companies prey on the ignorant, uninformed, and the irresponsible.

But what if I told you that if you are in fact educated, informed, and responsible that you can prey on them?

There are a few fundamental facts about the credit card business that mean that you can dominate them if you are shrewd and responsible.

The first fact is that we don't have debtor's prisons in America. Chase Bank can call you seven times a week to bug you, they can even sue you, but they can never put you in jail for non-payment. They also can't send a crew of 300-pound thugs to your house to collect. If you are savvy about credit card debt, the truth is, you have them over a barrel. Not the other way around!

The second, more important fact, is that credit card companies vigorously compete with each other to make what they hope will be high interest rate loans to you. This competition means that you can play them off each other to get the best terms and conditions for you.

The third and last important fact is that credit card companies now compete with all kinds of non-bank lenders, which will further lower the interest rate you pay if you are responsible and savvy.

The entire credit system is built to abuse and manipulate uneducated chumps. If you have invested the money and time to read this book, then you clearly do not fit that description. You can develop a strategy to use credit as a resource, but only in times of need.

Remember why rich people get richer? Because they don't need money. Perversely, the same apples to credit cards. The time to build up your credit is when you don't need the money. If you are wise about building up your credit history when times are good, you can lean on that good history when times are bad.

For example, let's consider Steve Smith. Steve makes $8000 a month as a junior executive and has been doing well at his job throughout most of his 20s and early 30s. Steve comes from a modest financial background, but he believes in investing and has been proactive. So, Steve has saved up $36,000 in a savings account and his stock investments currently total $100,000. He has worked very hard to get to this point. Of his $8,000 income, he only spends about $6500 every month. During his mid-twenties, he endured living with his parents for a few years until he could build up some savings. He drives a lightly-used car.

Steve pays a lot of his monthly bills on his credit card, because he likes to get the points. He pays his bill off in full at the end of every month. After a few years of doing this, he starts to get offers in the mail. He ignores them for a long time, but eventually he gets a very attractive, low interest rate offer on a second credit card, so he signs up. Even though he only uses a fraction of his credit limit every month and he pays off the card in full every month, once a year or so, he calls up both card companies and asks for a raise on his credit limit. As time goes by, they ask less and less questions and they just raise his limit. Before he knows it, his two credit cards have a combined limit of $30,000.

Steven continues in his job and does well, year after year. However, eventually, the economy crashes, the stock market crashes, and sales at his company start declining rapidly. On his desk, Steve has had an offer for a third credit card that has been sitting around for months. They want to lend him $20,000 at 0% interest for 18 months. He doesn't think he needs the money, but, fearing a layoff, he takes the loan. The credit card company sends him $20,000 within days that he will not have to pay off for 18 months.

Three months later, Steve's worst fears are confirmed and he is laid off. It's nobody's fault. The economy took a dip, the company has suffered, and there isn't enough work to go around.

During the same time, Steve's stock investments have tanked. His $100,000 in stock is now worth only $70,000! He has no job, no income, and his stocks are suddenly plummeting. Should he panic? Should he sell everything quick, now, while he still can?

Nope. Steve is a cool customer. He has been preparing for this day for quite some time. He currently has $36,000 in cash savings, plus $20,000 in the 0% interest loan from the credit card company, plus $30,000 in the credit limit on his credit cards.

Steve really worked hard on that job; he gave it everything he had and it still all went wrong. That's a tough pill to swallow. So he takes a month off. He goes to the beach every day. He plays with his kids more. He paints some stuff in his house that his wife has wanted painted for a while. He knows that he spends about $6500 in a month. He calculates that he has at least a year's worth of reserves before he would even have to touch his stock. Steve is relaxing and regrouping, instead of panicking and cringing in fear, because he is ready.

The next month, he starts looking for a new job. It's not easy! The economy is bad; few are hiring. He gets a few interviews, but they go nowhere. Three months later, he gets an offer, but it's for substantially less than he used to make and he would need to commute 1 hour every day. He turns it down.

After 8 months of looking, he finally finds a new job. He has spent about $52,000. First, he spent the $20,000 no interest loan. Then he started charging on his credit card. At the end of 8 months of unemployment, Steve still has $36,000 in emergency cash and hasn't touched his $70,000 in stock. He does now have $52,000 in debt that needs to be paid off.

Steve would have a lot of options from here. If the new job goes well and he starts to feel more secure, he could pay off the high interest credit cards immediately, applying a portion of his $36,000 emergency cash to pay off that high interest debt. After that, he can make monthly payments on the no interest loan that he took. They only start charging interest after 18 months. So much of that debt can be paid off with no interest.

Two years after the incident, Steve has paid off most of his debt, he has started to rebuild his emergency fund, and, the stock market has rebounded as the recession has slowly ended. His stock is now actually worth more than it was worth three years ago. Now his stock is worth $130,000. Because he never sold the stock, Steve has barely lost any money through the whole ordeal of being laid off during a recession. In fact, in just a few years, he will have made money, despite not working for 8 months.

Cash is King

Of course, there are a million different scenarios where the math would look different for all of the different people reading this book. But if there is one point to be made from the above example, it's the following: Money is power. Including the power to say "no". When the market crashed and buyers would only offer bad prices for Steve's stock shares, Steve simply said, "No", because he had cash in the bank. When he went on those first few job interviews and the job offers were low, he simply said, "No." Again, because he had cash in the bank. This is why the rich get richer. If they don't get the offer they like, they just walk away. Guess what? They tend to get better offers.

You can too. This isn't a book about hoarding cash. It's a book about building wealth through the stock market. But having ample cash in the bank gives you the intestinal fortitude to say "No" to bad deals. As an owner in many lucrative corporations, you would never want to sell those shares unless you got a great offer. Even then you might not want to sell. Setting yourself up so that you don't need the money to begin with makes all the difference.

The next time a friend takes you on a tour of the dream house that they just bought and they waste time babbling on and on about the pantry, the master bath, or the pool deck, just quietly ask yourself, "What is the foundation made of? How many hurricanes has the house survived? How many earthquakes can this foundation withstand?" These are the questions that make a difference. These are the questions that will make you rich.

Chapter 4: The Serenity Of The Roller Coaster

Why on earth would anybody go on a roller coaster? Before they even get on the ride, they can plainly see that it will fly up, then down, then sideways at gut-wrenching speeds. These days, they flip upside down, inside out, and move fast enough to exert enormous pressures on the riders. Given the white-knuckle ride awaiting even the bravest person in the amusement park, why would anyone voluntarily get on this ride?

Millions of people every year choose to ride roller coasters for two main reasons. Firstly, even though the ride will feel like a hurricane, they know ahead of time that the ride ends well 99.99% of the time. Secondly, they do it for the sheer thrill of a tumultuous rocket ride. Knowing ahead of time how the ride ends, the thrill seeker can just lie back and enjoy the sensory shock of all the ups and downs.

The stock market is no different. I love the stock market and I love what the stock market has done for me, but I would be lying if I told you that it has been a smooth ride. In my 20 plus years in the market, there have been some real nausea-inducing twists and turns. But I held on. I didn't hold on because I am smarter or braver than anyone else. I simply knew what the end of the ride would look like. Profit. Big profit. I didn't need a crystal ball or a religious level of faith. As we have discussed in earlier chapters, stocks have reliably made money for hundreds of years. There has been a lot of drama, a lot of ups and downs, but ultimately, just like the roller coaster, the stock market has delivered investors at a fixed destination decade after decade. That destination is profit.

The most important mental, and even emotional, lesson to learn is an exercise in vocabulary comprehension. Simply put: Volatility is not risk.

For some reason, the media tends to use these two words interchangeably, but that is an abuse of the English language. Again, think of the roller coaster. Of course, roller coasters are volatile by definition. But they aren't risky. They feel risky. That is what generates the excitement. But, ultimately, roller coasters are mostly thought to be a safe form of entertainment, which is why whole families often ride together. Kids ride roller coasters, grandmas ride roller coasters. They certainly are volatile, but they aren't dangerous, because the outcome is a lot more predictable and controlled than it appears from the outside.

You know what is actually very dangerous? Driving 2 miles down the street to your local convenience store to buy a loaf of bread. In fact, according to the Insurance Institute of Highway Safety, there were 33,654 fatal motor crashes in the United States in 2019, 70% of which occurred less than 10 miles from home! Considering this data, simply driving to your local school to pick your kids up should be an experience in terror. Unlike the roller coaster, there is, in fact, a real chance that you and your loved ones could die. Which seems scarier? Driving at a reasonable speed in good weather to your local Target to do some shopping or strapping into one of those massive roller coasters that makes you nauseous with fear before the ride even starts?

The point of this thought experiment is to demonstrate human fear and that the reactions to that fear are often not rational. Fear may not be data-based. It's just based on feelings. Your feelings tell you that a rollercoaster is dangerous, but driving a mile to pick up some milk feels safe. The cold hard facts would tell you the exact opposite.

It's just the same with investing. While stock markets are certainly volatile, study after study shows that, over time, they deliver reliable profit to those who are calm and patient. The fact that share prices go up and down has nothing to do with the end destination.

You might recall, every once in a while, reading some article about a freakish tragedy that occurred on a rollercoaster. In these rare cases, what typically goes wrong is that the rider exits the vehicle when they shouldn't. Something is wrong with their restraints and they go flying out of the roller coaster. Personally, I have never read about a roller coaster crashing. I have read the occasional article about someone slipping out of their seat.

It's the same with the stock market! If you just stay put, through ups and downs, twists and turns, you will arrive safe and sound at your destination. If you allow yourself to exit the coaster during one of its epic drops or twists, you'll have problems. Don't sell during the next market crash; just hold on tight and think of the drop as an inevitable and safe part of the ride. What is not safe is trying to exit the ride at the wrong time.

Chapter 5: Fear The Tax Man

Speaking of feelings that induce nausea, here is a feeling that most people hate: the feeling of writing a check to the IRS. Not just paying taxes; actually sitting down and writing a check to the IRS.

What would be the difference? Well, unless you are a small business owner, you probably work somewhere for a paycheck. In that case, the process of paying the Devil his due is automated. Most workers, even highly paid executives, simply get a cheque twice a month, with the taxes already deducted. If they go out of their way to check their pay stub, they may not like what they see. Otherwise, the pain is automated away. That is not an accident. Both Uncle Sam and Corporate America do better when the Average Joe doesn't fully understand what is going on.

However, if you own a portfolio of growing stock, then you are no longer a worker, but an owner. As an owner, the ritual around payment of taxes is much different and, in my opinion, much more painful. There is no automating away your yearly tax payments when you are a stock investor. On a yearly basis, you must actually sit down, look over what you have made that year, and actively "Render Unto Caesar" whether by paper cheque or electronic payment. This is akin to a patient being fully awake during surgery with no anesthesia.

Different people react differently to the unpleasant sensation of watching a large percentage of your money disappear into thin air. Some hem and haw and try cutting every corner. Others stamp their feet, curse Uncle Sam and the Stars Above, and just write the cheque. A few go to criminal tax avoidance lengths altogether.

Even those high net worth individuals, who believe in a more socialized form of society, in which the wealthy must "pay their fair share", still barely tolerate the pound of flesh that is extracted on a yearly basis. Even for the most idealistic, that yearly tax bill is kind of like eating your broccoli: necessary, salutary, but not something to look forward to. But if you want to be an owner instead of just an employee, you just have to pay the taxes on your stocks and get it over with.

Or do you? What if I told you that some of the richest people rarely pay taxes on stocks? What if I told you that the secret to keeping your taxes low had nothing to do with shady Swiss Bank Accounts or armies of accountants? If I could tell you a simple way to keep your taxes very low, wouldn't that be a better feeling than being mugged by Uncle Sam every year?

What Warren Knows

Here it is. The big secret to keeping your taxes low and feeling good about it. Don't sell. Do. Not. Sell. Your. Stocks.

As of 2020, wealth is not taxed in America. Income is taxed. So the paper value of your stock holdings can grow and grow (and grow), but until you actually sell the shares and convert them into cold, hard, cash, you pay very little tax.

Warren Buffett, perhaps the greatest investor who has ever lived, is very keenly aware of this. In fact, Buffett is famous for declaring, "I have a lower taxation rate than my secretary." In some ways, this is a gross exaggeration, but Buffett is only being honest. Whether or not this arrangement is fair or good for society is beyond the scope of this book. But I can certainly teach you why the American tax system is good for you.

Do you need to be a Certified Public Accountant to understand why stocks can (and should) be managed in such a way as to minimize taxes? No. All you need to understand are a few basic principles.

For a variety of reasons, rank and file employees actually pay a higher tax rate than owners of assets in America. The details on this vary depending on which political party is in power at the time, but, generally, taxes on Capital Gains and Qualified Dividends are between 15% and 22%. Taxes on the income you make as an employee can range all the way up to 37% and have historically gone as high as 90%! Capital Gains are the kind of cash produced when you sell a stock for more than what you bought it for. Qualified Dividends are dividends that are paid by a publicly-traded company that you own.

It certainly feels better to pay 22% than 39%. But what if I told you that the optimal taxation rate for most stock investors is 0%?

Once again, you only pay taxes on actual cash that comes out of your companies. This is why Berkshire Hathaway, the ultra-profitable company that Warren Buffett founded, has never paid a dividend in its half century of existence. Dividends are nice, but dividends means taxes. Instead Uncle Warren takes the prodigious free cash flow that his company creates and reinvests it right back into the company. This is why, if you had been lucky enough to invest $1000 with Buffett way back in 1965, you would now be sitting on $27,000,000, all without paying a dime of tax.

Of course, you only would have realized this return if you'd held onto the shares that long. If you had sold during a stock dip or a stretch of underperformance, you would have suffered in two ways. First, you would have missed out on stock price appreciation, which never seems to end. Second, you would have paid taxes for that privilege. Warren Buffett has rarely sold. The same should be true for you.

Trading vs. Investing

What if you buy and sell a lot? What does that taxation picture look like? If you dare, imagine the proverbial "death by a thousand cuts". That is what our taxation system does to the capricious trader.

Right off the bat, the active trader pays at least 20% tax on any profits, as opposed to 15%. Uncle Sam taxes you more if you sell a stock after holding for less than a year. Ok, so it's only a 5% difference. Who cares? What difference does 5% make?

It turns out, it makes a lot of difference. In fact, the more you trade, the more you get hit with that 5%, and the more the damage is compounded. Remember the concept of compounding returns? That was how Buffett turned $1000 into $27,000,000 over 50 years. Now imagine that very same mathematical phenomenon working against you. Ouch.

In fact, Goldman Sachs has taken the time to quantify the impact of tax efficiency on overall returns. They calculate that $200,000, invested in a tax-efficient manner in the stock market, should become $1,002,000 over 25 years. The same $200,000 invested in an account with more buying and selling only grows to $600,000. So, in this example, that 5% taxation difference added up to more than $400,000 in lost earnings over time (gsam.com, "The Power of Tax Deferral).

Say goodbye to your dream retirement beach house. That went to the Feds instead.

Of course, Goldman Sachs knows a lot about money and investing, but they also know a lot about getting money from you. Investment bankers are always trying to sell something. So maybe we should look for a more objective viewpoint?

Dr Stuart Lucas and Alejandro Sanz, of the University of Chicago Booth School of Business, set out to measure exactly the costs of over-active stock management, with a special consideration towards taxes. The resulting study was published in the Journal of Wealth Management in the fall of 2016. After studying reams and reams of data from thousands of investors, the authors' conclusions were:

In the hunt for investment value added, taxable investors need to think differently. A low-cost, low-turnover, equity-oriented strategy with broad, consistent exposure to the market is the most likely to succeed over long periods. The power of this simple approach lies in the interaction of investment strategy, tax management, and long-term compounding. After taking into consideration taxes, the cost of being wrong, and loss-harvesting capabilities, active strategies must generate 160 to 380 basis points of value added per year just to break even with this approach. If you want to fight the active management battle, do so in the knowledge that the odds are stacked against you.

Basis points are fancy finance talk for percentages. So, in this case, frequent buying and selling would cost you between 1.6% and 3.8% of your total returns over a long period of time. This isn't a small leak in your ship. This is the iceberg that sank the Titanic.

Balance Your Feelings

Active traders typically lose out due to a toxic cocktail of factors; taxation playing a big role. This is where the smart investor trains herself to turn bad news into good news.

Most investor behavior is driven by visualizations, and the feelings attached to those visualizations. Remember the two reasons why people buy and sell too much: either over-confidence that they "know what they are doing" or under confidence, claiming that "they must sell to avoid losses".

If you suspect that you sell too often because you fall into the confident camp, ask yourself, "Is the high I get from selling this stock going to be better than the pain I will feel when I have to send 20% to the Government?" Visualize yourself writing that big check at the end of the year versus owing nothing because you didn't sell any stock. If you sell a certain stock that has wavered up and down a lot, you may or may not have more money on paper in 1 year. If you hold the stock, you will very likely have more money on paper in 5 years. If you sell, for sure, the Feds will be going through your pockets this year. Even 250 ago, Benjamin Franklin knew that "The only sure things in life are death and taxes."

If you suspect that you are in the under-confident camp, try this thought exercise. If you sell a certain stock in a panic, you may avoid a loss in the short-term, but you will be exacerbating your long-term loss for certain. Remember Goldman Sachs' missing $400,000? Those were mostly investors who felt they had to sell to avoid a short-term loss. They may have saved themselves a few bucks in the short-term, but Uncle Sam wound up with the dream beach house, not the nervous investor. Paying taxes sucks. So, sell less, pay less.

People really hate the feeling of missing out on stock market profit because they bought or sold at the wrong time. So they feel compelled to do something, even when all of the data proves that what they should do is nothing at all.

However, most people also have a natural aversion to paying taxes. It gives the same wave of disgust you feel when a cockroach scuttles around your kitchen. Selling more, triggers more taxes. Harness this natural tax aversion to talk yourself out of excessive stock trading. Your portfolio will thank you for your fortitude.

Chapter 6: The Never Ending Story

It's been almost 30 years, but I can still feel the electricity flowing through my body. The pins and needles. The sheer excitement! That was the joy of stumbling upon an undervalued treasure at a comic book store or a comic convention. There it was, Spiderman #351. the debut of a certain bad guy or a special limited-edition cover art that should have been priced at $30 but instead it was marked for just $20. Even though I was only 11 years old, I knew to play it cool. I would take the book out of the bin, lay it down, and casually just pull out some other random books. I would walk around the store, check out a book over here, over there, pretending that my found treasure was nothing special; nothing special at all. Then I would bundle it with a few other run-of-the-mill books and see if I could get a little discount off the marked price. Sometimes I couldn't, but sometimes I could! It wasn't unusual for me to pay only $15 for a book that was listed as worth $30 in valuations that used to be published monthly.

After closing the deal, like any 11-year-old customer, what would I do? Would I go home, start working the phone to my knot hole gang of fellow comic nerds, and try to immediately flip it for a cool $15 profit? Or would I hold it for a few months and then try to sell it at a comic book convention?

Hell no. First, I would take it home and carefully remove it from its protective cellophane wrapper. I'd make sure that no dogs or annoying little sisters were around who could potentially damage the prize. Then I would carefully read the comic book, pane by pane, page by page, astonished by each stroke of the pen and outlandish plot twist. If the plot was average, I would then carefully resleeve the book and place it in a special safe place in my closet to be sold "when the time was right." But if it was a really good plot, if Spiderman had saved the day using some new tactic or vanquished a particularly loathsome enemy, then the book went up on the wall of fame. I had a cork board in my room on which I would suspend my most cherished books so that I could bask in their glory at all times. I reveled in the fact that they were valuable and getting more valuable all the time (well, at least from a kid's point of view), but really, I was just in love with the stories.

What if I told you that today, 30 years later, I behave much the same way with my equity investments?

Have you ever heard the expression, "John Doe has an addictive personality"? This phrase usually has a negative connotation. For example, John finally quit cocaine abuse, but then wouldn't stop gambling at the casino. He has "an addictive personality."

It turns out that I too have an addictive personality. But I am addicted to accumulating things of value. When I was a kid, those things of value were comic books. Now that I am a grown man, those things of value are equities. And, it turns out, 'value' is not defined just as a mathematical equation (although, as we have demonstrated earlier in this book, the math certainly pencils out). 'Value' also has an emotional, sub-rational appeal. In my case, I love a good story.

It turns out that this compulsion to compile things of value runs in my family. My octogenarian uncle made an outstanding living collecting and selling medieval arms and armour. Believe it or not, he is actually world-renowned for his collection, which has been featured in the Metropolitan Museum of Art, and he has sold antique weapons to sheiks and oligarchs around the world.

When I say that he has made a very good living dealing antique arms and armour, you need to take that with a grain of salt. I assure you that the value is real; I have witnessed him trade an ornate 17th century gun for a 6-figure check. But you didn't see the look of joy on his face that you would have anticipated. In fact, even with a 6-figure check in his hand, he seemed to be holding back a sour face as if he were sucking a lemon.

After 50 years of collecting, my uncle has the same problem that I had hoarding comic books as a kid. He loves these items and selling them feels painful. So, yes, he has built up a very significant net worth collecting antique guns. But it remains mostly a theoretical net worth, because he hates to sell.

Much like my old comic books, each antique is a finely-crafted piece of art that has a story and he will be happy to narrate the story of each piece: where it was crafted in Europe 500 years ago; the exact name and story of the craftsmen who forged the weapon; the story of the royal family who owned the weapon; even the origin of the precious metals and jewels that decorated weaponry fit for a king. Over the decades, his collecting business has become a habit so severe that he has purchased and accumulated real estate just to have secure places to store his beloved weapons. Guess what? The real estate has gone up in value as well. This is how an old crank living in rural America dies richer than many big-name corporate executives.

I'm not too different from my uncle. I have just made my life easier by accumulating things that don't have a physical presence. I have sold shares from time to time, just like I used to occasionally sell comic books and my uncle sells antiques when he must. But mostly I just freeze. Why? Each stock has a story and the story keeps me riveted. I want to see how it ends.

Once Upon A Time

The sooner you start thinking of yourself as the owner of a company and not just the owner of a simple commodity to be traded, borrowed, or bartered, the sooner you will become interested in the stories in your portfolio. And there are stories. The media never gets tired of pointing out that top corporate executives earn ungodly pay packages. But what is rarely considered is that many executives earn unusual pay packages because their lives have been journeys filled with tortuous high and lows, devastating defeats, and, eventually, outrageous good fortune.

Whether it was Henry Ford, who went bankrupt four times before finally becoming the Henry Ford, or a book dweeb named Jeffery Bezos, who quit Wall Street to found a little business selling books on the internet, there are some amazing tales hidden in plain sight right inside your brokerage account. Of course, more than anything, we seek value in the financial sense, but ownership in these companies also has value in the sense of the entertainment and learning that we can pick up by following the companies we own.

There are too many fascinating stories to recall in one short chapter: Steve Jobs, who was fired from his own company only to later resurrect both his own moribund company and his lagging career; Bill Gates, a social misfit who dropped out of Harvard because he thought desktop computers could change the world; of course, Elon Musk of Tesla, whose outrageous antics are also right on the border between inspirationally ambitious and just plain crazy.

Beyond mere individuals, as godlike as some of these larger-than-life executives may seem, there is also the world altering accomplishments that some of these companies have achieved. Gilead Science almost single handedly saved millions of HIV patients from sure death. The very same company cured Hepatitis C! Apple Computer put the power of the Information Age directly into your hand. As we speak, your utility companies are slowly but surely ushering in a new era of unlimited clean energy from the sun and the wind. As a shareholder, you have the power to actually participate in these stories. Every day is "choose your own adventure" when you invest in Corporate America!

The Kid Stays in the Picture

We have already established in previous chapters that selling your stocks is rarely the right move. Almost every scrap of data demonstrates that the real money is made by people who hold onto shares through thick and thin. As Warren Buffet is fond of saying, "Simple, but not easy."

Why didn't I sell my comic books even when I knew I could make a quick buck? Well, I thought they would be worth more later, but really, I just couldn't stand to part with them. Was I going to throw Captain America under the bus? Was I going to tell Batman to go fight crime somewhere else? How could I pretend that I didn't care if Wolverine died, was transported to another dimension, and was then resurrected with an all-new costume?

Leverage this story effect to strengthen your emotional resolve around your stocks. Do you really want to miss out on Elon Musk's latest antics? Gilead Pharma cured Hepatitis C. Don't you want to see what they (and you, as a shareholder) will come up with next? Ford Motor has been run by a member of the Ford family for almost a century. With all the changes coming in the automotive industry, isn't it interesting to see if a new generation of Ford motors will rise to the occasion?

This story effect is particularly powerful when the economy as a whole is in the dumps. If the market crashed by 30% in two months, don't sell! Would you walk out of the movie Superman when he is losing a fight to General Zod? Would you snap off the TV when Indiana Jones is surrounded by snakes? The most exciting part of Star Wars is when it looks like Luke Skywalker and his band of rebels are about to be extinguished. The point I want to make is: don't leave in the middle of the story!

It's the same thing with your stocks. If you build up an emotional relationship with the companies' stories and the stories of the executives who lead them, you will be less likely to bail out when the sailing gets rough. The data shows, again and again, that this reluctance to sell is a good thing.

When it comes to your own story as an investor, you are the one who gets to write that narrative. Will you be constantly buying and selling, often losing money, and wondering why you always seem to just miss the latest fad? Or will you slowly but steadily accumulate; taking joy from watching your pile grow almost as if by magic? It's up to you to decide. I can tell you that the second outcome takes a while, but eventually will feel better than you can imagine.

Chapter 7: The Way Of The Zagger

It's a sad fact that most Americans will struggle with poverty their entire lives. According to Investopedia.com, in 2017, the Government Accountability Office released a research report indicating that the average pre-retiree, aged 55–64, had just $107,000 saved for retirement. They did a lifetime of work to achieve about $6000 per year in passive income in old age.

Now, you might say that, when we use the word 'average', we are talking about folks that never went to college, folks born into poverty, folks that never did have much of a chance in life. But what about high income Americans? According to a study published by Magnify Money, using data from the Federal Reserve and the FDIC, the median high-income household has $500,000 saved for retirement. This means that even the top 10% of Americans would quickly run through savings if they were fired from their jobs or lost their health. Remember, $500,000 is the median. This means that 50% of the people who earn six figures for years, or decades, have little to show for it.

Most Americans are considered 'poor' their whole lives, and even Americans with six-figure incomes often wind up hovering around insolvency. But these must be people who foolishly spend their money on fancy vacations, flashy cars, and McMansions they can't really afford. If these high-income people invested, they would wind up rich. Not really! As we have discussed in several chapters in this book, even high-income Americans who use those high incomes to invest in the stock market tend to do badly.

The numbers are so shocking that they bear repeating. According to the DALBAR organization, a well-known financial research organization, between 1995 and 2015, the average investor underperformed the market by more than 3%. In other words, if you had simply bought a plain, vanilla index fund in 1995 and spent the next 10 years playing golf all day, you would have achieved a 7.31% annual return. But most people don't do that. They pay too much attention to their investments; buying and selling due to fear and unrestrained emotion. They only wind up with a 4.23% annual return over the very same period. However, that is the average person. In fact, many, many well paid, college-educated investors do even worse. Pitiful.

Suffice to say, the way that most people handle money is all wrong. Therefore, if you want better results than most people, all you need to do is behave differently than most people. Different behavior will bring different results. Since most peoples' financial behavior brings horrible results, you need to be different from the crowd on a regular basis to achieve good results.

You must become a Zagger.

Zaggerism: Defined

What the heck is a 'Zagger?' Very simply, a Zagger is a person who 'zags' while everyone else is zigging. The Zagger swims upstream, even though it would be easier to go with the current. While all the lemmings gather together for perceived safety and run off a cliff, the Zagger separates himself from the crowd and runs as far away from that cliff as possible. When a house is on fire and everyone else is fleeing in a panic, the Zagger runs toward the fire because he knows that there are unguarded treasures to be plucked out of the inferno.

Zaggers are often the people who make history. Galileo Galilei was thrown in jail for daring to observe that the earth revolved around the sun. Was Galileo risking life and limb to make a statement? Was Galileo making astronomical reports just to mess with the Pope's world view? No. Galileo was simply reporting what he observed, and if his carefully measured mathematical models didn't fit with society's version of reality, so be it.

Young Bill Gates was a Zagger. While all the other kids were out playing sports or trying to impress girls with mustangs in the late 1970s, Gates was scheming about how to gain access to the world's computers, which were quite primitive at the time. He dropped out of Harvard … Harvard! Young Bill did everything differently than most people and thus got better results.

America was founded by the greatest Zaggers the world has ever known. Throughout world history, most revolutions have been promulgated by desperate people with little to lose. The American Revolution was the exact opposite. The Founding Fathers were rich. George Washington was one of the richest men in all 13 colonies. Alexander Hamilton had overcome a lowly birth as a neglected illegitimate child to mount a promising career as a colonial official. Benjamin Franklin was not only wealthy, but a bonafide international celebrity. Sure, we see all kinds of Hollywood celebrities in the media today speaking out about pet causes and taking principled stands. But have any Hollywood celebrities been forced to tweet the following?:

"We must all hang together, or, most assuredly, we shall all hang separately."
—Benjamin Franklin.

By the way, hanging was only part of the punishment for treason against King George. George Washington, one of the richest men in the colonies, took the risk of being hung, then disemboweled, and then torn limb from limb, all because he got sick and tired of taking orders from a king that had never set foot on American soil. It really would have been a lot easier for George Washington to sit back and enjoy the life of leisure that he could afford. But at some point, he just had to do what he had to do. George Washington was a Zagger.

You know who is not a Zagger? The punk working down at your local organic brew fair trade coffee house with 20 tattoos and purple hair. That is someone small on the inside, willing to go to any lengths to get attention. Same thing for the jerk at the country club happy hour who wants to tell everyone how smart he is for playing the market with options, derivatives, and other unnecessary garbage.

The real Zagger doesn't seek attention or recognition for being different. The real Zagger often doesn't even feel any different from anyone else. They just consistently Zag while everyone else Zigs. That is just the reaction that feels normal for them.

The Original Gangster of the Zaggers

By now, you have probably noticed that I refer to Warren Buffett a lot. Warren Buffett is an icon in the investor world because he has been one of the few richest men in the world for damn near 50 years. He has also written extensively about his philosophy and personal journey, so the common man has an unusually high level of access to the mega tycoon's thought process. One of his many famous phrases is, "You must be fearful when others are greedy and greedy when others are fearful."

Warren Buffett is the original Granddaddy of the Zaggers. As of the writing of this text, Buffett is 89 years old and still highly active. From the moment we consider his career, his Zaggerism is obvious.

Think Rockefeller. What comes to mind? Oil.
Gates. What comes to mind? Computers.
Think Bezos. What comes to mind? Amazon.

Warren Buffett has been, at various times, just as rich (or richer!) than these legendary tycoons. But he is quite different. Each tycoon mentioned is associated with one big game-changing business that has generated a mind-boggling fortune. Buffett got rich by owning stuff … lots and lots of stuff. The publicly-traded conglomerate that he controls, Berkshire Hathaway, is a random hodgepodge of assets he has acquired over the decades. If Rockefeller, Gates, and Bezos were associated with the biggest innovations of their day, Warren Buffett is the financial titan equivalent of a crotchety old grandpa who accumulates stuff that he buys cheap at garage sales. What is the saying? "One man's trash is another man's treasure." In the case of Buffett, the emphasis is on treasure.

Of course, multiple tomes have been written documenting every aspect of Buffett's astounding rise to global prominence. But the gist of his success is the following: from the late 1960s to the early 1980s, the American Stock Market vastly underperformed. Due to a variety of geopolitical factors, the market crawled along like a sickly turtle for what seemed like a very, very long time. It got so bad that no one even wanted stocks anymore. No one except Warren Buffett.

Realizing that common stocks had fallen drastically out of favor, Buffett actually found ways to use other people's money to acquire more and more shares at better and better prices. Berkshire Hathaway acquired GEICO (sound familiar?), an insurance company. He used those millions in insurance premiums to just keep piling up unloved stocks that no one else wanted.

Whether it was luck or genius, or some combination of the two, Buffett turned out to be right. Just as the 70s had been a nightmare decade for stocks, the 80s and 90s handed in year after year of scorching outperformance. By 1996, everyone and their mother was buying stocks, often at overinflated prices. It didn't matter to Buffett. He had amassed a mind-boggling stockpile of shares decades before when they were still cheap. When the world was Zigging, Warren Buffett Zagged. He behaved differently from most people, thus, he wound up with very different results. Very different results.

The Zagger is You

None of this is to say that you must risk execution by hanging (like George Washington) or control a publicly-traded international mega-conglomerate (like Buffett) to be successful. Washington and Buffett are simply famous examples that illustrate a point.

If you have sought out and paid good money for this book, you probably already have something of the Zagger in your personality. The trick is to harness that natural contrarian tendency and hone it into a razor-sharp advantage.

The most fundamental application of the Zagger mentality is to realize that stock market crashes are good, not bad. When you hear about a flash discount sale on Amazon or with your favorite retailer, do you react with dread and palpitations? No, you get excited, because a whole lot of great merchandise is about to be sold cheap for a limited time. It's just the same with stock market crashes.

Better yet, don't do anything at all! Sometimes, a Zagger can stand out from the crowd by simply not engaging in the hysteria of the masses. Go ahead, plow large amounts of money into some simple, broad index funds and spend the next 20 years going to the beach and playing with your kids. The data clearly show that, while everyone else is busy running around with their hair on fire, buying, selling, shorting, and optioning, you will very likely be making more money by just doing nothing. How easy is that?

Zaggerism also helps you achieve a rich sense of humor. I view financial media, such as CNBC, as more of a comedy show than anything else. Sure, Jim Cramer and his colleagues are entertaining, but they have no idea what they are talking about. We will discuss this more next chapter. It is clear that even the most grisled Wall Street veteran or the number one graduate from Harvard Business School does not have a crystal ball to predict the future. Take a look at your friends or neighbors who breathlessly hang on the words of these charlatans and enjoy a good chuckle. As PT Barnum once said, "There is a sucker born every minute." Every two minutes, a sucker calls into "Mad Money," on CNBC.

It's common knowledge that many people take pleasure in behaving differently than others. Think about the term "sexual deviant." In a literal sense, it only means someone with a different flavor of sexuality than most people. But of course, the phrase "sexual deviant" has a bad connotation. The phrase connotes two things. First, it implies that being different is dirty, or wrong. Second, most importantly, it connotes that being different feels good.

Of course, it would be irresponsible for me to promote sexual deviance in these pages. But sex is just one way to feel good. I will wholeheartedly promote "financial deviance." Go ahead; be different, be unique, be you when you invest. You might be surprised by how good it feels.

Chapter 8: Become An Expert

Quick review question: What are the two reasons why people typically buy and sell stocks too often? Confidence. Either too much confidence or too little. The overconfident investor "knows what he is doing" and therefore believes that his constant buying and selling will add value. Of course, the data firmly indicate otherwise. The underconfident investor feels that he doesn't really understand what is going on and therefore he is exposed to a disaster that could strike at any time. He believes that his constant buying and selling is the best way to shield himself from his lack of knowledge. Again, the data prove that, typically, rather than avoiding a disaster, the buying and selling is the disaster.

The number one way to avoid either overconfidence or underconfidence is to become an expert in the companies you own. That way, when you think you know what you're doing, you actually do know what you are doing.

Warren Buffett calls this concept the "Circle of Competence". While Buffett is famous for the deals he has done and the success he has had, he is equally famous for the deals he has not done and the disasters he has avoided. He attributes a lot of success to his extreme reluctance to invest in businesses that he does not understand. Before he puts his capital (and the hard-won capital of his shareholders) at risk, he wants to make sure he understands the business. You should do the same. It's not nearly as hard as you think. In fact, you probably already understand a lot more than you think you do.

Jack of All Trades, Master of None

You may have already noticed that I have a low opinion of most financial media, especially financial 'personalities'.

Falsehood #1: 'Stock' experts know everything about every kind of stock and can be consulted, just as if you were gazing into an omniscient crystal ball.

Falsehood #2: If you don't have the same kind of expertise as these 'stock' experts, you should either not be in the game or you should be hiring and paying an expert who knows all things 'stocks'.

Above, I put the word 'stocks' into quotation marks because 'stocks' are not stocks, they are companies; little slices of companies that you own. They are no different than if you owned 100% of a local dry-cleaning chain, except, in this example, you own 0.01% of a national dry-cleaning chain with thousands of locations. When you put the investments in that context, we easily see why financial personalities are nothing more than circus performers. Who could possibly know about every kind of business around the world?

During every single show, Jim Cramer does his 'lightning round', for which people call and ask questions about their holdings in dozens of different kinds of businesses. Dozens! This would require Cramer to have expert knowledge about dozens of different kinds of business and industries. In a typical week, Cramer comments on the prospects of at least 20 different companies in 20 different industries. How could anyone be an expert in industries as diverse as defense, pharmaceuticals, software as a service, and construction?

Let's go back to the dry cleaner example. Let's say you own 100% of a small chain of local dry cleaners. Let's say you have built up ownership of 10 dry cleaners over the years. Now you have borrowed a million dollars and you want to acquire other small businesses that would be complementary to your current dry cleaning holdings. Who would be a better consultant/advisor for you? Someone who has 20 years of experience in dry cleaning/chemistry/commercial real estate or someone who barks out random predictions about 30 unrelated businesses every week?

This is why the Financial Media can provide value to equity investors, but those investors have to be choosy about who they listen to. If CNBC is running a segment about biotech companies, then they should be engaging with a noted expert on biotech companies. Likewise, if they're running a special on agriculture investments, then they should be interviewing someone who has a lifetime of experience in the farm business. I don't want to hear someone who sells stocks for a living spewing forth diatribes about ratios, value creation, or PE multiples. Get me someone who knows about the specific type of business in question.

The Expert is You

You can do very well as a long-term shareholder even if you never watch one day of CNBC and you don't even know where Bloomberg TV is on your cable package. You already know a lot more about business than you think.

There are generally two ways somebody becomes an industry expert; both are perfectly viable and worthy. Firstly, consider the knowledge you acquire over the years by working for a paycheck. In my particular case, I have been a champion salesman in the medical field for almost 20 years. Pharmaceuticals, pathology services, medical devices; I have sold it all. I have spent thousands of hours in doctors' offices, hospitals, and outpatient clinics. I have seen things from the point of view of the doctor, the medicine maker, and the hospital owner. For me, focusing on biotech and medical devices makes sense. The healthcare world is my automatic 'circle of competence'. This was why I started www.sickeconomics.com and published my first book, Your First Biotech Million. I had already earned the knowledge through decades of work; I just chose to lever that knowledge to achieve maximum value for myself, and my readers.

You're probably no different. Whether you are an architect, advertising salesperson, or attorney, there is probably a constellation of publicly-traded businesses that you already know a lot about. If you concentrate your equity holdings in these names, you will be a lot more competent and less likely to suffer from overconfidence or underconfidence.

Secondly, another way to become an expert in a sector is with pure passion. Let's say you're a dentist. You trained hard to become a dentist and, month after month, you make a nice, steady living this way. There's nothing at all wrong with your solid career. But drilling cavities and extracting molars has never been what really gets your heart pumping. What really makes your blood rush is the roar of a brand new Mustang or the brand new leather smell of a Porsche. You love cars. Ever since you were a kid, you dreamed of sports cars, trucks, limos … basically anything with wheels attracted your attention like a magnet. You read all of the relevant industry blogs and subscribe to some newsletters. You would do it all for free; the thrill of the open road is that powerful to you.

In this example, you would probably already know a lot about companies such as Ford, BMW, or Fiat. You probably also know the names of more obscure players, like companies that manufacture car parts. In this example, you could probably be a very successful investor in equities related to the automotive industry. Your years of research will help you make wise, patient choices related to your holdings; you're unlikely to be rattled by bumps in the road, because you know the players and you understand the evolving economics of that particular industry. In this example, who would be more fit to comment on automotive businesses? An 'expert', who just looked at his computer screen for 10 minutes or you, who have followed every new car release over the last ten years?

Holding onto your shares for the long term requires a level of emotional comfort. You need to feel comfortable in the story, mission, and management of each of the companies you own. It is a lot easier to achieve this Zen-like state if you know the industry. Pick a few industries that appeal to you. Get good at understanding them.

Chapter 9: Get Busy! The Other Compounding

As we have discussed throughout this book, the data show again and again that you are very unlikely to add value to your stock portfolio through constant buying, selling, and other manipulations. Stock investments were simply built to be passive investments. Your Board of Directors and CEO already oversee the company that you own. Adding an additional layer of oversight is just like trying to drive a car while you are upside down. Sure, if you really want to, you can push the gas and brake pedals with your hands and steer the wheel with your feet, but the machine wasn't built to be used that way. You can pervert the manufacturer's design intention, but it's highly likely that you won't like the results. Your stocks drive themselves; for goodness sake, leave them alone!

But, of course, this is easier said than done. Those two psychological factors, overconfidence and underconfidence, are powerful forces that compel otherwise sound decision makers to errors in judgement. How do you block out those compulsions that creep up on so many otherwise rational people? Simple: fill up your time with other productive endeavors. The less spare time you have, the less time you have to wander around your stock portfolio looking for things to mess up.

We have already examined in detail how a little extra activity in your stock portfolio can sabotage your returns over the long term. Now let's consider how a little extra activity in the real world can turbo charge your stock returns over time. Let's look at the facts; then you can decide how best to invest your precious time.

Meet Mr. Average Joe

For the sake of this example, I am going to assume that our Average Joe is like most middle class or upper-middle class people in America. We will say that his earnings (or the earnings of himself and his spouse) are just enough to cover monthly expenses and even save a little. We'll assume that his primary money-making occupation takes up about 9 hours a day of his time.

Let's say our Average Joe earns about $90,000 a year at a job. After taxes and expenses, he manages to pay his monthly bills and save about $5,000 a year.

He's about 40 years old, and he's been diligently saving for 20years, so between savings and compounded investment returns, he currently has a $200,000 nest egg. Not bad at all for an Average Joe!

Joe likes to get about 8 hours of sleep a night, which leaves him with 16 waking hours per day. Joe labors for a paycheck about 9 hours a day, which leaves him with about 7 hours of free time per day. He's married with two kids, so his domestic responsibilities eat up a lot of that free time. After all is said and done, Joe has about 3 hours of 'me time' per day. He rarely has to work for his company on weekends. So Joe may have up to 10 hours of 'me time' during the weekend. This 'me time' is the danger zone for a stock portfolio.

If you are truly the Average Joe, you may get bored or anxious during your 'me time', which would lead you to crack open the stock portfolio and begin the process of screwing yourself out of large profits. But, in our example, our Average Joe is just a bit better than average.

Joe Gets Busy

Instead of fooling around with his stock portfolio, he sells affordable antiques online. On weekends, he prowls garage sales and estate sales, looking for things of value that people have forgotten about. He reads the obituaries and calls up families when he knows that Grandma has passed on. After a few years of this, he actually gets to be known around town and sometimes people call him, looking to sell items they no longer want.

The extra money Joe makes this way is a nice bonus, but he mostly does it as a hobby. He likes antiques, he likes the stories behind the objects he finds, and, mostly, he loves the rush of stealing a good deal. He makes about $1000 a month this way.

A lot of people would take that $1000 and spend it on vacations, a fancy car lease, or home renovation. Not our Average Joe. He spends $250 monthly buying something extra for his kids or wife and the other $750 goes right into his stock portfolio.

Ok, so what? A lousy $750 per month into his stocks is never going to transform our Average Joe into 'More Wealthy than Average Joe', right? Well, let's see. We will use Nerdwallet.com to crunch some numbers.

Prior to Joe getting his side gig going, his family was saving about $420 per month. Let's just assume for a moment that he never did get a side gig. At age 40, he already had $200,000. So, if he attained a 6% annual return on his stock portfolio and his new monthly investments, by age 65, Average Joe would be looking at $1,185,000. Not bad at all, but not enough to afford a dream retirement.

But, starting at age 40, Joe is now going to invest $1170 per month, which is the sum of his previous $420 plus the $750 from his side gig. You'll also remember that, statistically speaking, the average 'active' investor underperforms the market by 3% every year. Between his regular job, his side gig, and his family, our Joe simply hasn't had time to obsess over his stock portfolio. The man is busy; as he acquires more and more stock, it just sits there and does its own thing, the way it was designed to do. Instead of earning a 6% annual return, Joe achieves a 9% annual return, which has been the average return of the market for many decades. In this scenario, Joe sails into age 65 with a whopping $3,200,000 in his stock portfolio!

How could there be such a huge difference in these two scenarios? How could Joe's little side gig make such a difference over time? One word: compounding.

It turns out there is a reason why Albert Einstein called compounding, "The 8th wonder of the world." Very simply, when compounding works in your favor, it's an incredibly powerful tailwind. When compounding is working against you, it's like trying to run a marathon wearing sneakers made of lead.

In our example above, Joe's little side gig actually delivers the power of double compounding. By being so busy that he has little free time left, he is likely to realize the full value of the market, which is about 9% annually. If he had time to mess around with his stock portfolio in a sad attempt to imitate Gordon Gekko, he would most likely achieve a lower return over time.

Secondly, Joe's little side income has added up over time. Joe is working hard, but Joe is also working smart. He does enjoy some of his extra income every month in the form of fancy meals out or baseball tickets. But most of it just goes into growing his net worth, month after month, year after year. The result? Some real gold in his Golden Years.

The important principle here is twofold. First, "idle hands are the Devil's workshop," as the saying goes. Too much spare time leads the mind to wander, which often leads to a stock trading habit that will cost you more than a cocaine addiction over time. Secondly, extra income steered into your investment accounts grows like wildfire over time. In our example, Joe built a side gig selling antiques online. How he attained the income is irrelevant. You could work part time somewhere; you could paint houses or work as a handyman. Just do what you must to make sure your income exceeds your monthly expenses by a wide margin and you too can wind up rich.

Harnessing the full power of compounding is certainly not as sexy as founding Tesla or writing a best-selling novel. But the simple arithmetic will get you where you want to go. The question is: How badly do you want to get there? If you want to be rich, it will require a little discipline and a lot of hard work.

Chapter 10: Birds Of A Feather

The net lesson of the last chapter was that small changes in behavior can make huge differences over time. Our Average Joe was just a little more disciplined than average, just a little more hard working, and displayed just a little more initiative. Yet he wound up with a net worth over $3,000,000; a number that will remain just a fantasy for 95% of Americans.

Maintaining that kind of financial discipline over time is not as easy as it seems, but I can tell you the easiest way right now; avoid bad influences, by which I mean certain people. Many perfectly good people are bad influences. They may be perfectly nice, ethical, decent people, but more than likely, they know nothing at all about the accumulation of wealth. These are good people with bad ideas about money. Avoid them and you've already taken the first step towards retiring with $3,000,000 while most Americans struggle to make ends meet well into old age.

To be clear, I am not advising you to suddenly cut off all contact with friends and family who are unwise about money. Simply take what they say with a grain of salt and make a concerted effort to surround yourself with people who think the way you do.

Let's return to the case of our not-so-Average Joe. Over Joe's lifetime trek to wealth, who did he likely avoid and who did he likely embrace?

Well, first and foremost, he tuned out all of the people who told him he didn't need a side gig because stock trading should be his side gig. If Joe told anyone that he had a substantial stock portfolio (he may very well have just kept that information to himself), I can guarantee that dozens of people over the years either gave or requested advice on what to buy or sell. Joe may well have engaged in some entertaining discussions about the long-term trends that he likes or a few particular companies in his portfolio that he cherishes. But he certainly avoided talking about chart patterns, short selling, trading options, buying on margin, and all of the other nonsense habits that destroy value for the 'suburban day trader' set.

Joe also very likely avoided people who insisted that he needed a new luxury car or a brand new kitchen every 5 years, or even those who insisted that his kids needed to go to an out-of-state private college. Not only did Joe show tremendous initiative and gumption in mounting a side gig, he invested the extra money instead of spending it. He may have had iron discipline, but investing instead of frivolous spending is a lot easier when your friends don't drive Mercedes and a week of camping is considered to be just as much fun as flying the family to Paris. If most of your friends are on the thrifty side, then there is no consumption pressure to begin with.

Who would Joe have embraced? Well, he probably would have a lot of fun socializing with other antique collectors and dealers. After all, it was mostly his passion for antiques that drove him to work nights and weekends; the money was just a bonus. Assuming that Joe mostly dealt in items that fit his price range ($100-$1000 dollars), he would most likely have come into contact with antique traders in the same financial range. They, in turn, would be likely to have personal finances akin to Joe's family. Thus, Joe would naturally be socializing with people whose habits he could afford.

Another place where Joe could have found companionship with like-minded individuals would be online. If you go to a smattering of real-world social events and the topic turns to investing or share purchases, you remain a victim of chance. You could find yourself amongst shrewd, disciplined investors, such as yourself, or you could be forced to listen to your 19-year-old nephew boasting about his big financial adventures on the Robin Hood trading app. If you don't control your environment, you may wind up having to filter out a lot of world views and opinions that don't fit your financial worldview.

Online, there are hundreds, if not thousands, of financial clubs and conversation groups that are divided by investing style, age group, or even industry (biotech clubs, real estate clubs, etc). If Joe chose to join an online investing community, this would give him the power to control the environment he enters. By choosing a group of conservative value investors, he has automatically screened out 90% of the absurd opinions out there. Of course, the internet is notorious for giving soap box platforms to cranks and crooks. But Joe can simply exercise the same good judgement that he has used in his day-to-day life and screen it out with the press of a button.

How to Not Be a Jerk

Even if Joe applies all of the techniques listed above, it's still likely that he will be cornered by a lot of financial idiots over a lifetime. The stock market just has a weird mystique that attracts all kinds of people, many of whom are fools. I guarantee, they will want to push some of their foolish ideas on you.

How to gracefully handle these situations? Well, one great way is to downplay your level of expertise. Joe can present facts as ideas or theories, which makes him seem more humble. Here is a list of time-honored phrases that will help you reject idiocy with grace:

-"My understanding is …"
-"I had read that …"
-"I wonder if …"
-"Is it possible that …"
-"Some people say …"
-"Just one man's opinion, but …"
-"In my experience …"

Another outstanding way to refute moronic ideas about money, without sounding preachy, is to simply attribute the ideas to other people.

"I read a book by Warren Buffett, one of the world's richest people ..."
"There is a great book by an author called Benjamin Graham ..."
"I used to have a rich aunt that used to say …"
"My old college roommate has done great and he is always saying that …"

By this point in the book, you know how I feel about the writings and guidance provided by Warren Buffett. His ideas have influenced me a lot. So, when some young punk wants to talk about the benefits of rapid stock trading, I hardly offer my opinion at all. I just phrase it as something that I read by a famous author. The kid can take the hint or not. But the important thing is that I am not positioning myself as some kind of superior person or investment authority. I'm merely passing on some information that was shared with me and now I'm trying to help the next guy.

Feeling Good

So why do people trade so much? Why do people buy fancy cars and shiny watches? Ultimately, logic has very little to do with these financial behaviors. People are driven by feelings, and feelings cause people to throw away the earnings of a lifetime on items that bring a momentary rush.

It's very likely that our not-so-Average Joe is wired a bit differently than most. He probably couldn't have maintained that level of initiative and discipline all those years unless he took a kind of pleasure in watching his brokerage balance go up and up. While others take pleasure in watching their shoe collection grow and grow, for whatever reason, Joe is motivated by watching his stock collection skyrocket over time.

Joe is likely to get the most pleasure out of life by hanging around people who feel the same way he does. If he finds himself amongst the BMW set, he may feel lost. While they are droning on and on about the various features of their fancy new vehicle, Joe is just daydreaming about owning stock in BMW.

The point of this chapter is not to encourage a life devoid of pleasure. The point is to help you define where you find your pleasure. If you have purchased this book and read this many pages already, it's very likely that you will take mental pleasure from knowing that you could purchase 10 BMWs. Actually purchasing one will likely disappoint you and feel like a waste.

Additionally, the point of this chapter isn't to judge people who prefer to accumulate goods rather than profits. If most people really enjoy a luxury car or a fancy house, then by all means let them find their own pleasure in life. But don't be surprised when they seem stressed out and depressed, even while tooling around in their luxury automobile. Remember that bad compounding is just as powerful as good compounding. The long-term price tag of the lux lifestyle is far more than what was written on the original invoice.

Choose your friends and acquaintances wisely, control your environment, and speak with humility when possible. Accumulating wealth through shareholdings actually gets easier when you follow those principles. Good people and good surroundings will help you build the healthy mental habits that will make you rich in money and in spirit.

Chapter 11: If You Must: Part I

Most of this book has been dedicated to exploring psychological tricks and tactics to help you avoid being a frequent, overactive investor. I do believe many of you will have good success with these tactics. If you commit to practicing these mental strategies, they will become habits, and everyone knows that habits are hard to break, for better or worse.

But there are a certain percentage of people who just can't help themselves. Some people just have to be 'in the game' and no amount of rational explanation or psychological conditioning will be able to control the urge to become an active player in what should essentially be a passive game.

If you bought this book and have read this far, you probably buy into the logic of disciplined, methodical stock market investing. But that doesn't mean you will be able to control yourself. If you suspect that you just won't be able to keep your dirty hands away from your keyboard and you could trade stocks at any moment, this chapter is for you.

Afterall, everyone is human. The following two chapters will teach you how to channel your natural human impulses into positive action. If you must treat your stock portfolio as an active affair, you still have a chance to benefit. You just have to do it right.

Cash Flow

As we have discussed throughout this book, owning a sliver of Corporate America is an astoundingly lucrative proposition. Most of America's largest corporations (and many smaller ones) produce excess cash year after year, decade after decade. One of the tasks of the managers you have hired to run your corporation is to decide what to do with the torrents of cash that gush from your remunerative business.

Typically, there are three ways to leverage excess cash flow to create even more value for shareholders. **Option #1** is via mergers and acquisitions. If you own a company that makes tires, you may choose to use excess cash flow to buy a company that manufactures tire hubs. The theory would be that combining the two businesses at the right price will result in an even more profitable entity. M&A sounds great in theory, but in reality, corporate empire builders have had a very 'hit and miss' track record over the last 50 years.

Option #2 is to simply take excess cash and buy back the company's own shares. The theory would be that, by reducing the number of 'free floating' shares on the open market, each share will be worth more. The company is leveraging excess cash to create scarcity in its own shares. This approach has become a very entrenched tradition in Corporate America, but the practice has been controversial for two reasons. First, buybacks don't always raise share prices; there has often been a gap between theory and reality. Second, a lot of critics see this practice as essentially building a bonfire fueled by excess cash. It feels like an unproductive use of capital to a lot of business professors and progressive government critics.

Option #3 is the oldest, most established method of rewarding shareholders. Simply pay a dividend. Excess cash, which is produced on a predictable and methodical basis, is paid out to shareholders just the same way. Corporations have been rewarding shareholders this way since the 1600s.

Just like any other practice that has lasted 400 years, dividends have come in and out of vogue over the years. While many investors rejoice at the feeling of cold, hard cash in their hands, the practice still has its critics. For very wealthy people (who increasingly control the bulk of shares in America), any extra income creates extra taxes. Therefore, there is a class of share owners out there who actually advocate to minimize income.

Another criticism of dividends is that any extra cash should be put towards growing revenues. If cash is paid out, it often appears that management haven't been able to think of anything better to do with it. This is why, over the last several decades, high growth companies, such as tech startups and biotechs, have tended to eschew dividends. At some point, the mathematical implications of dividends become less important than the 'signal' they send to investors. Companies that want to be considered 'young guns' don't pay dividends, because they have so much more growing to do. 'Grown up' companies with mature business tend to cultivate and grow their dividends with great care; they are looking to attract a slow but steady group of owners.

When dividends are paid out to you, typically, you would have three choices to make yourself.

Option #1: spend the dividend. You could spend the dividend on something frivolous or fun, because, hey, life is short. Or you could just live off the dividend. Millions of senior citizens around the world depend on quarterly corporate dividends to pay for food, electricity, and even rent.

Option #2: set up automatic reinvestment at your brokerage. This program is sometimes called a DRIP program; if you own stock in Coca-Cola and Coca-Cola pays you a dividend four times per year, that dividend never shows up as cash in your brokerage account. Rather, the dividend immediately goes toward buying more shares of Coca Cola.

This way, you are harnessing the power of compounding automatically. You can go about your life, spending your time as you please, and one day you could come back and you own a huge chunk of Coca-Cola stock. You planted the vine long ago, and one day you came back and it had taken over the whole yard. Except now you have a vine that grows money.

Option #3: take those quarterly dividends and reinvest them yourself. In this example, you are still planting seeds that will one day lead to a verdant garden. But now you'll get to play the role of Master Gardener. Each quarter, four times per year, your dividends come in, and you'll decide where to invest the cash. Sometimes, you may put it right back into the company it came from. But you may think the cash would be better invested in another company in your portfolio. In this example, you will lovingly tend your garden quarter after quarter, year after year. One day, you will also wind up with a lush garden filled with money trees. But this is more like a manicured English Garden. Nature certainly did its work, but this time she did it in partnership with a horticulturist.

If you absolutely, positively must take an active hand in your stock portfolio, the reinvestment of dividends, patiently and with discipline, is a great way to leave your mark on your money garden.

The Power of Dividends

We rarely hear about dividends in the media. Right now, we are going through a phase in which dividends are not seen as sexy, cool, or even very lucrative. In the era of the Robin Hood speculator, everybody is about quick trading profits based on price appreciation. The underlying fundamentals of a company barely seem to matter to millions of 'momentum' traders. A momentum is someone who buys the most popular stocks of the moment, betting that "momentum" will push prices from high to even higher.

However, for our patient financial gardener, cash flow matters over time. It really matters. Again, this isn't my opinion; this is the data speaking. Dr. Ian Mortimer and Matthew Page, CFA, published a study on this topic. They asked the question, "What percentage of total returns over time are related to the compounding of dividends?" The findings were shocking:

For an average holding period of 1 year, dividends accounted for 27% of total returns of the S&P 500 since 1940. If we increase the holding period to 3 years, dividends account for 38%, 5 years it increases to 42%, over a 10-year period it rises to 48%, and with a 20-year holding period, dividends account for some 60% of total returns. It is important to note, too, that here we are not just looking at the S&P 500 as a whole and not focusing purely on companies that actually pay a dividend. If we did, we think these results would likely be even more striking. (Why Dividends Matter; GAFunds.com)

Dividends matter. A lot. You may remember the three options we discussed for the investor who receives a dividend deposit. One option was to simply spend the dividend. After all, all we hear about in the media is share price. Did it go up? Did it go down? What has the share price done over the last month, the last year? You might think you could just spend the dividend with minimal consequence. Mortimer and Page did some research on that idea, as well.

If you had invested $100 at the end of 1940, this would have been worth $174,000 at the end of 2011 if you had reinvested the dividends, versus $12,000 if dividends were not included.

Of course, turning $100 into $12,000 is a neat trick, but you would wind up leaving some $160,000 on the table by ignoring the importance of the dividend compounding effect.

If dividends and dividend compounding is so important, why don't we hear about the phenomenon more? Instead, we only hear "What went up today?"; "Which sector is hot right now?"

Plainly put, people are impatient and lack vision. They want profit now. Sitting around and watching a garden grow is not very sexy.

But it is sexy to the horticulturist. Millions of people across the United States pay great money towards the hobby of making things grow and making things grow the way they want. If you choose to reinvest your own dividends, you are no different.

Where is the pleasure for a horticulturist? Do they have some kind of magic button they can push to make shrubs and vines grow more quickly? Nope.

They take pleasure in knowing that their actions today will lead to greater results tomorrow. The pleasure is actually three-fold.

The first, mental pleasure, comes from building the vision. Remember, most champion gardens begin with a vision in mind: they want a proper English Garden with stiff rows of hedges that stand like soldiers; they want a tropical garden that looks like a permanent Hawaiian vacation. There is a certain pleasure in envisioning the goal.

The second mental pleasure is the physical act of working the soil. Some people use gardening as a light form of exercise or even a way to tan. Plus, sticking your hands in the dirt has certain primal appeal for a lot of people.

The greatest pleasure is watching your vision slowly become a reality. Yes, after planning and planting, the waiting is tough. But it isn't long before tender sprouts start to take root and the gardener can see green shoots arising. Bit by bit, these green shoots grow, and eventually, our patient gardener arrives at the big payoff: his vision has become reality. He has harnessed the power of nature to realize his vision.

Leveraging the power of dividend compounding is just like gardening, in that both photosynthesis and exponential compounding are forces of nature that were discovered by man, but not invented by man. That is why Albert Einstein called compounding, "The 8th wonder of the world". Compounding is a natural law that mankind discovered, and the exponential math works in all kinds of scientific and business disciplines. As the patient dividend gardener, you are planning and executing a vision to make sure that this natural law works for you.

Christmas in July

Why do holidays exist? If you love someone, why wait for their birthday to buy them a gift? Why wait for the pageantry of Christmas when you could just order something from Amazon today?

Holidays exist for two reasons. First, to enforce a kind of discipline. You may love someone, but if you buy them gifts all the time, you may well wind up broke. If you only buy during designated times that are commonly accepted throughout society, you have a better chance of keeping your spending healthy.

Second, to increase the pleasure of buying. There is just something satisfying about waiting until exactly the right moment to purchase. Think about your childhood. How much of your pleasure did you get from the actual birthday gift you got and how much did you get in the waiting for that gift? Daydreaming of what the gift could be, the suspense of it all, the ritual. Random gifts lose their meaning. Gifting as a calendar-based ritual is more pleasurable for most people.

It can be the same for you and your dividends. Most companies pay dividends quarterly; some monthly or yearly. Either way, most companies that do pay dividends strive to maintain a clockwork regularity. This means that you can mark on a calendar, one year in advance, exactly when your pay days will be. Even better than your annual birthday, now your birthday comes four times a year!

The skills you learned as a kid still work today. If you think you are going to get your dividends in the last week of April, then in March you'll start thinking about how best to

75

invest those dividends. Again, you don't need to do this. This reinvestment can be fully automatic if you desire. But many people get pleasure out of the ritual. Just like the expert green thumb that gently clips a vine here or plants a new bush there, you are tending your garden to get to your ultimate goal, except your green thumb is the kind that blossoms dead presidents.

Patient, methodical dividend reinvestment is a great way to get your hands in the soil without becoming a mad day trader. For an investor who generally understands that your involvement in your own investments should be minimal, this is a way to have some fun without taking a chainsaw to your own money garden.

But what if this just isn't enough? You see so many good companies out there: you must buy to capitalize! You see so many bad managers: you must sell to avoid disaster! All of my data, all of my real-world stories, all of my analogies, are a tepid defense against the raging bull that lives inside your head. "Buy!" It screams. "Sell!" It moans. "Data be damned, we need action!"

If you have read this whole book and you still realize that you are the unlucky person who cannot resist the compulsion to buy and sell stocks on a regular basis, I still have one last trick for you. This last technique has worked for even the most hopeless day traders. I know, because it has even worked for me.

Chapter 12: If You Must: Part II (The Gambler)

So far, you have been reading all of my tips and tricks regarding self-discipline and long-term investment, and you'll already have a distinct gut feeling. That gut feeling says either, "Yeah, I can make this work" or "This is never gonna work, I've got to trade. Got to!" If you fall into the first group, just skip this chapter and go on to the next. If you feel the pit of your stomach growling "Must trade … must … trade," don't worry, there is still hope for you! Read on.

If you must trade stocks, buying and selling frequently based on news, rumors, or supposed insights you have had, just go right ahead and do it. Afterall, some forces of nature simply cannot be contained. Just make sure you are gambling at a level you can afford.

I will teach you a specific trick to save you from ruin. It helps to visualize a casino. As we have explored in depth, long-term investing is a game of skill; you need intellectual prowess to pick winning enterprises that will thrive for decades and you need the emotional discipline to hang onto those shares through thick and thin. Buying a stock for a month and selling on a whim becomes a game of chance, just like those in a casino. But casinos are fun. Las Vegas and Macau are some of the largest tourist attractions in the world. Millions of people visit for a casual thrill every year; only a small fraction fall into the corrosive life of a gambling addict. This chapter will teach you how to enjoy it with moderation.

Low Stakes, High Thrills

What if I told you that the amount of money a gambler wagers is often irrelevant? In other words, wagering $10 can be just as exciting as wagering $1000. There are a few reasons for this.

The first reason is that at least 50% of the thrill of gambling is not based on the wager itself, but in the ritual and the pageantry of the casino. Vegas Casinos go to extraordinary lengths to create an all-encompassing, 360° sensory experience; flashing lights, sparkling crystal, card dealers wearing special uniforms. There is a certain pulse-accelerating effect merely entering Lady Luck's lair. Then there is the ritual of approaching and seating yourself at the table, looking around and sizing up the other players at the table, picking up a vibe from the card dealer; the feeling of rubbing your fingers over the chips in your hands. Money rarely has such a physical manifestation in our world anymore, so holding it directly in your hand spikes the adrenaline a bit more.

The highly sophisticated corporations that run major casinos know that over 50% of the thrill comes from the overall experience. That is why the lower stakes gambling tables often look just the same as the higher stakes gambling tables, except the super high rollers gamble in their own rooms, which creates an air of exclusivity and makes sure that low stakes gamblers don't accidentally seat themselves with the big gamblers. I know this, because I've done it myself by accident. I thought I was going to the $10 table and instead I wound up at the $100 table. They look just the same. The pageantry, the uniforms, the gamblers themselves. All the same. If the $1000 table hadn't been behind a velvet rope, I may well have wandered over there by accident.

The point is, you can still get a pretty big jolt of adrenaline from low stakes gambling. The other way of thinking about this arrangement is by considering that 'low stakes' could mean something different to everyone. Have you ever read one of those finance articles with a headline that reads: "Jeff Bezos loses $10 billion in one day." Oh my goodness, what is going on with Amazon? Are they somehow suddenly falling behind? Is the online shopping king about to lose his throne? No, the media just loves to play games with math. To 99.99% of humanity, $10 billion is an unfathomable amount of wealth. But to Bezos, it's actually a rounding error. If his holdings of Amazon stock come in at $200 billion, a small fluctuation in the share price could make it look like he 'lost' $10 billion in one day. Is this low stakes poker? Hell no. Is this low stakes poker to Jeff Bezos? Astoundingly, yes.

It's no different for you. If you are truly of modest means, then gambling $10,000 on risky stock trading might feel like a fortune to you. But if you are a mid-career executive and investor with a growing net worth, you might be able to put $100,000 or more into a stock trading portfolio and still only be playing with a manageable percentage of your net worth. This is actually the exact technique that I recommend for the 'must trade' crowd.

Safety First

A Porsche sports car is a speed machine that simply was not built to drive at the speed limit. Show me a Porsche owner who claims that they only drive 65 miles per hour and I will show you a liar. Some people just feel the need to own a dream machine and drive faster than what is prudent because we only live once.

A smart person enjoys their Porsche while taking a few basic precautions. They will wear a seatbelt, they won't drink and drive, they don't take their Porsche over 80 in a school zone. This is called responsible enjoyment. Well, mostly responsible enjoyment. You can do exactly the same with your stock portfolio.

"If you're going to gamble, be prepared to lose." My uncle, a very accomplished business person, once told me that. That statement has been one of my operating principles for decades. So, if you know yourself and you know that you just can't resist buying and selling stocks, no matter what the data say, you need to first sit down with a spreadsheet and ask yourself the honest and answer this tough question: "How much could I afford to lose without triggering disastrous consequences for my family or my retirement?"

Everyone will have a different answer to that question, but I will help guide you. You absolutely should not be trading stocks with more than 20% of your total net worth. I would really advocate for about 10% of your net worth; enough to give you that thrill you're looking for, but not enough to really damage the golden future that you have worked so hard to build.

One of the greatest elements to this strategy is the fact that the market will evolve with you. In just the last few years, the market has changed to accommodate small investors. It used to be that if you were only trading $1000, or even $10,000, any potential profits would get eaten up by fees. But, now, most people, even at the lowest levels, can trade for free. So, if 10% of your net worth equals $100,000, then put that money aside. If 10% of your net worth equals just $1000, then put that aside. This technique works equally well for Big Shots as well as Aspiring Big Shots.

After this separation, you should have two pots of money. 90% of your money will go into plain, vanilla, conservative index funds and big name 'blue chip' stocks. This is your "slow but steady" portfolio. Choose a brokerage, park the money, and forget that you own it. Read your statements a few times a year. Other than that, ignore this portion of your wealth. This is the portfolio that will really make you rich over time.

Then take your remaining 10% and put that in a separate brokerage. Note, I didn't say a "separate brokerage account." I said, "a separate brokerage." What is the difference?

One individual investor can easily have multiple accounts at the same brokerage. Let's say you have three accounts at E-Trade. When you log into E-Trade, the home screen will show all three accounts next to each other. This is no good! Leaving everything in the same place increases the temptation to trade it all (by the way, the brokerages only make money when you trade, so they do this on purpose to stimulate trading).

Having separate brokerages solves the temptation problem. In this case, perhaps you might put 90% of your assets in plain vanilla index funds with Vanguard and 10% of your assets with Robinhood. That way, you are checking your Robinhood 10 times a week or 10 times a day, but the bulk of your wealth will quietly compound over at Vanguard, year after year, safely out of the limelight.

Human Beings: The Social Animal

Think back to that casino for a minute. How much of the fun and excitement is simply about numbers, odds, and chips and how much is it about other people? Sizing up the other players at the table, trying to read the dealer, reporting and comparing gambling outcomes with friends. People like to win money; but, more importantly, people like other people to know that they won money.

The same thing happens in today's fast-paced stock trading culture. Now that people can trade dozens of times per day from their cell phone and report those trades to friends, family members, or anyone who will listen, huge online communities exist, dedicated exclusively to the 'Fast Money' crowd. These communities exist supposedly because trading is serious business. Hopefully the statistical analysis provided earlier in this book has convinced you that frequent stock trading is, in fact, more like monkey business; it is unlikely to be productive, but is a lot of fun while you're doing it. And, hey, enjoyment needs to be a part of life.

So, now, you are ready for responsible enjoyment. Most of your money is safe in a brokerage account that you rarely check; "Out of sight, out of mind," as the saying goes. You can excuse yourself from a boring meeting at work, go into the bathroom, and use your cell phone to scoop up shares in the latest hot tech IPO. You can post notes on Twitter telling the world about your big score. You can text your WhatsApp chat group to let them know that the High Roller is at it again. Using the 90/10 separation technique, you can enjoy the social and gambling elements of trading, without mortgaging the golden future that you have labored to build.

The idea that people build psychological walls in their lives is well established in pop culture and social science. Bruce Wayne is Batman. Jekyll is Hyde. In post WWII America, many stone cold killers on the battlefield came home to build lives of peaceful suburban normality, never again to discuss what happened on the killing fields of the South Pacific or Europe.

You will build a dual identity for yourself: The Fast Money Wall Street player constantly rearranging his portfolio on his smartphone and the disciplined, judicious, long-term investor, who rarely sells solid blue chip stocks.

But even the judicious, long haul business owner will occasionally need to sell a stock holding. The whole point of this book is to show that you should rarely sell shares. But not never. Nothing in this life is never. There comes a time to sell a business. I will leave you with some critical guidance on this rare event.

Chapter 13: When To Sell

As I've stated dozens of times throughout this book, a successful investor should sell stocks very rarely. However, those rare moments that do emerge are critical. In order to establish a firm framework around the concept, let's return to our dry cleaner analogy.

You and your two siblings own a small dry-cleaning chain. Your Dad started the business decades ago and, through diligence and good fortune, you three siblings have managed to build a local chain of 10 stores. At this point, you have a general manager who does most of the heavy lifting for you; the main tasks of the three owners are to provide high level oversight, high level direction, and count the money that comes in. And the money does come in; quarter after quarter, year after year, for decades on end.

But lately, something has happened. Something new. A friend of yours in the textile business told you about a new kind of fabric technology that means that clothes will rarely need to be cleaned. This new chemical technology means that a shirt could go months without being wrinkled or stained. This is not good for someone who owns a dry-cleaning business.

You do some independent research and find out that this report is true. Although the new fabric technology is just now emerging from the lab, it is possible that in five years or so, the stain-resistant, wrinkle-resistant technology will be worn by millions of people.

You convene a private meeting to discuss the situation with your fellow sibling owners. After much discussion and debate, a division opens up between the three of you. You feel that the value of the business is in grave danger; new clothing with better chemistry means less dry cleaning. Your two siblings think this technology will be just another bump in the road of a lucrative business that has remained almost the same for decades; they want to hold on and attempt to adapt to the change.

So, ⅔ of shareholders don't want to sell the business. Effective control of the business won't change hands. But they do offer to buy you out. Since the business still produces strong cash flow, your sibling partners make you a fair, perhaps even generous, offer. In addition to your serious doubts about the future of the dry-cleaning business, the truth is, you have had your eye on a construction business for a while, which the proceeds could be put towards. After careful thought and some soul searching, you sell out to your sibling partners. This principle and scenario would be similar if you owned ⅓ of a dry-cleaning business or 0.003% of a Fortune 500 company that makes dry cleaning chemicals. A shareholder is a shareholder.

Who got the better deal in the example above? Is it the remaining sibling shareholders, who now have one less shareholder to worry about? Or is it the sibling who liquidated and who now doesn't have to fret about fundamental core changes to the dry-cleaning market? Only time will tell. Two groups of rational people analyzed the situation and came up with two different answers. But the key is, the sale was prompted by fundamental changes in the overall market. You would never sell your shares in a profitable, established business on a whim or a rumor.

Fundamentals, Fundamentals, Fundamentals

As we come to the end of this book, I will leave you with one last Warren Buffett quote. This one is a real zinger.

"Try to invest in a business that an idiot can run. Because, believe me, eventually, an idiot will run it."

With the flick of his sharp tongue, Uncle Warren delivers just as much business knowledge as you might get from a Harvard MBA. In fact, he probably gives you, for free, knowledge that you would never get from a Harvard MBA. This is because Harvard is in the business of charging big bucks to teach people how to manage businesses. How much would they be able to charge if they openly admitted what Buffett already knows? Management hardly matters for a good business.

But how could that be? When we say a 'good' business, we mean one in which the dynamic of supply and demand is in favor of the supplier. There are many reasons why this imbalance may occur and persist, but it's a clear and obvious pattern over time. Successful long-term corporate businesses actually have surprisingly little competition. They sell goods and services that are, for a variety of reasons, scarce. Therefore, they can be run by an idiot and it won't really matter.

Ouch! But think about it. If you're going shopping online, you will likely be using Google to search. Of course, they mint money; they have a 90% market share. You may well buy from Amazon. If you don't like Amazon, perhaps Target or Walmart. But, statistically, you will be buying from the 'Big Three'. All other competitors are minnows next to these three giants.

Even legendary technology upstarts have grown like wildfire and then slowed dramatically as competition emerged. IBM and GE were the high-tech wonder kids of the 60s and 70s. Now? Not so much. I'll let you in on a not-so-little secret. In the 60s and 70s, there was little competition on the global stage. Half of Germany was still occupied by a nightmarish communist regime and the rest of Germany had to live in constant fear of invasion. Japan was just emerging from the smoldering wreckage of WWII. Communist

China was known more for starving children than building iPhones. IBM and GE emerged to provide cutting edge technology, in the form of products and services, that few others could provide at the time. Now dozens of different companies from around the world compete to provide similar services. Guess what? Investors who sold IBM and GE decades ago got the better end of the deal.

The growth of Tesla has been a phenomenon for the record books. Elon Musk and his team created a brand new market for electric cars out of thin air. Against long odds, investors have been hugely rewarded with a return on investment. But, up until now, Musk and Co have had virtually no competition. Now that a firm market for the vehicles has been established, everyone and his brother is coming to grab a slice of it. It could get a lot harder from here for Musk. Will he eventually go the way of IBM and GE? Who knows? But the market is changing in a big way.

The number one reason to sell a stock is if there is a major change in the competitive landscape. It doesn't matter what kind of super MBAs you may be employing to run your company. If they suddenly have double or triple the number of competitors and the overall demand for goods and services remains the same, investment returns will be weak for years or decades ahead.

Another reason to sell would be if there was a core change in the demand for a product that has nothing to do with competition. It wasn't great to be in the horse business when Henry Ford introduced the Model T car. This is like our dry-cleaning example.

Another example of this change in underlying demand could be seen in the energy business. About 10 years ago, I sold all of my oil stocks and I bought into Tesla. It just seemed to me that oil was a necessary evil in society, but as that evil became less and less necessary, demand would drop. Tesla, while risky and unproven, seemed to me to be the technology of the future. As of the writing of this text, my prediction has come true. Major oil stocks have struggled for years. As the saying goes, "The stone age didn't end for lack of stone."

Personal Choices about Personnel

If top management hardly matters in your typical Fortune 500 company, would that mean that personnel changes should not be a reason to sell a stock? The not-so-simple answer to that simple question is "it depends."

Financial history is filled with many examples and counterexamples. For example, when Steve Jobs was unceremoniously fired from the company that he founded, it didn't take the corporate dimwits who replaced him very long to run the once-thriving concern directly into the ground. When a desperate board of directors coaxed Jobs to return years later, the company's fortunes began to turn around almost immediately. In this case, the change in management really did matter.

On the other hand, some of the biggest names in Big Pharma have thrived for a hundred years or more with a constant rotation of top executives. Pfizer, Merck, Eli Lilly … they have ground out profits for decades with such machine-like efficacy that probably the village idiot could probably run the company and still produce a decent return on investment. Ultimately, developing and bringing to market major new pharmaceutical innovations is a very expensive proposition that requires highly specialized knowledge and contacts. About 10 large companies split up a global market of 7,000,000,000 people. That's not a lot of companies serving an almost incomprehensible number of people. The chief executive could probably play golf 7 days a week and still churn out boku bucks for you, the investor.

Perhaps the biggest factor that should be considered is the situation surrounding personnel changes. Mega Corporations, such as Big Pharma, tend to have very well-orchestrated succession plans that are announced well ahead of time. When you are paying an executive $20,000,000 or more each year, and they are a substantial shareholder in the firm, any sudden departure under less than transparent conditions is a major red flag. As we've stated, you can get away with almost anything at the top of Corporate America. If your CEO has just not gotten away with something, you need to investigate the circumstances.

While the CEO that you employ to run your company may or may not be highly competent, they are very likely to be highly ruthless. They have put in decades of 80-hour work weeks to arrive at the pinnacle of Corporate America and demand the same grueling work schedule from their (and your) top executive team. This is great news for you as a passive shareholder. You can sit by the pool with a pina colada because some vice president somewhere is missing his kid's birthday to make more money for the shareholders (you). But sometimes ruthless goes over the line into criminality and corruption. Sometimes way over the line. When this happens, it may be a time to sell.

A great example of this is Wells Fargo Bank. Wells Fargo was one of the most established venerable banks in the world. Millions of Americans were touched by Wells Fargo in one way or another. It turns out, millions of Americans were also screwed raw by the very same Wells Fargo.

The saying "A fish rots from the head down" was true for Wells Fargo. After a storied career climbing the corporate ladder of major American banks, John Stumpf, MBA, was promoted to the role of President of Well Fargo in 2005. Within a few years, he had consolidated his power over the giant bank, achieving the title of Chairman and CEO. Stumpf proceeded to build one of the largest fraud machines the world has ever seen. Subsequent investigations by the SEC, the United States Congress, and just about every other governmental agency, concluded that Stumpf and his team had methodically required associates to fabricate accounts and create millions of credit card accounts that no one had asked for. The response from the Board of Directors was to fire Stumpf and promote his Chief Operating Officer, the very same executive who had partnered with Stumpf for years in the creation of his fraud machine. Of course, this didn't go over well with the media, investors, or the legions of government investigators who proceeded to nail Wells Fargo to the cross. Investors lost billions in fines. Investigations are still ongoing today, 5 years after the fraud was uncovered.

From Stumpf's appointment as President in 2005, through the Great Financial Crisis, to the eve of his downfall, the executive produced a 150% total return for investors. That is a stellar number for a classic, slow growth S&P 500 behemoth. If investors had sold at the first hint of corruption, they would have walked away in good shape. Subsequently, poor Wells Fargo has still not recovered. From 2016 to August 2020, the shares produced a cumulative return of -44%. Just for comparison, Apple produced a return of +450% during that period. In this example, leadership mattered!

You'll have to make your own judgements about leadership and leadership changes in the companies you own. Think about it just as if you owned that dry cleaning chain and you were hiring or firing a general manager.

So, the three main reasons to sell a stock are:

-Meaningful change in a competitive market place
-Meaningful technological and societal change that transforms a market.
-Abrupt or suspicious leadership change.

Tuning Out The Dumb Dumbs

About 95% of the time, the three reasons listed above are the only reasons to sell a long-term stock holding. However, there are all kinds of people who claim to see all kinds of signs and portents that will supposedly allow them to predict outcomes. Most of these analysts are about as reliable as a gypsy palm reader.

Do NOT sell a stock based on an analyst's recommendations. You should be your own analyst. You may choose to watch an analyst interviewed on CNBC or Bloomberg, but this is mostly for entertainment and to get your own ideas flowing. You may occasionally choose to read analyst reports if you get them for free through your brokerage. But mostly, analysts are just people with the very same human limitations as everybody else. They may have more formal education than you, as we have discussed, but some of that education may actually be a liability in terms of accuracy.

Do NOT sell a stock based on chart patterns that some trading 'expert' swears will predict the future. You may have heard terms such as 'support levels', 'golden cross', or 'momentum breakthrough'. These are simply Wall Street translations of the old incantations, 'Hocus', 'Pocus', 'Dominocus'. If it sounds like nonsense, that's because it is nonsense.

Do NOT sell a stock because the company has faced a temporary setback. We have already discussed examples of fundamental problems. These are actually somewhat rare, which is why S&P 500 companies tend to churn out cash decade after decade. An example of a temporary setback would be: A big pharma company suffering a failure in a clinical trial; a car company with a poorly selling new model, a Hollywood studio that releases a bomb of a film.

In all three of these examples, the company has temporarily underperformed. However, these failures do not necessarily indicate an overall failure of the business model. If a Hollywood studio is constantly birthing still-born movies, then there may be something systematically wrong. But a certain amount of episodic failure is just part of business, even big business. Ultimately, there just aren't that many entities out there that have the massive capital base, deep knowledge, and contacts to create and distribute major motion pictures. Most studios can easily shrug off a dud and move on. Instead of you selling shares at a temporary low point, you might actually want to consider buying more.

Money Mind

Ultimately, human beings live in a world shaped and formed by our psychology. Societal ideas that are widespread become accepted as objective facts. People have worked themselves to the bone for money. They have crossed oceans, dug mines, and even harnessed the powers of nature for money. Sadly, many have even killed for money. All for some little green pieces of paper!

The architecture of our mind makes things real or not real. The goal of this book has been to help you draw a mental blueprint that will result in a solid financial house. I already know that you are smart enough, because you don't have to be very smart. I already know that you are educated enough, because you don't have to be very educated. I already know that you have enough money to get started, because you don't need much money to get started.

The questions are:

"Are you disciplined enough?"

"Are you focused enough?"

"Are you ready to become the master of your own emotions?"

Saying "YES!" to these three questions will help you to build your Money Mind. The very same Money Mind that will put real money in your pocket.

Financial Freedom

Retire Now With Dividend Stocks

"I work like a slave to become a master."
-Big Daddy Kane

Introduction: Jailbreak!

Have you ever noticed how many popular films and books tell the story of a man who escapes from jail? Typically, the hero of the story has been imprisoned for a crime he did not commit. When the hero relies on perseverance and intellect to escape his confinement, the audience cheers. If you simply Google "Escape from jail movie," hundreds of entries pop up. One of the more prominent listings is an article entitled, "19 Best Prison Escape Movies of All Time" by Screenrant Magazine.

19? I could see one or two great flicks, but the 19 Greatest of All Time?

In fact, the obsession with men (and it is mostly men) who escape from jail is not even just an American obsession. Hundreds of years ago, one of the hottest selling novels in Europe was The Count of Monte Cristo, the tale of a good man who is wrongly sent to the gulag and, you guessed it, busts out of that place and proceeds to mete out righteous justice to the men who framed him. These tales permeate most cultures and times. Some might even say that the Exodus of the Israelites from Ancient Egypt, as transmitted to billions of Jews, Muslims, and Christians through the holy texts, is in fact the greatest jailbreak of all time! Of course, the Israelites weren't technically in jail, but rather enslaved, which is sort of like being in jail forever through no fault of their own.

Why are tales of imprisonment and self-actualized freedom so appealing across most cultures and epochs?

Could it be that an enormous number of people see themselves as serving a sentence for a crime they didn't commit? Could it be that many, many people live lives of quiet desperation, where they very much feel in bondage, even if no physical chains or bars hold them back? Could it be that, even though we pray for divine help to release us from our servitude, who we really wish would help us…is us?

If you are reading this book, it's very unlikely that you are reading it from an actual jail cell. It's also very unlikely that you are literally kept as a slave (although, even now, some people still endure physical bondage).

But something still ain't right. Society learned a long time ago how to control us, dominate us, and exploit us without a single whip or chain. Money may or may not be the root of all evil, but it certainly does make a lot of people do things that they don't want to do. Every day, millions upon millions of people across this Earth squander their precious time doing things they really don't want to do, because they need the money.

I wrote this book to help you increase the freedom in your life. I wrote this book to help you stand up to organizations or people in your life who have been exploiting and abusing you. I wrote this book to help you take your life back, whether you are 25, 55, or 75.

The way that you take your life back in the modern world is to make sure that money is working for you, rather than you working for it. As Sir Francis Bacon is famous for saying, "Money is an excellent servant, but a cruel master." I am going to teach you how to create passive income through dividend stock investing. It won't be quick, and it won't be easy, but I wrote this book to help you make a plan to become the master of your own life.

I know I can teach you how to do it. Because I broke out myself. If I can go from financial servitude to mastery of my money and my life, then you can, too.

My Story

I will admit right off the bat that I am a lucky guy. I was born to a well-to-do, if not rich, family that provided an outstanding education for me, and allowed me to graduate from a prestigious college debt free. I even got an inheritance in the low six figures, bestowed upon me over a series of years. But sometimes, when you are high born, that just means you have farther to fall.

I had inherited enough money to do something, but not enough to do nothing, so I did what most kids in my position did after college; I got a job. It was horrible. In exchange for what was considered high pay for a new college graduate, the owner of the company had figured out a way for him to get rich by setting up a white-collar sweatshop. Me and my fellow graduates worked seventy to eighty hours a week month after month, year after year. We got 10% of the value we produced while the owner of the company got 90%. That didn't seem fair to me, so I quit. Got another job. Guess what? Same thing.

It soon became clear to my young self that I was never going to make the kind of money that I dreamed of, or live a lifestyle I thought was fair, working for someone else. So, I started a business. And failed. And lost a lot of money. Chastened, and scared, I went back to having a job. Once again, it just gave me a nauseating feeling to watch someone else reap most of the benefit of my long hours and hard work. So, I tried to start another business. I failed again. And lost a lot of money again. This pattern repeated itself often throughout my 20s. I was substantially poorer at 29 then I had been at 21. I frequently woke up at night in a cold sweat, overwhelmed by feelings of frustration, desperation, and shame.

By age 30, I had settled into a "good" career in medical sales. I was lucky by most measures. I made good money. I didn't have a boss directly on top of me. I got to spend time around refined people. But it still felt wrong. No matter how much I sold, the company only wanted to know how much more I was going to sell the next month. I won various awards and honors, but within weeks of winning my little gold star, my boss only wanted to know how much more I was going to bring in. I would routinely see older sales people laid off; decades of faithful service to the company would be rewarded by one month of severance pay and over-priced COBRA health insurance. Even when times were good, it all just felt wrong to me. After losing so much money in my various failed entrepreneurial ventures, I needed a job, but I hated having a job. My existence as a mouse in a corporate maze made me sick every day.

So, I did the only thing that I thought that I could do. I saved. And saved. And saved. I drove used cars. I lived in neighborhoods that were so "up and coming" that I couldn't let people visit me after sundown. I shopped at Marshalls.

This frugal lifestyle was very expensive in other ways. I once broke up with a girl when she started crying after she saw the "new" used car I had procured. One girl dumped me when a homeless man defecated on the sidewalk outside my building with us just a few feet away. Apparently, she didn't like the neighborhood I was living in, and had fears about the kind of future that I would be able to provide for her. I had a marriage that lasted less than a year when it became clear that I had foolishly wed a woman who just didn't understand my burning desire to break away from Corporate America. I can look back at all of these incidents now and laugh. But it was far from funny at the time, and I limped through my early 30s in an anxious and depressed state.

As time went by, it became clear that I was much better at owning businesses than starting or running them. What I mean about that is that my stock market investments started to win. There were frightening times like the great financial crisis of '09, but somehow I just kept going. When everyone else was selling, some little voice inside me said, "keep going," and I would put almost all of my hard won sales commissions into stocks. I don't know if I was any smarter than anyone else; I was probably just more desperate. Every day in my corporate job, my invisible chains felt heavier and heavier; after failing so many times as an entrepreneur, the accumulation of stock market wealth seemed like the only remaining route of escape.

One day I turned around, and I had been saving and investing for twenty years. Much like that prisoner breaking rocks in the sun, the weeks had turned into months, and the months had turned into years, and I was still taking orders from corporate bosses who regularly demonstrated that my happiness meant nothing to them. But my assets were growing. On some level, I knew that I was approaching a financial space where I might not need that corporate paycheck anymore. But, how? I knew lots of rich people from my privileged upbringing. It was quite obvious that most of them did nothing every day. It was also quite obvious that it was purely a financial equation that allowed them to live a life of leisure. But how, exactly, did they do it?

The question became more and more pressing as time went on. In the aftermath of the 2009 financial crisis, the Federal Reserve, the government agency in charge of regulating our currency and our interest rates, had lowered rates to historically unprecedented levels, and then just left them there. Despite endless debates and the hand wringing of pundits and financial analysts, as I write this book today, interest rates are the lowest they have been in a thousand years or more. What I had always learned was that stocks were for accumulating wealth, and bonds were for retirees who wanted to reap safe income from that wealth. Now the Fed had broken the equation by taking away those safe interest payments.

That means that in order for me to quit working for a corporate paycheck and start living off my assets, I would have to start selling stock. That idea certainly felt bad! I had toiled for more than twenty years to fill up my "money bucket" and now suddenly, at only age 43, I was supposed to slowly but surely empty my "money bucket" over the rest of my potentially long life? The thought gave me a feeling of dread that slithered out of my guts and wrapped around my mind like a boa constrictor. I didn't want to keep running on my gerbil wheel, but I didn't want to start selling the stocks that I had so lovingly collected over the years. I needed to find a way to generate income from my investments, without endangering my wealth too much.

Earning money for a company that didn't care about me gave me a terrible feeling, and the only action that seemed to make that feeling go away was to study personal finance. I knew that all of those rich friends of mine still did just about nothing every day, even with interest rates at 1%. If they could do it, there had to be a way for me to do it. So I studied, and I studied. For the first few years of my 40s, in fact, you could say that I really had two jobs. During the day I worked in medical offices, hospitals, and clinics selling products for whatever commission I could wrangle, and at night I learned all about stock dividends. What exactly were dividends? Where did they come from? Why did a company pay them (or not pay them?) What could go wrong? And was it really true that most companies only paid 2 or 3% dividends?

It was my investigation around this last question, and my resulting mastery of the topic, that finally set me free. After a lot of investigation, a lot of learning, and a lot of scary trial and error, I found more and more investments that could pay me quarterly or monthly dividends of 5%, 7%, 9%, or even 11%. Instead of waking up every morning and dreading a job that I didn't want to do, I started to look forward to mornings, because mornings were the time when my dividends appeared in my brokerage account. It started out small, as if the tooth fairy had visited and left me a $20 bill when I was sleeping. But as my knowledge of dividend investing grew, and my confidence in my knowledge grew, so did my dividend income. Instead of waking up to find $20 in my bank account, it became $40. Then $140. Then $400. Then.....you get the idea.

Of course, one of the most famous jailbreak scenes of all time is from The Shawshank Redemption. After years of laborious and risky work, our hero, Andy Dufresne, crawls through the hole he has chiseled in the jail wall, through a sewer pipe, and emerges to dramatic freedom outside of the jail. We savor the drama as Andy is drenched in cleansing rain. For the first time in years, Andy feels like a free man.

After all of the anxiety and disgust that my corporate career caused, you would think that I would have had a dramatic Andy Dufresne moment when I realized that I didn't need a paycheck from my bosses anymore. You would think that the day that the dividend fairy left me enough to pay my bills outright I would have seen the heavens open up and heard the singing of angels. But I didn't.

It's hard to know why. Perhaps because my impending financial freedom wasn't a surprise. It just slowly happened, bit by bit. Just like the way Andy Dufresne slowly chipped away at the tunnel in his jail cell. When I finally crawled out of my hole, I had a feeling of disbelief, as if I were watching a movie called The Corporate Redemption, with me as the star. But I knew how the movie would end. I had done the math thousands of times.

Who I Can Help

I only tell this story about me to give you an idea, an inspiration, about what is very possible for you. Maybe your story is somewhat different. Maybe you actually do have your own business, but it's not what you hoped, and you need to find a way out. Maybe you're in a bad family business and you need to establish some independence. Maybe your corporate career has been good enough, but, as you age, you know that it's time to look to a new, more independent time in your life. You can use the very same techniques that I did to amass dividend stocks that will create passive income for you.

I took a lot of financial beatings over the years so that you don't have to. In the chapters that follow, I will help you understand each kind of dividend-paying security, and how the security may fit into your overall financial plan. Towards the end of this book, we will examine some specific life scenarios and apply what we have learned to create model portfolios that will increase financial freedom in each of the following scenarios.

-If you are just starting out in life, but you already have a creeping feeling that Corporate America is not for you, I can help.

-If you are already middle aged, have some funds saved, but only have a vague notion of how those funds can benefit you, I can help.

-If you are approaching the end of your career, or have been told that your career is over whether or not you want it to be, I can help.

-If you are already retired, and wondering how on earth you are supposed to generate income when bonds only pay 2%, I can help.

Who I CANNOT help are readers who just want specific stock tips handed to them. There are plenty of investor services that will do that for you, and plenty of financial advisors who will be happy to pick specific stocks for you. That's a fine route to take, but it's not the route I offer in the pages that lie ahead.

This book is more of a training manual to help you fend for yourself. As the saying goes, "Hand a man a fish and you feed him for a day; teach him to fish and you feed him for a lifetime."

My goal is to turn you into an outstanding fisherman of passive income. I want this book to be your first step on your journey to waking up in the morning and finding "magic money" in your bank account. Except for you, it won't be magic. It will be something that you made happen because you had a burning desire to be free.

Let's get down to business.

Part 1: Essential Concepts and Core Holdings

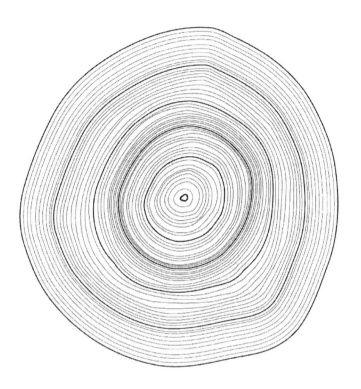

Chapter 1: The Good Old Days

Are you familiar with the term "The Greatest Generation?" This term refers to the wave of Americans born roughly between 1900 and 1930. This demographic of Americans earned this moniker by surviving the Great Depression, grinding to victory in World War II, and fending off nuclear disaster while halting the global advance of Communism. Great indeed!

But what a lot of people don't realize is that the Greatest Generation also enjoyed the greatest retirement of all time. They lucked into the greatest scenario for retirement the world had ever known. If you were born in 1920, then you were 65 in 1985. Financial conditions in 1985 were the exact OPPOSITE of today. Any moron could retire with ease, and millions upon millions of morons did.

What was the special sauce that made retirement so easy for that generation of Americans? Simple. Sky high interest rates. Just as today's interest rates are uncommonly low, from 1980 to the turn of the century, American interest rates were historically high, even though inflation was low. The result was that an unprecedented number of modest, middle class individuals could stop working at 55 or 60 and live off passive income from very secure bonds until 75, 80, or even longer.

When I say "secure" I mean rock-solid secure. The typical conservative retiree would have an assortment of CDs (certificate of deposits), treasury notes, and municipal bonds. All of these were insured by the government in one way or another, and as of 1985, any old grandma could earn 6, 7 or even 8% guaranteed interest for decades to come. If grandma got a little more daring and bought corporate bonds, even bonds of well-known, blue-chip corporations, she could reap 9 or 10%!

Today, the same grandma would be lucky to earn 0.9% interest on the same bonds. Same grandma, same fixed income securities, literally 1/10 of the income that she would have collected 35 years ago. No wonder people today feel screwed! Just to give you an idea of the magnitude of the generational difference in interest rates and what it means in a practical sense, check out this chart:

Expected Cash flow from $1,000,000

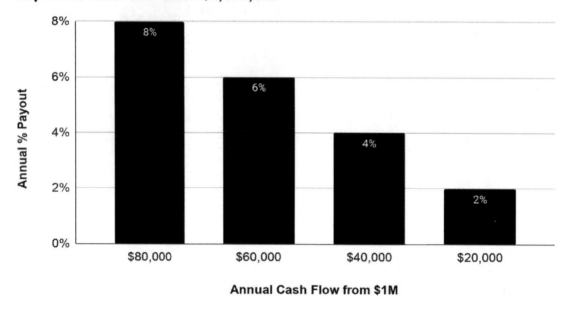

Figure 1

As you can see, the percentage of passive income that you can earn on your investments can make a dramatic difference to your lifestyle. The Greatest Generation had the greatest luck of all time when it came to options for passive income. Today's investors face a transformed landscape.

What Happened?

In life, all kinds of things happen for no reason at all, but in economics, everything happens for a reason. This book is mostly about solutions for today's passive income investor, but before we get to solutions, it's good to understand the problem, and how that problem came to be.

America went through a rough patch in the 1970s. A very rough patch. Inflation soared out of control, almost reaching levels that are commonly associated with developing markets. It got particularly bad in the late 70s and early 80s, when annual inflation hit 12%.

There are a lot of reasons why inflation flew out of control this way. An arab oil embargo against the United States had shocked energy prices. Strong labor unions had the power to constantly ask for higher wages. Some think that the advent of big government social programs like Medicare helped unchain the inflation beast.

Suffice it to say, when President Reagan was elected in 1980, he made it his solemn mission to win the war against runaway inflation. The chief general that he chose to wage this war was Paul Volcker, who became head of the Federal Reserve.

Volcker was quite a character and 100% committed to doing whatever was necessary. If you like history at all, I would recommend looking up images of Paul Volker on the internet. You'll immediately realize that the world of 1982 was a different galaxy because you'll see Volcker chomping on one of his trademark cigars in the middle of an indoor congressional meeting. Volcker meant to rein in inflation, and he wasn't messing around.

So the new Fed chair applied radical shock therapy. He raised interest rates even higher than the rate of inflation. Volcker hit rates so hard that the ten-year treasury note, a bellwether for these kinds of measurements, actually hit 15.68% in 1981! This means that you could lend Uncle Sam $100,000 in 1981 and he would owe you payments of $15,680 each and every year for the next decade, guaranteed by the full faith and credit of the American Federal Government. How is that for passive income?

Of course, it didn't all feel like such a great deal in 1981. Receiving interest payments of 15% isn't so great when annual inflation is running at 12%. But that is where the luck came in.

Volcker's radical shock therapy worked. The aggressive approach caused two sharp recessions, a lot of controversy, and a lot of gnashing of teeth, but Reagan and Volcker held fast. By 1986, annual inflation in America had fallen to a mere 1.9%.

You know what didn't fall? The interest rates that the federal and municipal (local) governments were obligated to pay when they issued bonds in 1981 for ten or thirty years. An entire generation of lucky geezers purchased guaranteed government bonds at 10% or more, while inflation fell to just 1.9%. These payments were locked in for decades. No wonder one of the most popular shows of the 1980s was "The Golden Girls."

One of the laws of physics is that objects in motion tend to stay in motion. The laws of economics are similar. Even with inflation dead, interest rates stayed high for almost two decades. They slowly drifted down and down, but as late as 2000, you could still get 6.58% on a ten-year treasury note. Compare that to less than 2% today. The environment of high interest rates from 1980 to the early 2000s lead to certain pieces of financial advice becoming canonized as financial gospel.

The first piece of financial advice that became gospel is that bonds are almost always safe, and thus a core product for most conservative passive income investors. As Warren

Buffett used to say, "stocks are a great way to get rich; bonds are a great way to stay rich." There are a few reasons why this advice became the norm.

With interest rates so high, you could easily achieve durable passive income through the purchase of bonds guaranteed by the government. Treasury notes are guaranteed by the full faith and credit of the Federal Government. Certificates of Deposit, which in that era paid ample interest, were guaranteed by the FDIC, a federal agency. Municipal bonds were tax free, and guaranteed by state and local governments. Even corporate bonds had legal restrictions called "covenants." Covenants were financial guidelines that borrowing companies were legally bound to follow that acted as protections to investors. Covenants were like guard rails on a road. Even though corporate bonds were not guaranteed by the government, these covenants would make it harder to drive a corporate car off the cliff without investors getting plenty of warning. Today, most corporate bonds have been stripped of covenants. If management drives the corporate car off the road, that's just too bad for investors.

The second piece of conventional wisdom that became ingrained in financial advice was not only that bonds were safe, but you could still make good money on the bonds themselves. In other words, not only would the interest payments be lucrative for an investor, but the price of the bond itself would probably go up on the open market. Why would that be?

Well, think about those 15% notes from 1981, and think about the same ten-year treasury notes earning just 6.8% in 2000. If you had bought notes at 12 or 13%, and a few years later the only new notes available on the market paid 7%, then your older treasury notes would be worth more. A lot more. Year after year, decade after decade, interest rates slowly went down, meaning that legions of "golden girl" retirees actually made a killing on the mega high interest bonds they had purchased in the 1980s and 90s.

If bond income was always safe, and the market price of the bonds typically appreciated as well, that meant that everyone should own bonds. Everyone. I personally know many older, ultra-conservative investors who retired for decades only on bonds. But the standard advice that most financial planners would have given would have been for a youngish retiree to own the "60/40" portfolio. In other words, 60% stocks for growth, 40% bonds for income and security. The idea was that bonds would often go up when stocks went down. In fact, this advice worked great for decades. According to portfoliocharts.com, the "classic" 60/40 portfolio returned in excess of 8% for many years throughout the 80s and 90s. This means that, even with a large portion of your assets being in guaranteed bonds, you would have doubled your money every nine years.

You may have heard the term "black swan event." While it's not a common term in everyday language, it's a critical term in economics. Remember when I said that in economics, much like physics, objects in motion tend to stay in motion? The black swan event is the occurrence that causes that motion to come to a screeching halt. The Black Swan is an unexpected event that crashes the system and changes everything. In the world of geopolitics, the 9/11 attacks were a black swan. In the world of economics, the first major black swan of the 21st century was the great financial crisis of 2008/09.

The causes and results of the financial crisis, which started with mortgages and spread to everything, everywhere, run deep enough to merit a book all in themselves. Suffice it to say, things got bad, fast. Instead of inflation, which had been the bete noire of the Reagan generation, for the first time in modern history, America was confronted with deflation. The crisis crushed our economy so badly that people and organizations were not spending at all. They were nursing huge losses and hoarding any money they could get their hands on. The result could have actually been falling prices, the opposite of inflation. This phenomenon had occurred in Japan at the end of the 20th century, and did tremendous damage to the Japanese lifestyle for decades. Economists knew that deflation, once it takes root, is very hard to exorcise.

So America had a new boogeyman. Deflation. And in order to banish deflation, the Federal Reserve radically lowered interest rates. Interest rates dropped like a rock from 5.25% to effectively 0% in less than a year. It was shock therapy again, except just the opposite of what Volcker had done. The Fed really, really wanted individuals and organizations to borrow money, and spend money, and they were willing to go to almost any lengths to keep the Titanic from sinking. Many critics of the radical new policy felt that such low interest rates were unnatural, and worried about collateral damage. The Fed luminaries replied that the micro rates were just temporary, and more normal rates would quickly be restored when the ship righted itself.

That was twelve years ago. In 2008, the ten-year treasury note (a bellwether interest rate that the Fed only controls indirectly) hit an all time low of 2.16%. Between then and now, it slowly crawled back to a high of 3.05%, only to plummet again to 0.64% during the worst of the coronavirus crisis. At the dawn of the 21st century, that same rate was 6.39% (Data from macrotrends.net).

That Newtonian law of physics had made its weight felt in the world of economics. Micro interest rates that were supposed to be temporary just kept going.

Looking Forward

No one has a crystal ball, but it seems very likely to me that interest rates will remain very low for many years to come. A lot of experts agree with me. One reason is simple momentum; society has reorganized itself around ultra low interest rates, and business people are used to paying 2 or 3% on a loan. Without a black swan event, nothing changes. But there are two more fundamental reasons why I would guess that we will be living with micro rates for a long time.

The first principal reason is that micro interest rates have been very, very supportive of share prices. Asking if low interest rates are good for stock prices is like asking if the Pope is Catholic. There is a very simple acronym that explains why this is so.

TINA. There Is No Alternative. Prior to 2008, stocks and bonds competed with each other for investors. If many portfolios had been historically geared as 60/40 stocks to bonds, that meant that at least 40% of all of the capital in the world, trillions and trillions of dollars, was allotted to bonds. The drastic reduction in interest rates made bonds much less appealing. This meant that an investor looking for anything better than a 2% return actually HAD to invest in stocks.

The TINA effect has resulted in some world-beating returns for stocks since 2009, when the new low interest rate regime really took hold. A simple investment in the S&P 500, a basket of stocks that represents the 500 largest companies in the world, would have delivered an annual return of 13.7%, for a total cumulative return of 312% in just eleven years. In other words, an investor would have turned $10,000 into $31,200 in the past eleven years.

Nothing wrong with that! Or is there? The problem with TINA is that it took choice away from investors. Investors come in all shapes and sizes, with all kinds of different goals, and when you take away options, you are forcing a lot of people into solutions that may not meet their needs. If you have been an aggressive stock market investor who focuses on share price, the last eleven years have been heaven. But if you are a more conservative investor looking to live off the wealth that you have accumulated with care and love over a lifetime, you have been living in hell.

Another way to think about the problem is by noting that, traditionally, investors fell into one of two general categories: investors who were still in accumulation phase, and investors who were in payout phase.

The traditional profile of an accumulator was someone who was still working every day in a job or business, and was interested in growing her savings as aggressively as possible. She would have been willing to take on more risk in exchange for that growth; after all, she was still working every day, so any temporary losses could still be made up through salary and/or active business earnings.

The payout phase investor was someone who now depended on those assets to pay her bills. Whether 45 or 75, the payout phase investor was, by her nature, more cautious and conservative. Because she didn't have an active day to day income, losing capital on risky investments would be more dangerous. These are traditionally the kind of investors who liked to buy safe, steady bonds at 6 or 7%.

At some point, the Greatest Generation faded away, and the Baby Boomers grabbed the wheel to guide society. And in case you haven't noticed, the Baby Boomers are not big on ageing gracefully, and never were into slow-but-steady anything. In fact, many of our most powerful business leaders today are in their 70s or even 80s! They will retire when they are dead; the more powerful or upwardly mobile they are, the more the Baby Boomers seem to want to work forever. So, many of today's "Super Seniors" are stuck in the accumulation phase. They are making more money in their 70s than they ever did. Too much is never enough, so they would never consider taking their foot off of the accelerator and converting their growing fortunes to less aggressive strategies. On a fundamental level, they don't understand the concept of sitting back and relaxing, so they have little regard for older people who are suffering today due to a dearth of traditional passive income options. This is the "Me" generation we are talking about here! If they have to put a gun to grandma's head and force her into the casino of stock market investing in order to make their own equities continue to rise, they will happily do so. The "Super Seniors" who you see leading the government and big business today have grown enormous stock market fortunes over the last eleven years, and they have no intention of letting anyone take away the punch bowl.

The second reason why I would foresee micro interest rates remaining for many years to come is even more scary: Uncle Sam is flat broke. Every year, the Federal Government must borrow more and more money to keep the lights on for the United States, and it is much easier to keep treading on thin ice if interest rates are very low.

Just how and when our national finances began to fray is a robust topic that easily could be a book, or several books, all on its own. In fact, I would recommend the work of Danielle DiMartino Booth. She spent substantial time working at the Federal Reserve, and she has written extensively on the topic of our proud nation's descent into voodoo economics. Suffice it to say, we have been living beyond our means for decades, and it's getting worse all the time. According to Thebalance.com, our national debt in 2008 was $5.8 trillion. By 2020, that debt had skyrocketed to $17.8 trillion! We certainly haven't felt broke during that time. In fact, public services have been mostly the same. As far as I know, we haven't seen any aircraft carriers hawked at garage sales and they haven't pawned the Liberty Bell yet. So how can these numbers work?

The Fed's black magic has been the only thing keeping us out of the poor house. Even though our debt has ballooned over time, our interest payments have barely changed at all. In 2008, our total interest payments due were $253 billion. In 2020, even though our national debt had tripled, our total interest payments were only $375 billion. In terms of our national budget, our interest service actually went down. In other words, in 2008, 8.5% of our national budget went towards interest payments. In 2020, even though our debt had tripled , we spent only 7.8% of our national budget on interest.

One heck of a neat trick, don't you think?

In economics jargon, this phenomenon is called "fiscal dominance." Basically, we may well see low interest rates for a long time, because the Federal Government can't pay its bills any other way. The Fed, the government body in charge of setting interest rates, is supposed to be deciding rates based on the "dual mandate." This refers to the dual goals of creating and protecting maximum employment for Americans while also maintaining stable prices. In reality, the Fed's low interest rates are the only thing standing between our nation and insolvency. It is going to take a jumbo sized black swan for interest rates to ever go back to "the good old days," when a conservative income investor could loan money to Uncle Sam and live off of the interest.

So now we have described the problem that today's passive income investor faces. We have explored the root causes just enough for you to understand some of the forces at work. Bonds haven't paid decent interest rates in years, and it seems highly unlikely that they will anytime soon. And yet, my rich private school friends haven't suddenly gotten jobs or sold the family jewels for income. Somehow they still get monthly or quarterly payments that provide income to pay all of their bills.

How?

Let's find out.

Chapter 2: Common Advice; Commonly Wrong

If there is one chapter of this book that could be considered the most important chapter, this would be it. The concept we are about to discuss can change your life.

It changed mine.

Two false statements separate millions of investors from the passive income they deserve.

Fallacy #1: Average dividends are 2-3%. If a stock pays much more than that, something is wrong.

Fallacy #2: Stocks with high dividends must be more risky. After all, more reward always comes with more risk.

Both of these statements are commonly believed, and not just by amateur investors. Many experienced financial advisors also believe these two statements. To be fair, they seem logical. But the logic is based on a profound misunderstanding about what goes on in corporate boardrooms across the United States.

The reason why these two statements are false is because corporate America is much more lucrative than most people realize. By now, you probably understand that I am not a fan of working in corporate America. But owning corporate America? Now that is another story entirely. Owning corporate America in the form of being a common shareholder is one of the greatest bonanzas in human history.

It turns out that most big name corporations only pay dividends between 1 and 3% because they feel like it. In fact, they could pay more cash to shareholders. Much more.

According to research done by Goldman Sachs, and cited in Barrons's magazine, in 2021, analysts expect the S&P 500 companies to pay out $524 billion in dividends. At the same time, Goldman Sachs expects the very same companies to buy back $602 billion of their own stock. In 2019, a bumper year before the coronavirus crisis, the S&P 500 companies actually bought back $750 billion of their own stock!

So, that "safe" corporation that is safe because it only has a 2% dividend? Turns out, it easily could have paid a 5% dividend. Instead, management chose to spend that money on share buybacks instead. That 3% yielder? Actually, it could have been 6%. Again, management chose not to pay out that much in cash dividends. And this doesn't even begin to take into account all of the money that was spent building corporate empires. According to statista.com, $3.9 trillion dollars changed hands in corporate mergers and acquisitions in 2019. If even a fraction of that money had been paid back to shareholders in dividends, rather than spent gobbling up other corporations, we could easily see dividends of 5% or more across the whole S&P 500.

But we don't. For some reason, corporate boards in the United States tend to think of dividends last when considering how to allot corporate funds. Why?

Dividends Vrs Stock Buybacks

Figure 2 (Source, Goldman Sachs Estimate for 2021, as per Barron's Magazine)

The Rich Are Different From You and Me....

The way that corporate cash flow gets allocated simply comes down to priorities, and the priorities of the corporate Masters of the Universe are quite different from your average mom-and-pop investor.

Theoretically, each publicly traded corporation is overseen by a board of directors composed of shareholders. By law, a majority of the board members must be "independent" shareholders, meaning they hold a certain amount of shares as a passive investment and are not employed by the corporation they govern. The theory is that these people should have interests that are very similar to you and me.

The one thing that separates most S&P 500 corporate directors from you and me is that they are fabulously wealthy. I don't mean well to do, or upwardly mobile. I mean filthy stinking rich, tens or hundreds of millions of dollars rich. This changes their priorities whether they realize it or not.

Oceans of ink have been spilled over the growing gap between the "haves" and the "have nots" in America. It has been pointed out ad nauseum that the top 1% of Americans control an ever growing chunk of the economic pie. Most directors of large corporations are themselves highly accomplished executives, entrepreneurs, or ex-government officials. They have been chosen to direct the most complex, most prestigious corporations in the world based on their stellar record of prior corporate achievement. That means that most major corporations are being guided by people who have been in the 1% for years, if not decades.

It may seem counterintuitive, but the very rich in America do not seek to maximize their income. In fact, quite the opposite. Most very rich people in America spend substantial time and effort attempting to minimize income. Because in America, income means tax. Less income, less tax.

Try this thought exercise. Take a trip to fantasy island for a minute, and let's say your net worth is around $100,000,000, not an unusual achievement for today's high ranking corporate executives. Let's say that most of that net worth is in stocks. It's important to remember that even with that massive net worth, you are still employed. You get a paycheck in excess of $1,000,000 every year that pays for most of your needs. If you want an extra vacation home now and then, you simply cash in a million or two of stock and buy it. But mostly, your $100,0000,000 in net worth just sits there and grows, month by month, year by year. It's simply too much to reasonably spend, and you're not retired anyhow.

Let's look at three scenarios and think about which scenario you would favor if you were in this position. In scenario #1, your $100M is invested mostly in high yield dividend stocks, and you get about 6% in dividends every year. This means that your passive cash income from your investments is a massive $6,000,000 per year. You need to pay tax on that. Currently you would be looking at something in the range of 23% tax, so a cool $1.5 million would have to go to Uncle Sam. You're so rich it doesn't make a difference but....ouch! Who likes sending more than $1M to the feds?

In scenario #2, your $100M fortune is invested in a simple basket of S&P 500 stocks, which yield around 2% in cash dividends every year. So, in this case, you get $2M in passive cash every year and you pay about $450,000 in taxes. Still, ouch, but less ouch.

In scenario #3, your $100M fortune is invested primarily in high flying tech stocks and biotech stocks, most of which don't pay dividends. In this way, your fortune grows, on paper, as much as 12% per year. That amounts to $12,000,000 in paper profits each and every year. You get $0 in cash dividends, which means you pay $0 in tax every year. Your wealth grows by approximately $12,000,000 each and every year, and what you send to Uncle Sam is... nothing. Not bad, right?

Now, if you dare, multiply those numbers in your head by a factor of 10, or even a factor of 100. Many major corporations have directors and shareholders who would laugh at $100M. A lot of tech founders and executives have amassed fortunes well into the billions. What if those stocks paid hefty dividends? Who wants to pay tens, or even hundreds of millions, in tax?

So there you have it. The #1 reason why most major corporations in America pay only modest dividends is because the tycoons that run them don't want to pay tax on cash flow they don't need anyhow. Yes, they vaguely recognize that millions upon millions of small mom-and-pop investors could use enhanced dividends to pay for a modest existence. But most corporate directors are so rich that they live in their own world of wealth and privilege. Everyone they know wants lower income to pay less tax. Low corporate dividends are a symptom of our nation's growing wealth inequality.

Managers In Paradise

In theory, each public corporation is overseen by an independent board of directors who hold the c-suite accountable. In reality, many board members find it more profitable and easier to just go along with entrenched management. A lot of the largest corporations in America are run more for the benefit of the CEO than anybody else. In addition to the reasons discussed above, the c-suite may have a few distinct reasons for shunning dividends and choosing corporate buybacks instead.

Dividends are considered to be "sticky." This means that if a company runs into hard times, and has to cut its dividend, shareholders notice, immediately. If a corporation has paid a 3% dividend for many years, runs into some kind of problem, and is forced to cut that dividend, many long time shareholders will sell, and the stock price may start to fall. From the point of view of management, this makes the situation worse.

However, corporate share repurchases are sort of an invisible force. In theory, each share repurchase increases scarcity of shares, thus making each remaining share more valuable. In reality, there is only a fuzzy relationship between stock buybacks and share price. It's not like shares immediately increase in market value as soon as a buyback is completed. However, if a dividend is cut, the punishment in share price can be harsh and immediate.

Simply put, share buybacks are seen by most corporate managers as more low risk to them. If a dividend is cut, bad things start to happen immediately, and corporate managers can be blamed. Share buybacks are more flexible. Since their tangible benefit is mostly theoretical anyway, buybacks can be cut with few repercussions for management. How is that for twisted logic?

Another reason why some corporate managers choose stock buybacks over dividends is because they can use share buybacks to directly rig their pay packages. Many high level corporate executives earn multi-million-dollar bonuses based on a measure that is called "Per Share Earnings." This is the total earnings of the corporation, divided by the number of shares outstanding. So, if a company makes $100M and has 1 million shares outstanding on the market, then the earnings per share are $100. However, if the company makes the same $100M, and buys back 10% of its shares, then we divide $100M by only 900,000 outstanding shares. Shazam! Now the company earns $111.11 per share, even though the total earnings stayed the same. Cue massive bonus and third vacation property.

Why is this bit of financial chicanery allowed to happen in broad daylight? Remember, the CEO chooses the board of directors, and then the board of directors oversees the CEO. If that seems like an incestuous little arrangement, it is. But somehow corporate America hands in massive profits decade after decade, and share prices go up and up, so few people complain.

Speaking of massive profits: there is one last reason why many brand names and major corporations pay out much lower dividends than they could. They are so grotesquely profitable that they really don't need to draw any attention to the cozy racket they have set up. According to research done by Rakesh Shamra at Investopedia.com, the iPhone 7, which retailed for about $649 in 2016, cost about $5 in labor to assemble. Major corporations have piled up billions and billions in excess cash that is just sitting around, even after buying back countless billions of stock AND paying a dividend. If Apple paid out a 6% dividend, instead of its current 1% dividend, do you think people might start to wonder if they were paying too much for an iPhone?

Again, the people who make big decisions at Apple are so unfathomably wealthy that they will never spend the vast fortunes they have accumulated. So, given that cash flow is the last thing they need, why draw unneeded attention to the fact that they found a way to mint money by exploiting foreign labor? They would prefer to squirrel away hundreds of billions of dollars, which is what they have done, rather than drag it into the light where it could be scrutinized. Small dividends mean small transparency and small accountability for the corporate titans who reign over today's S&P 500 companies.

Saved By The Bell

You can think of the investing ecosystem like a high school. In that high school, the S&P 500 stocks represent "the cool kids." Rock stars like Tesla, Google, and Facebook are the center of all of the attention, and they set the tempo that everyone else moves to. But if you ever went to high school, you know that there are all kinds of other cliques, many of which provide unique value. You had the drama kids, the band nerds, and the technogeeks. You had the grade grubbers, the stoners, and the foreign exchange students. If there is one lesson that many of us learned as the years have gone by, it's that a lot of those less popular kids have done just fine as they have gone out into the world.

I am going to teach you to do just fine by ignoring what the cool kids are doing and looking for value in other parts of the equity ecosystem. The S&P 500 is just one subset of publicly traded companies. In reality, there are thousands of different investments to choose from.

Stocks that pay high dividends are not necessarily dangerous, and there may not be anything wrong with them at all. They're just poorly understood, like that computer nerd back in high school who is a tech billionaire today. He was overlooked in high school because he thought differently than others, and he didn't give a flip about what the cool kids were doing. But anyone with a discerning eye back then would have known that shunned kid was going somewhere.

How can we gain a discerning eye? How do we identify value? How do we figure out which stocks will keep pumping out passive income forever, and which ones are duds?

In the next chapter we will begin to build your research toolkit, so you can find the answers to these investment questions and reap the corresponding profits.

Chapter 3: Fallen Angels

The first way to look for exceptional dividend stocks is to find the ones that are hiding in plain sight. These are a group of stocks that I call "fallen angels": Well-known companies who have a high dividend yield because they have fallen out of favor. When a stock becomes unpopular, its share price can fall, even though the underlying business still generates plenty of free cash flow. This can lead to a situation where a stock that used to yield 2% now yields 4%, or a stock that used to yield 3% now yields 6%. The math works like this. If your shares trade at $10, and pay a $0.25 dividend, then your dividend yield is 2.5%. Very average. But if your share price falls to $5, and you still pay the same $0.25 dividend, all of the sudden your stock boasts a 5% dividend. Better than average. Of course, if you owned the stock at $10, and now it's worth $5, you won't be happy. But if you find the stock after the fall, when it's trading at just $5 and paying a meaty 5% dividend, you may well have just found yourself a deal.

Sometimes, these former belles of the ball have been eschewed for a good reason. Maybe something is wrong in their industry or with their specific product. Often, they simply sell a product or service that has gone out of style with Wall Street.

Was there anything wrong with those Z-Cavaricci pants that you used to wear with pride to the best parties? No, they worked just fine. At some point, however, you stopped wearing them because everyone else did. They just went out of style. That is what happens with a "fallen angel stock.

GILEAD SCIENCES: A Case Study

As I write this, one excellent example of a fallen angel is Gilead Sciences. Over the last five years, Gilead's share price has slumped from $100 per share to just $58 per share. For reference, the S&P 500 returned a total of 97% for those same five years. So, if you had bought almost any other stock, you could have doubled your money in five years. If you bought Gilead, you actually cut your money in half. Wow! This must really be a company in trouble, right?

Not really. In 2019, as the company's shares plumbed all new lows, Gilead still produced $9 billion in positive cash flow! In fact, that $9 billion was more than the previous year's positive cash flow of $8.4 billion. The company had $24 billion in cash just laying around, and only very modest debt at very low interest rates.

As Gilead has seen its share price shrivel, the dividend has only gone UP. In 2015, the biotech firm paid roughly a 1.5% dividend. As of 2020, that dividend has approached 5%.

This huge rise in the dividend yield has happened for two reasons. First, as the share price has fallen, even if management had only maintained the same dividend, the dividend yield would have grown as a percentage. However, management did not just hold the dividend steady. They actually grew the dividend reliably, year after year. In 2015, the dividend was $0.43 per share per quarter, and today that dividend stands at $0.68 per share per quarter.

Many investors, even professional investors, see this kind of situation and immediately take a pass. If a company has faced headwinds, and the stock price has fallen, but the dividend has actually gone up, they assume that the company is paying out money it doesn't have in order to keep investors from abandoning ship. The assumption is that a desperate company is paying out whatever it can now, sacrificing future growth by paying out cash that it shouldn't. Sometimes that is the case. But often, it isn't, and that is where the opportunity comes in.

While Gilead's revenue has gone in the wrong direction over the last few years, the core business is still a prodigious cash generation machine, and we can see that Gilead can afford it's dividend raises with ease. In 2019, the business generated $9.1 billion in free cash flow, but only paid out $3.2 billion as a dividend. Over the years between 2015 and 2020, while Gilead was busy hiking its dividend, the company invested an average of $4 billion a year in research and development, and ended the period with a massive $24 billion cash balance in its bank account. A company with a constantly rising dividend, a constantly rising bank account, and a steady commitment to investment in research and development. Does this sound like a sinking ship to you?

So why was the share price punished so viciously over the last few years? Poor Gilead just got its story wrong. Perhaps you have heard the phrase "story stock?" An example of a story stock would be Tesla. A charismatic founder, a clear mission to save the world, legions of nerdy fans. Wall Street has paid little attention to the mathematical fundamentals of Tesla, because the story is just so compelling. Gilead used to be the Tesla of biotech, until, one day, it wasn't. Turns out that pundits and fanboys who fall in love with a stock can just as easily turn sour. If you have ever experienced a love affair gone bad, you may know the feeling.

Gilead's original claim to fame was that they pioneered the first effective treatment for HIV. If you lived through the 80s and 90s, you know that HIV had an all pervasive effect on the global cultural conversation, in the same way climate change does today. Gilead rocketed from obscurity to dazzling fame by taking a dagger to the heart of the boogeyman who haunted millions of nightmares around the globe.

Gilead didn't cure HIV, but they did get the epidemic under control by creating a medical regimen that has helped millions of patients live healthy lives for decades. For their next trick, they aimed even bigger. No more indefinite treatments. Gilead was aiming to use their hard-earned scientific knowledge to slay some viruses, once and for all.

Amazingly, they did. Starting in 2013, Gilead found a way to cure hepatitis C. Although not as visible as HIV had been, the Center for Disease Control estimated that formerly incurable hepatitis C killed as many as 19,659 Americans per year by 2014; that's more than all other infectious diseases combined.

Gilead had an instant phenomena on its hands; revenue and profit skyrocketed overnight. So did the share price. The value of the company quadrupled in just a few years.

In one of the more cruel ironies in the annals of American business history, Gilead cured its way into a stock crash. It's hepatitis C treatment has been so effective that less and less people contract and spread hepatitis. According to the CDC's National Progress Report on Hepatitis C, the mortality rate of the disease had dropped from 5 per 100,000 Americans to 3.72 per 100,000 Americans just between 2013 and 2018, with the trend pointing to further declines heading into the 2020s. Great news for patients. Great news for humanity. Terrible news for Gilead.

The result at Gilead was falling revenue. Just as the company had enjoyed a massive boom in revenue from 2013 to 2015, they have endured a slow but steady decline as their own medical breakthrough has brought America's hepatitis C epidemic under control. Talk about a victim of your own success!

The important thing to remember in this case study is that Gilead still makes money. A lot of money. Gilead still has cash on hand. A lot of cash on hand. And Gilead still pays great dividends. Lately, Gilead has decided to deploy these impressive resources in the quest to reignite growth. They have brought in a new CEO and made a string of big name acquisitions. It may take years for them to return to the glory of their hepatitis C days. But in the meantime, that dividend just keeps growing.

Gilead was kicked out of investing heaven because their profit and loss statement, prepared under Generally Accepted Accounting Principles (GAAP), no longer told the sexy biotech growth story that many impatient investors demand. However, Gilead's rock solid cash flow and balance sheet tell a different story. It's this chasm between theoretical accounting for growth and real world accounting for cash flow where the skilful dividend investor finds the best opportunities. We will go over this technique in more detail at the end of the chapter, but just remember the following principle: while everyone else is running out the door in a stampede, you just remember to double check and see if they dropped anything of value. Sometimes in their panic to move their money to the latest hot stock, they leave some juicy dividends ripe for the taking.

Sectors In Exile

In the case study above, we explored one particular stock with specific problems that have led it to be shunned by investors who have missed the value that lies just under the surface.

However, it's not uncommon for entire sectors to fall out of favor. Traditional Wall Street analysts are very big on categorizing stocks so that they can compare "like" with "like" companies. One reason for this is because in an apples-to-apples comparison, all of the inputs and outputs are theoretically the same for all of the players, therefore analysts can focus on a narrow set of factors that might differentiate one company from another. For example, Wall Street analysts would typically group all gold mining companies together. The theory would be that they all have similar raw inputs (there is the same amount of gold in the world for everyone to discover) and similar outputs (gold demand is the same for every seller of gold….gold demand is global). Therefore, if company X did better than company Y, it would mean that company X had better management, or better partners.

While these kinds of groupings may make life easier for Wall Street, they often lead to a phenomenon where entire sectors fall out of favor all at once. If the fundamentals of a sector no longer seem appealing, then all of the companies in that bucket are just ignored. Sometimes whole sectors should be ignored. But often, the fact that an entire sector comprised of dozens of companies has been painted with the same brush means opportunity for the astute investor.

One example of a sector that is currently on the outs' is oil. This may be an example of a sector that has fallen out of favor for some good reasons. Some people won't touch oil due to moral concerns related to climate change. Others feel that oil is simply yesterday's resource. Either way, it has led to a situation where massive international energy corporations are selling for dirt cheap. At some point during 2020, Exxon Mobil, one of the largest energy companies in the world, had seen it's share price drop so far that it was yielding 10%! Exxon, like all oil companies, had a terrible 2020 as the coronavirus created historic turmoil in the energy markets. Exxon may struggle as we move through the 21st century and renewable energy becomes dominant. However, according to Industr.com, there are currently 2,000,000,000 internal combustion engines on the road, and, as of today, 95% of new vehicles still need gas. The oil industry will continue to churn out cash flow for many years to come, and may be a suitable investment for a senior citizen who isn't overly concerned about climate change. A reliable 10% yield from Exxon Mobil would go a long way towards helping grandma squeeze a decent income from a modest nest egg.

Another example of an industry that has been left for dead is the tobacco industry. As the link between tobacco and cancer has been more and more firmly established, smoking rates have plummeted, which you would think would have made tobacco a terrible investment. You would be wrong. The corporate scoundrels who run Altria, one of the world's largest tobacco companies, found a way to produce $4.9 billion in free cash flow in just the first six months of 2020, a time period that witnessed one of the worst economic contractions in history. Of that, Altria pays out a whopping 77%, leaving the stock with a massive 8% dividend. You might have very good reasons to stay away from investments in tobacco, but the sure death of the tobacco industry shouldn't be one of them. If Altria could produce bountiful cash flow during one of the worst economic crises of the last 100 years, you can be sure that the earnings are more than just smoke and mirrors.

So you might understand why an industry that profits by accelerating death might have fallen from grace in the investment community. But what about an industry dedicated to preserving life? The pharmaceutical industry, or Big Pharma, is a classic example of a sector that has gone in and out of style dozens of times over the decades. Often accused of exploiting the vulnerable through questionable pricing practices, in 2020 Big Pharma was America's knight in shining armor, delivering a raft of coronavirus treatments in record time. Based on Big Pharma's heroic performance during our time of national crisis, suddenly the industry was invited back into the country club of "hot" sectors. But this hasn't always been the case.

As recently as 2018, the Wall Street Journal published an article entitled, "What is Ailing the Drug Industry?" (June 22, 2018). The WSJ described Big Pharma as the definition of an out of fashion industry:

U.S. health-care spending regularly grows faster than inflation and has reached about 18% of gross domestic product. Prescription drugs are a major component of that sum. The Centers for Medicare and Medicaid Services projects that total U.S. drug spending will rise by 68% to $600 billion by 2026. Meanwhile, the Food and Drug Administration is approving new medicines at a brisk rate and venture capitalists have poured billions into biotech startups.

Yet the stock market is treating drugmakers as a struggling industry. The NYSE Arca Pharmaceutical Index has underperformed the S&P 500 by nearly 30 percentage points over the past two years. Not all drug companies are suffering. Over that same time frame, an index of small biotech stocks has beaten the S&P 500 by more than 50 percentage points.

You may notice in the quotation above that the WSJ took pains to point out that not all components of the drug industry were underperforming. In fact, biotech, a risky sub-sector famous for a casino-like ethos, was booming. Society was spending on medicines at a growing rate. But big, established pharmaceutical companies like Pfizer, Eli Lilly, and Johnson&Johnson were left out in the cold, like a bunch of nerds refused entrance to the hottest dance club in town.

The Wall Street Journal went on to offer all kinds of theories as to why biotech was piling up high returns while it's more mature cousin, Big Pharma, languished. But the real reason was a lack of sex appeal. As time goes by, memories of the Trump years may start to fade. But when the host of The Apprentice swept into Washington like a tornado, it awakened what many commentators call "the animal spirits," the idea that any risk is a good risk, and the sky's the limit. The early Trump years were what analysts call a "risk on environment." Unprofitable young biotech companies with big futures just seemed a lot more alluring than stodgy, established Big Pharma companies with a century of dividend paying credentials under their belt.

This mismatch between what was in style in 2016 and what would meet the needs of an income-oriented investor meant a huge opportunity. Many brand name pharmaceutical stocks, which had been reliably pumping out dividends for decades, could be purchased with a dividend yield between 4 and 6%. Compare that to 2% on most bonds. In the "Go Go" beginning of the Trump era, Big Pharma was the dowdy older sister who wasn't invited to the party. But contrarian dividend hunters found plenty to value, and today they enjoy plentiful dividends that show up like clockwork every three months.

Accounting and You

This is the part of the book where I dispense some unpopular advice. If you want to be able to identify the best fallen angel opportunities for yourself, you need to learn some basic accounting. This is advice coming from a guy who was a mediocre math student who never made it past basic algebra in school. In fact, accounting is less like a complicated math discipline and more like a language. Maybe you are slapping your forehead with your hand and groaning right now; maybe you struggled through two years of high school French and quit. Learning a language, even the language of business, is not popular for most people. But it may not be as hard as you imagine. Think of the example of Martin Luther.

You may remember from history class or religious school that Martin Luther was the founder of Protestant Christianity in the 16th century. Luther's ideas upset a lot of the Powers that Were, and as such, he spent a lot of time in jail. How do you pass the time if you are stuck in a hellish, medieval jail filled with rats and plague? If you are the founder of a major world religious movement, you study religion. In Luther's time, that meant studying in Latin, Ancient Greek, and Hebrew. His native language was German. I remember being dazzled at the revelation. How on earth would a 16th century German have mastered languages that had been dead for a thousand years? In an era when most people couldn't read at all, how was pious Martin Luther mastering three different obscure languages from his jail cell?

It turns out that Luther, and religious scholars like him, only had to learn a very limited form of each language. Luther learned to study biblical texts in their original languages, but he wasn't about to start having long conversations in Ancient Greek with his German cellmates. Luther only needed to understand these languages in certain, very specific contexts, contexts that are mostly fixed and predictable. Learning the language of accounting would be the same for an income-oriented investor. You don't need to earn an accounting degree or become a Certified Public Accountant. To find the best fallen angel investment opportunities, you just need to learn to identify certain specific numerical situations.

One example of these kinds of opportunities is the dichotomy that often exists between a company's accrual accounting and its cash accounting. By law, each publicly traded company must publish a profit and loss statement, which is governed by the rules of accrual accounting, and a cash flow statement, which is governed by cash accounting. The company must also publish a balance sheet statement, which is a summary of the company's assets and liabilities at a particular moment in time.

Accrual accounting is a kind of accounting that factors in theoretical costs and revenues, and gives tangible numbers to intangible concepts. For example, if your company hands out a billion dollars in stock options, that is noted as an expense in the accrual accounting of the profit and loss statement. That $1 billion in stock options cost the company $0 in actual cash out the door, but by law it still shows up as an expense in the profit and loss (P&L).

The cash flow statement only factors in the tangible cash that goes out and comes into the business. If you were running a lemonade stand as a kid, you were concerned with the cash flow statement. You factored in the money you put in, you factored in the money you took out, and if you took out more than you put in, you were making money.

The opportunity arises because 90% of investors only pay attention to the P&L statement. The P&L statement is what grabs all of the headlines in the financial media. A shocking number of growth stocks somehow manage a soaring share price with no cash flow at all. The fantasy world of the P&L statement can have a very real effect on share price. You are looking for the instances where the share price crashes because of an unattractive P&L, even though the cash flow revealed on the cash flow statement remains hearty.

Let's circle back to the example of Gilead that we discussed earlier. From a P&L perspective, Gilead looked bad. Revenue went down a few years in a row. That is the headline that the world saw. But remember what we found when we dug a little deeper and we scrutinized the cash flows? We found a company that was still minting money like clockwork. We found a company that could easily maintain its hefty dividend while still reinvesting back into the business. All of this bounty was lost on investors who only focused on the P&L statement.

If you take a basic accounting class, available for free or cheap online, or you read *Accounting for Dummies*, you will already be ahead of 90% of investors. Investing in fallen angels is all about finding opportunities that others have missed. The reward is a lucrative, income-producing equity that you bought on sale.

Chapter 4: Dividend Growth Investing

A lot of people view dividend stocks as a way to preserve wealth. A way to gain safe and regular income from wealth that has already been accumulated. But did you know that income stocks can also be an effective way to get rich? Although many dividend stocks lack the panache and media buzz of "growth" stocks such as big technology names, there is a method of dividend investing that can help you grow your wealth at an exponential rate.

This method is referred to as "dividend growth investing." The idea may seem counterintuitive at first, but some basic arithmetic reveals the awesome compounding power of boring stocks.

The basic concept is the following: don't focus on stocks with the highest dividend yields, focus on stocks that grow their dividend at a very high and sustained rate. In other words, don't worry about scoring a stock that currently yields 10%. Rather, focus on finding a stock with a modest dividend yield that is growing at an annual rate of 10%.

This methodology is recommended for anyone who will measure their retirement in decades rather than years. If you are a 75-year-old retiree, you would probably be better off just choosing stocks that have high dividend yields now. However, if you have just quit your corporate career at age 45, and want to live off your dividend income for decades to come, dividend growth investing makes sense for you. Dividend growth investing is also a recommendable technique for people who either can't or don't want to do a lot of research. This is a very popular method, so it's easy to find lists online of brand name stocks that grow their dividend rapidly.

Simple Math. Shocking Math.

As I mentioned earlier, I was never great at math in school. But even some basic arithmetic can demonstrate the amazing outcomes that are possible through dividend growth investing.

To start with, let's ask ourselves the following: what constitutes above average dividend growth? Wyo Investments recently published a piece on this topic on the website Seeking Alpha. The author is a young retiree with eleven years of dividend growth investment under his belt. Here is his criteria for "high dividend growth. "My current goal is twofold; Maintain 7% dividend growth without reinvesting dividends. Achieve 10% dividend growth with reinvesting dividends." (Seeking Alpha, 1/5/21). The author goes on to list a portfolio of 40 stocks, many of which are household names, that have met that criteria.

What has been the practical implications of that growth? Between the years 2016 and 2021, his overall dividend income increased from $8,000 per year to $12,500 per year. That is without him investing any additional capital; sometimes he spent his dividends, sometimes he reinvested them. Either way, he grew his passive income by over 50% in just five years. How many of you have gotten a 50% raise at your job over just five years?

Another way of thinking of the growth potential is simply to compare your rate of dividend growth to the rate of inflation. During the time period referenced above, inflation hovered somewhere around 2% annually. That means that Wyo Investments easily found investments with passive income streams that grew at four times the rate of inflation. You can see the powerful results achieved in just five years. What would the results look like over longer periods of time?

I'd Like To Buy The World a Coke

Typically when we think of millionaire-maker stocks, we imagine high flying growth stocks like Tesla, Google, or some biotech firm. But what if I told you that you walk by liquid gold every time you go to your grocery store? Plain, old, boring Coca-Cola has made a mind boggling fortune for Warren Buffett and many other investors.

Before we go into the specific math of Coca-Cola, we need to discuss a key vocabulary lesson. Typically, when we are talking about income producing stocks, the term used to discuss the current dividend is "dividend yield." This is a percentage-based measure of how much the current dividend is. So, for example, if company X has a share price $10, and is paying a $0.50 annual dividend, then company X currently has a dividend yield of 5%.

But the key concept to remember is that dividend yield is a fluid measurement that changes with market conditions over time. Your costs do not. So, if company X's share price slowly rises to $20 over time, and the dividend slowly rises to $1 as well, then your current dividend yield remains 5%. But you bought the stock at $10 years ago. Now the dividend has risen to $1 per year. That means that your base cost has stayed the same, and your yield has doubled. So, your current dividend yield is 5%, but your "yield to cost" is a whopping 10%. This is the secret formula that makes boring companies like Coke so lucrative over time.

Author Sean Williams explained how Buffett has profited immensely from his long term investments in Coke and American Express:

Buffett also holds true to his winners. For instance, Coca-Cola has been a Berkshire Hathaway holding for more than three decades, while American Express has been a consistent holding for more than 25 years. As these two companies have appreciated in value and grown their payouts over time, Berkshire's annual yield based on the original cost basis for Coca-Cola and American Express has soared.

Paying out almost $261 million annually, yet with a cost basis of only $1.287 billion, AmEx is providing a roughly 20% yield each year. Meanwhile, Coca-Cola's $656 million in annual dividends, relative to its $1.299 billion cost basis, means it provides a 50.5% yield from its initial cost basis every year. (Fool.com, 3/5/20)

Boring old Coca-Cola has made a fortune for Warren Buffet. It can do the same for you.

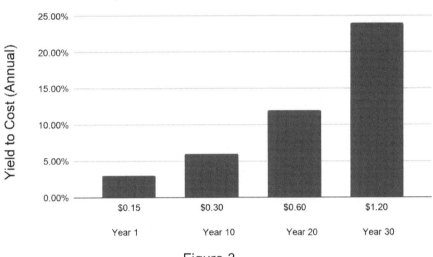

Figure 3

You buy shares in a theoretical company at $5. Even if they raise the dividend by 7% annually, the cost you paid for those shares will always remain fixed. Thus, your "Yield to Cost" as a percentage just goes up year after year, no matter how big the dividend grows. Although not pictured in this illustration, the investor likely benefited from share price appreciation as well, which would further boost overall returns.

Money For Nuthin' and Divs For Free

Perhaps the best thing about dividend growth investment is that it's uncommonly easy. If you found the search for fallen angel stocks to be intimidating and exhausting, then the relative ease of dividend growth investing may appeal to you.

A great place to start shopping for dividend growth is the "dividend aristocrats." A company is dubbed a dividend aristocrat if it has grown its dividend every single year for 25 consecutive years. Think about all of the challenges that have arisen over the last 25 years! The tech bubble crash, 9/11, the Great Recession. For 64 very special publicly traded firms, all of these blows barely put a dent in their armor. They just kept paying more and more no matter what was going on in society.

According to Moneyinvestexpert.com, amongst these 64 companies, the average dividend growth rate was 6% annually, or three times the rate of inflation. But that was just the average. Of the 64 dividend aristocrats, the top had often grown their dividends at an annual rate of 12% or more over the last decade. That means that these "boring" companies doubled their dividend payout every six years! Have you ever had a job where you could double your salary every six years for decades on end?

It's easy to identify great stocks for your dividend growth portfolio. Just Google "dividend aristocrats" and "dividend growth rate" or "DGR" and numerous lists will appear.

If you don't even want to do that, you can easily harness the power of dividend growth investing through exchange traded funds. Here is a list of five different exchange traded funds that will help you harness the power of dividend growth without ever losing a night's sleep (from Investopedia.com):

- ProShares S&P 500 Dividend Aristocrats ETF (NOBL)
- ProShares S&P Technology Dividend Aristocrats ETF (TDV)
- SPDR S&P Dividend ETF (SDY)
- SPDR S&P Global Dividend ETF (WDIV)
- ProShares S&P MidCap 400 Dividend Aristocrats ETF (REGL)

This is a powerful strategy considering the small amount of effort required. If you had bought one of the more established exchange traded funds above, SDY, in 2010, you would have turned $46 into $109 even if you spent the dividend every year. If you invest in dividend aristocrats and hold onto these stocks through thick and thin, you will be the one who winds up feeling like a king.

Chapter 5: European Stocks

Ah, Europe, sweet Europe. French baguettes and Spanish tapas. Beer and wine ripened in the Old World sun. Six-week vacations. Certainly a continent known for easy living and a penchant for the high life.

But did you know that it's also easy to find high dividend paying stocks in Europe? This doesn't require special knowledge, or even much work at all. Many Euro stocks simply pay higher dividends than their American equivalents. For example, the EuroStoxx 50, a broad index of the fifty largest European companies, has paid a median divided yield of 3% over the last five years; at times that yield has gone as high as 4.22%. By comparison, the S&P 500 in America has typically yielded around 1.8% during the same time period. With no skill at all, you could earn double the dividend yield of American stocks just by buying a European exchange traded fund.

Many critics could say that companies that pay "too much" dividend are not growing. They say something must be wrong if they pay double the dividend of their American competitors. This is a wrongheaded notion. Remember the math we went over in earlier chapters. Most major American companies have enough cash flow that they could easily pay much higher dividends. They choose not to. Instead, they typically choose to buy back their own stock. Europeans prefer plain old dividends.

Math is math, and greed is greed. History shows that all human beings, whether they be from Philadelphia or Flanders, like to get paid. So why would Europeans choose to receive payment in the form of dividends rather than share buybacks?

A different history and a different culture lead to different choices. Let's take a look at three reasons why European capitalists prefer dividends.

The Noble Dividend

One of the most important reasons why large, publicly traded European companies tend to reward shareholders with dividends rather than buybacks is the ownership structure. Many large, brand-name Euro companies are actually still controlled by founding families. This arrangement would NOT be like Walmart now, which is controlled by Sam Walton's four children. This would be like Walmart circa the year 2100, when it is controlled by Sam Walton's 25 great grandchildren.

In the Old World, everything is, well, old. So, large, well-known corporations that have been in business for hundreds of years are still controlled by families. Because it's been so many generations, the family shareholdings themselves are often split between dozens of cousins, which, as you can imagine, can lead to some migraine-inducing ownership structures.

One example would be Roche. Roche is a global pharmaceutical giant with around 95,000 employees. The company was founded in Basel, Switzerland in 1896, and is still domiciled in Switzerland. The total value of the company's shares on the open market is $300,000,000,000, of which half are still owned by dozens of cousins descendent from the founding Hoffmann family.

So, a private family still controls the third largest pharmaceutical company in the world. Nice work if you can get it. The way they got it was by never selling shares. Roche has shunned share buybacks in comparison to it's American counterparts because selling shares would not be in the interest of the controlling family. The only way that share buybacks work is if someone wants to sell shares. The members of the Hoffmann family haven't sold in over a century.

In the world of Euro stocks, selling shares means selling control for some very, very rich families. So, dividends become the preferred method of rewarding shareholders. According to moneyinvestexpert.com, Roche has raised the dividend for 32 consecutive years. Every shareholder gets the same dividend payout, whether you are a member of the Hoffmann family, or just a plain Deiter in the cobblestoned street. That annual cash payout has quintupled since the year 2000. As I write this, the current share price is $43 and the dividend yield is 1.7%. But remember, the Hoffmann family has owned the same shares since they were worth just $4 or less. So they could easily be reaping a 20% annual yield to cost, or even much more. Who needs the aggravation of share buybacks? Meaty dividends have funded a regal lifestyle for Roche's controlling shareholders for the last century.

Another reason why founding families would be reluctant to dilute their corporate control by selling is because of who their other shareholders are. In Europe, most major companies have several large blocks of shareholders. In Germany, for example, by law labor unions must have a certain percentage of representation on the board of directors. At the same time, it's not uncommon for local or even national governments to own a large block of shares. So, a controlling family that sells shares to get quick cash risks handing corporate control to the labor unions, or worse still, the government.

Due to these baroque shareholder structures, founding families are often in a tug-of-war with other large shareholders. Lately, this has been a very hot topic at Volkswagen, the largest manufacturer of cars in the world. On the company's website, the Board of Directors is described as the following: "The Supervisory Board of Volkswagen AG comprises 20 members and conforms to the German Co-determination Act." This means that, by law, labor unions must be represented on the board. The State of Lower Saxony owns 20% of the company, so the government has representatives on the board. The government of Qatar owns 17% of the company, so they have representatives on the board. The founding family owns 35% of the company, but controls 50% of the votes due to special share classes, so they have representatives on the board. The unwieldy nature of this ownership structure was laid bare in 2020, as the industry wide shift to electrification caused private power struggles to burst into into the open:

FRANKFURT, Nov 27 (Reuters) - Volkswagen's Chief Executive Herbert Diess has asked the company's owning families to back a contract extension in a bid to break a management deadlock at the world's largest carmaker, two people familiar with the matter told Reuters.

The appeal for support from the Piech and Porsche families, who control a majority voting stake at the carmaker, comes after Diess was forced to relinquish management responsibility for the VW brand in June to retain his job as group CEO.

"He is bringing the issue to a head," one of the sources said.

Volkswagen declined to comment. The owning families declined to comment, the company's works council and the German state of Lower Saxony, which owns a VW stake, declined to comment.

To American investors, this scenario seems bizarre, but it's a common situation on the European continent: at some of the world's largest, best-known companies, it's hard to tell who's really in charge. If you were a member of a controlling family, and you were legally forced into a constant, uncomfortable tango with labor unions and the government, would you want to sell shares? Does it look like anyone at Volkswagen wants to give up an ounce of control? In these kinds of situations, steady and growing dividends are the way that shareholders can reap cash flow without ceding control.

Speaking of uncomfortable, isn't it surprising to learn that Europe, a continent now renowned for a socialsitic way of life, is still home to many mega corporations that are still controlled by what is essentially aristocracy? How can a continent that taxes workers' incomes at up to 60% still be home to Lords and Ladies who have owned major corporations through passive vehicles for a century or more? How is France, the home of "Liberte, Egalite and Fraternite" also the home of Bernard Arnault, a world-famous billionaire whose family controls publicly traded LVMH-Moet-Hennesy, the legendary purveyor of luxury goods?

The answers to these questions are beyond the scope of this book, but suffice it to say that big business in Europe struggles with dicey publicity. They wouldn't want to attract the negative attention that big share buybacks can bring in America.

When a company is swimming in cash, many observers feel that share buybacks hurt workers and "stakeholders", i.e. people who depend on the company for their livelihoods, even if they aren't shareholders. For example, cash burned on share buybacks could instead be invested in factories that create new jobs, or invested in cleaning up a company's environmental footprint. In America, the cultural attitude that prevails is that companies exist to build wealth for shareholders alone; lip service is provided for other stakeholders, but when push comes to shove, American culture is all about getting paid.

Many Europeans may secretly feel the same way, but the prevailing culture is very focused on fairness and social well being. The fact that France taxes workers at double American rates, yet also provides Dior and Hermes luxuries to the world, is just a careful balancing act that corporations must navigate. In this environment, the quiet regularity of dividends draws less negative attention than share buybacks.

We're All Euro Now

Studies show that many investors suffer from what researchers call "home country bias." This means that Americans are more comfortable buying American stocks, Japanese more comfortable buying Japanese stocks, etc. While there are many great reasons to accumulate American stocks (which we will go over in the following chapters), some allotment to European stocks is recommendable if you want to live off of dividend payments.

Some investors hesitate to purchase European stocks due to technical concerns. Maybe this would have been a barrier thirty years ago, but today it's very easy. Whatever brokerage you use in America is likely to offer a wide variety of ADRs from major companies all over God's Green Earth. An ADR is an American Depository Receipt. It is a ticker symbol that trades on American stock exchanges mirroring the share listing of stock in its home country. I own dozens of ADRs; they are just as easy to buy as an American stock.

Another rational concern might be accounting and standards. Most Americans are familiar with financial regulatory bodies like the SEC (Securities Exchange Commission) and the IRS. How can we trust stocks from foreign lands? What if the accounting is different, adding complexity? Is anyone regulating these stocks at all?

The good news is that the very rich people who own the majority of stocks are typically citizens of the world. They often travel widely and own assets on every continent. As such, you can usually expect similar standards in accounting and financial regulation across major global financial markets. Would I recommend buying stocks based in Latvia? Perhaps not. But core, Western European countries have been doing this a long, long time. You can expect accounting and financial rules to be similar to what you would find on this side of the Atlantic. Regulatory documents will almost always be available published in English.

Some investors who pay attention to current affairs and global economics might have one last, common sense question. If European economic growth is sluggish, why would an American want to invest in European stocks?

It's been well documented that European economic growth has been sub-par for many years. Double digit unemployment is common in the southern half of the EU, the birth rate is the lowest it's ever been, and growth of Gross Domestic Product has been anemic for most of the 21st century. If European companies only sold goods in Europe, I would tell you not to invest.

However, that very sluggishness is what has caused long established European large capitalization companies to become global powerhouses. VW, despite it's chronically dysfunctional ownership structure, remains the largest car manufacturer by volume in the world. They certainly didn't sell all of those cars in Germany! VW has operations in almost every country on the map. Wherever growth is on the globe, VW is there. The same goes for Roche, and most other companies that make up the Euro Stoxx 50.

The only reason we categorize these companies as "European" is because a disproportionate number of shareholders and upper management are European citizens. This leads to decisions that can be different than companies primarily owned by Americans; for instance, the decision to pay out dividends rather than buy back stock. But make no mistake; these titans of global commerce do business in any country that has a solvent currency. As a shareholder, we simply sit back, relax, and enjoy our quarterly dividend checks. How to make those dividend checks grow is the problem of Claus or Francois back at headquarters.

How To Choose

How to find good dividend stocks headquartered in the Old World? The process is very simple. 90% of Americans don't even bother to look across the pond due to that home country bias phenomenon. Just by looking, you can instantly beat out 90% of your competitors.

If you don't want to put in the time and effort to do research, you can always buy a broad based exchange traded fund, just like the Euro Stoxx 50 that we discussed earlier in the chapter. Pretty much every flavor of American exchange traded fund has a European equivalent, which can easily be procured from companies like Vanguard or iShares. Very often, these ETFs will yield more than their American counterparts, because of all the reasons we reviewed earlier in the chapter.

Even if you prefer individual shares, the process can be simple. In the next few chapters, we will be reviewing different industry sectors in the American stock market that tend to offer high yields. If you decide, for example, that you want to invest in oil, first check

American companies. Then look up European counterparts. For example, as I write this text, Chevron, a legendary American oil company, offers a dividend yield of 5.6%. BP (British Petroleum) has nearly identical operations across the globe, but offers a dividend yield of 7.67%. These two companies aren't clones, but in reality they are very similar. One yields 30% more than the other. Making the trip across the Atlantic may well be worth it.

You can repeat this comparison in most major sectors. Energy, pharmaceuticals, consumer goods, even real estate investment trusts. Comparing European companies to American companies is just like checking out both Amazon.com and Walmart.com before you buy. Good shoppers find good deals. So can you.

Why do both Europe and America host mega corporations that compete over the very same markets globally? Because some businesses are so good, that everyone wants in. In the next chapters we will review two businesses that you, too, may want to own.

Chapter 6: Big Pharma, Big Dividends

If you want secure and growing dividends, then the pharmaceutical industry offers the good medicine you seek. In the good old days that we discussed earlier in the book, your average retiree would have a large allotment of bonds in her portfolio. The idea was that bonds offered predictable, regular income that would help a retiree sleep well at night. In today's desert of micro interest rates, large pharmaceutical companies, or Big Pharma, offer the next best thing to the security of bonds. Big Pharma pumps out generous dividends with machine-like regularity, while also offering growth that Grandma never could have achieved with bonds.

Many big name corporations have come and gone over the decades. Remember Montgomery Ward? RadioShack? In contrast, America's pharmaceutical giants have remained evergreen. Johnson & Johnson was founded by... you guessed it, the Johnson brothers, all the way back in 1885. In Indiana, they grow both corn and pharmaceuticals. Eli Lilly was founded all the way back in 1876. But all of these youngsters pale in comparison to the granddaddy of them all... Pfizer. If you can believe it, Pfizer was founded by two German Immigrants in 1849. 1849! When Pfizer was founded, owning slaves was legal, there was no such thing as a camera, and electricity hadn't been invented.

Needless to say, investors in Pfizer, Eli Lilly, and J&J have enjoyed generations of prosperity while poor Sears shareholders have been passing through the nine levels of hell. In fact, had you invested $1,000 in Johnson & Johnson in 1977, the year of my birth, today you would have a mind boggling $85,999. The company went public in 1944, and, somewhere out there, there are families who have been reaping outsized benefits for more than 70 years.

Innovate or Die

So, America's pharmaceutical titans have somehow stayed forever young while corporate giants in other sectors have not stood the test of time. What is the magic trick?

I believe that the trick to achieving solid longevity in the business world is to feel your own mortality every day. Big Pharma draws strength from its smash hits; world beaters such as Prozac, Lipitor, and Viagra come to mind. But each billion-dollar baby is born to die; due to our very well established legal system related to patents, every high ranking pharma exec understands explicitly that no one pill or potion will last forever.

Big Pharma is notorious for employing every legal and semi-legal method for extending medical patents, and wringing every last penny from blockbuster drugs. However, behind closed doors, executive teams know, down to the month, exactly when their golden goose will stop laying eggs.

You could call this "innovate or die." This is the genius of our American creative machine. As much as the scoundrels running Big Pharma would love to ride one or two big products forever, they just can't. Due to the laws of our land, Big Pharma has an unquenchable thirst for new products and new technologies.

Let's contrast Big Pharma's situation with the more typical scenario in other sectors of the economy. There are too many sad stories to count. The pattern is typically that a Fortune 500 company has a huge hit product on its hands, that reliably prints cash year after year, and perhaps even decade after decade. On some level, they know that the party can't last forever, but they don't know it in their bones. Who wants to be the vice president who greenlights big corporate spending on R&D when that very same R&D threatens to replace the company's existing cash cow? For example, did you know that Kodak engineers actually invented the digital camera?

"It's no exaggeration to say Kodak invented digital photography. In 1975 Kodak engineer Steve Sasson created the first digital camera, which took photos with 10,000 pixels, or 0.01 megapixels — about a hundredth of the resolution that low-end camera phones have today. Kodak didn't stop there; it worked extensively on digital, patenting numerous technologies, many of which are built into the digital cameras of today......"If you want to point back to the most pivotal moment that caused this," says Hayzlett, "it was back in 1975 when they discovered the digital camera and put it back into a closet......In 1995 the company brought its first digital camera to market, the DC40. This was years before many others would get into the digital game, but Kodak never took advantage of its early start. Philosophically, the company was steeped in the film business, and to embrace digital meant cannibalizing its own business. "It's a classic business strategy problem," says Miriam Leuchter, editor of Popular Photography. "Their whole business was tied up in film and in printing. So while they're developing this business technology, there's not a big incentive to push it very far." (Mashable.com, Pete Pachael, 1/20/12)

This same sad story has been repeated hundreds of times across the Fortune 500. On the most basic level, major corporations are filled with people who don't fully control their own businesses, and who aren't big risk takers anyhow. That's why they work for a Fortune 500 company. Big Pharma certainly doesn't like risk. But they have no choice.

Even in the glory days of Viagra, when Pfizer was swimming in cash, they knew that Viagra would one day go generic. They could predict Viagra's death down to the month. If anyone was about to bumble into any good new innovations in the lab, shoving that nascent innovation into a closet would be the last thing Pfizer would want. Of course there are no guarantees in life. But so far, Pfizer has outlasted many nations, so the steady cash flow should help a retiree sleep well at night.

Getting The Right Rx

How do you know which Big Pharma stocks are the right ones? Well, the simple answer is that they are almost all the right ones. As we discovered above, most of the big household brands that you know were founded before your grandfather was born. They were good investments for your grandpappy, and they'll be good investments for you.

That being said, a few words of caution. First, not all pharmaceutical stocks are Big Pharma stocks. The world of pharmaceutical investing is roughly divided between Big Pharma and biotech. While both of these groups are dedicated to the discovery and commercialization of new medicines, they are very different kinds of companies with different investor groups.

The world of biotech is for swashbuckling investors who want maximum share price growth. These are typically young, high risk companies that pay no dividend. In fact, many have little if any cash flow at all!

Big Pharma companies are very large, multinational firms that take a more "slow but steady" approach to winning in business. Many medicines start life in the laboratory of an upstart biotech innovator, but wind up being marketed, distributed, and sold by a Big Pharma concern.

The world of biotech is an exciting place for an investor who wants to see his money grow as fast as possible. It's so exciting that I wrote a separate book on that topic (*Your First Biotech Million: How to Earn Your Fortune in Biotech Stocks*). However, if you want to live off dividend income for an indefinite period of time, what you want is a proven, long established business that functions like an ATM machine. That would be Big Pharma.

How do you know which companies are Big Pharma, and which are biotechs? There are a few where the line gets blurry. For example, Amgen and Gilead are often referred to as biotechs because twenty years ago, they were scrappy upstarts. Today, they are behemoths that churn out dividends. Yesterday's biotechs are often today's Big Pharma firms.

According to Becker's Hospital Review, here are the largest global pharmaceutical firms:

The top 10 pharmaceutical companies, ranked by revenue:

1. Pfizer — $51.75 billion

2. Roche — $50 billion

3. Novartis — $47.45 billion

4. Merck — $46.84 billion

5. GlaxoSmithKline — $43.54 billion

6. Johnson & Johnson — $42.1 billion

7. AbbVie — $33.27 billion

8. Sanofi — $27.77 billion

9. Bristol-Myers Squibb — $26.15 billion

10. AstraZeneca — $23.57 billion

Of these, five are based in Europe (Roche, Novartis, GSK, Sanofi, AstraZeneca). The ten pay between 2 and 6% dividends, and those dividends have grown between 5 and 10% each and every year for decades. This means that almost any pharmaceutical stock has grown its dividends at three to four times the rate of inflation. Most of these ten have a total return in excess of 200% over the last decade. Novartis, the laggard of the bunch, has still returned 143%. Good medicine indeed!

Big Pharma is a great business. But it's not the only great business. In the next chapter, we will explore another appealing option.

Chapter 7: Energy Stocks - Powering Your Retirement

Here is a confession for you. I know very little about how the modern world works. When you press the ignition button on your car, why does it start reliably? When you flick your light switch, why do the bulbs suddenly illuminate? I have a very rough idea based on 6th grade science, but if you really pressed me, I would have to admit that it's all black magic to me. The black magic behind modern power generation, distribution, and consumption isn't so important to us as investors. What is more important is how we turn that black magic into green magic; however energy works, it typically works great for dividend investors. Big energy companies have reliably churned out dividends for decades, just as the sun rises and sets with predictable regularity.

An amazing aspect of the energy sector is that, no matter what the inputs, the outputs remain just about the same. That is why I use the term "energy" rather than "oil," "gas" or "wind." It turns out, the more things change, the more they stay the same from the point of view of the income investor. Oil, gas, wind, are all different inputs that lead to the same output; energy that millions of consumers can summon on demand. The science and politics are different depending on how energy is being harnessed, but the underlying business isn't so different. Energy is needed around the globe on a constant and predictable basis; that constant, predictable cash flow lends itself to the sowing and reaping of dividends.

You can literally earn money for yourself every time you start your car or turn on your home oven. Whether you prefer "old school" hydrocarbons or "new school" renewables, this sector produces generous dividends that can power your lifestyle for decades to come.

Black Gold

The most traditional place to look for dividends is in oil stocks. Oil "supermajors" like ExxonMobil and Chevron have pumped out reliable cash flow for decades. According to Dividend.com, in the thirty-year period between 1990 and 2020, Exxon has grown its dividend by roughly 700%. In other words, a yearly payout of $0.48 per share in 1990 became $3.37 in 2020. These kinds of cash flow bonanzas have not been unusual; British Petroleum (BP) grew it's dividend from $0.05 per share per quarter in 1998 to $0.63 per share per quarter just before the coronavirus hit. So, a BP shareholder who had simply bought the stock and then done nothing for 22 years would have seen her annual cash flow grow by 1,260%. By the way, this is during a time period in which BP caused the greatest environmental disaster in history and paid record fines into the multi billions. (The DeepWater Horizon).

Bottom line? Nothing could slake the world's thirst for oil over the last hundred years. Almost any large oil company would have been a great investment for a retiree who wanted to live off of the income.

But is it still a good investment? You may have noticed, the world is starting to change. As I write this, Tesla, an electric car company, has seen its stock surpass every other car manufacturer combined. The United Kingdom has pledged to stop selling internal combustion cars altogether by 2030. More and more people feel that the pollution and geopolitical turmoil that oil causes makes it an unethical industry.

The answer to this question is that oil supermajor stocks remain great investments for the right kind of investors. These stocks are not for everyone. Ironically, there are two specific, opposite groups of retirees that might benefit the most. The first group is risk averse, elderly retirees. The second group, paradoxically, are younger, more aggressive investors who are willing to take a risk.

If you are a traditional retiree trying to navigate a world of micro interest rates, you are looking for companies that will provide steady, predictable income for the rest of your life. At 70 or 75 years old, the "rest of your life" may mean twenty years or so. According to Policyadvice.net, in 2020, electric cars only achieved a 2.2% market share of new cars sold. This means that, of all the new cars sold, 98% were still internal combustion engines. Even if many nations ban internal combustion after 2030 (and that's a BIG "if"), that 98% of new cars sold today will remain on the road for many years to come. It seems clear that electric cars are the future, but sometimes the future can be stubbornly slow in coming. In the meantime, our traditional retiree can kick back and enjoy many more years of steady dividends. If you are currently in your 70s, and you suspect that your investing timeline isn't more than twenty years, oil supermajors may be a good source of income for you.

How could the very same stocks appeal to a younger, thrill-seeking investor? Why would a forty year old want to buy stock in oil companies when oil may be gone by the time she reaches traditional retirement age?

Lately, even some of the most established oil companies in the world have publicly and dramatically committed to transforming into "energy" companies. Slowly ramping down investment in hydrocarbon production, while slowly ramping up investment in wind, hydrogen, and biofuel projects. While this seems shocking at first (as the leopard doesn't often change his spots), there is a certain logic to it.

One of the most promising and rapidly growing fields of renewable energy is offshore wind production. This involves installing massive wind turbines in deep water far off shore. Not an easy task, and one that requires a company with deep pockets and substantial ocean-oriented infrastructure. The argument goes that oil companies have a long history of massive projects deep at sea due to their many adventures and misadventures in deep water oil drilling. Installing windmills the size of the Eiffel Tower may actually be considered easy work compared to the great lengths these companies have gone to extract oil buried under miles of ocean and rock hard ocean floor. The same argument applies for hydrogen. Even though hydrogen is in its infancy, the thought is that liquid hydrogen would function much the same way that oil and gas do today, except in a much more sustainable and eco-friendly manner. The oil supermajors know a thing or two about flammable liquids that need to be transported over vast distances.

The potential for transformation is real, but it won't be quick, and it won't be easy. The risks are large. Many mammoth global corporations simply can't overcome their own bureaucracy to enact effective change. Also, many of these companies have made noises about this kind of transformation before, only for the wheels of change to get stuck. Is the commitment real this time? Both BP and Total, two of Europe's largest oil companies, have publicly pledged to become carbon neutral organizations by 2050. This would mean slowly but surely shifting investment away from oil and gas, and truly becoming energy companies rather than oil companies.

In the meantime, oil companies across the globe are being shunned by investors. BP is yielding between 7 and 8%, Total has hovered around 7%. Exxon Mobil, which has been more reluctant to get on the eco train, has yielded as much as 10%! These are examples of where the sector has fallen out of favor, causing share prices to drop. As cash flow has remained roughly the same, these new energy companies are now deeply discounted. This is why they might appeal to a younger investor who is willing to take a gamble. If they do succeed in weaning themselves off oil and moving into renewables in a big way, there is a lot of upside that other investors have ignored. If these ancient lumbering giants are surpassed by more nimble, more youthful competitors, then they will wind up in the dustbin of history, along with Sears, RadioShack, and Kodak.

The New Kids On The Block

Some people just don't want to go near oil and gas stocks. They feel that hydrocarbons pollute the earth, or they simply don't want to get involved in yesterday's energy technology. If you feel this way, no problem! Wall Street has cooked up something tasty for you. I present: The yieldco. If you need a mean green machine to pump out reliable dividends without pumping oil from Mother Earth, a yieldco investment could be for you.

If you ever were to get involved in the oil business, you might hear terms such as "upstream," and "downstream." These terms revolve around the idea that finding oil, starting up an oil field, and operating an established, profitable field are really separate businesses. It turns out that the dynamic is no different when the source of the energy is renewables.

Yieldcos are companies that are related to large developers of renewable assets. These entities contain the mature, established, cash flow positive assets of these development companies. Yieldcos offer predictable, long term cash flow to investors, while allowing the developers of the renewable assets to "recycle" the capital that they initially deployed to develop the project. Every time a large developer of renewable energy projects successfully stabilizes a wind farm, for example, they sell an interest in the future revenues of that wind farm to a yieldco. The developer can then, in turn, use the same capital again and again to build more and more wind farms. As an investor, you get the income for decades to come.

One example of a yieldco is NextEra Energy Partners (NEP). Although the vehicle is technically a partnership, you can buy and sell shares just like anything else on E-Trade or whatever brokerage you use. NEP is the little brother of NextEra Energy (NEE), a utility and one of the largest developers of renewable energy projects in the United States. NextEra started out its corporate life as Florida Power and Light, a sleepy, government-regulated energy utility that mostly used traditional energy sources to provide regulated electricity to millions of Floridians. About ten years ago, the company radically changed course and embarked on an aggressive program to develop renewable assets around the US.

The strategy worked. Over the last decade, NextEra's share price has rocketed from $12 to $84. The stock currently trades at a price to earnings ratio of 44, which would have been impossible when the company was merely another government-regulated utility.

This legendary share growth is certainly appealing to a wide swath of investors. However, it might not appeal to investors who seek dividend income. Currently, NextEra only yields 1.6%, a far cry from the 3-5% it would have yielded when it was just another utility stock. Never one to leave money on the table, NextEra devised a solution: NextEra Energy Partners, a yieldco that will provide less share price growth, but more current yield. In this way, NextEra management can engage and please two different shareholder constituencies, while recycling capital as described above. NextEra Energy Partners yields 2.81% and is just getting started. According to management, a shareholder could expect this dividend yield to grow by 12-15% annually for the foreseeable future. At that rate, you would double your income every five years. How is that for green energy?

According to the US Energy Information Administration, as of 2020, only 11% of American energy is considered to come from renewable sources. But costs associated with solar power and wind are falling dramatically, while battery technology is constantly improving. Many hope that the United States will extract 100% of its energy from renewable sources by 2050. So that would mean that the epoch of the renewable yieldco is just now beginning. If you want a reasonable dividend that grows quickly and is derived from the latest cutting edge technology, look at names such as NextEra Energy Partners (NEP), Brookfield Renewable Partners (BEP), and Atlantic Yield (AY).

Old School Meets New School

If you don't quite know whether you want tried and true, traditional hydrocarbon stocks, or you want to bet on the new technologies of the renewable world, you can always outsource that decision to experts. You can achieve balance and safety by simply investing directly in electric utility companies. These are publicly traded companies that provide energy as a service directly to consumers and businesses across the United States. Although they trade on the stock exchange just like any other security, they often function in a unique business ecosystem. Often, electric utilities enjoy a monopoly over a certain defined geographical territory in exchange for being regulated by an alphabet soup of different governmental entities. The result is a world of investable companies that are conservative by definition and highly scrutinized by the general public, both good things if you are a retired investor seeking reliable yield. In fact, these companies are so reliable that they have been termed "window and orphan" stocks. Meaning that they are good purchases for unsophisticated, vulnerable inventors who just need steady cash flow.

These electric utilities have a mandate to deliver reliable energy to citizens and reliable dividends to shareholders, so a broadly diversified portfolio of energy assets is the safest approach for them. This means that, as a shareholder, you automatically get "the best of both worlds," a mix of reliable traditional energy sources (natural gas, coal, nuclear) and more cutting edge technologies (solar, wind, biomass). As time goes by and technology progresses, most utilities are using less and less dirty coal and more and more clean sunlight. When you buy shares in these utilities, you are hiring a team of seasoned energy professionals to handle this transition for you. These are the ultimate "set it and forget it" stocks.

That being said, not all electric utilities are the same. Some are more aggressive than others in terms of transitioning to 21st century energy. Some actually own natural gas pipelines. Some, like NextEra, both develop new projects around the country, and own a regulated local utility. Some just provide stodgy old day-to-day energy for specific locals. They may have different dividend yields and different dividend growth rates that reflect some of these distinctions. Below is a list of the ten largest (by market capitalization) utilities so that you can shop and compare:

1. NextEra Energy, Inc
2. Duke Energy Corp
3. Southern Co.
4. Dominion Energy Inc.
5. American Electric Power, Inc.
6. Exelon Corp.
7. Sempra Energy
8. Xcel Energy
9. Eversource Energy
10. Public Service Enterprise Group

(Data: Vanguard.com, February 2021)

Whether you choose the high dividends of oil stocks, the high growth of renewable energy yieldcos, or the balanced approach of electric utilities, energy equities can reliably deliver dividends between 2 and 6%, year after year, decade after decade.

But what if there was a way you could earn more? Much more, without incurring much more risk? What if there were reputable, established businesses that could pay you 7%, 9%, or even 11% on your money? Would that have a dramatic effect on how early you could retire, and on your lifestyle in retirement?

Read on to learn all about these enhanced income options…..

Part 2: Special Vehicles

Chapter 8: REITs - Trustworthy Dividends

Have you ever gone for a ride in your car, looked around at the buildings that you pass, and wondered to yourself, "who owns all this?" The gas station where you filled up, the strip center where you dropped your dog off for grooming, the warehouse that you passed on the highway. We each pass thousands and thousands of buildings every year. Who owns all of that? What if I told you, that "who" could be you?

Most people understand on one level or another that real estate can be a great investment. Yet for many people, the world of real estate seems time consuming, risky, and, more than anything else, complicated. It can be all of those things. If you wanted to own a hundred-unit rental building, you would have to line up millions in financing, find some way of managing unruly tenants, and find methods of maintaining the property without breaking the bank. Imagining those kinds of challenges, too many people stay away.

There is an easier way to enjoy the benefits of real estate ownership without all of the hassle and complication of directly owning strip centers and apartment buildings. A Real Estate Investment Trust, or REIT, is a special kind of investment entity expressly crafted to suit the needs of a passive income investor. A REIT is a simplified vehicle for owning real estate; there are dozens upon dozens of different kinds of REITs that specialize in different kinds of real estate. If you want to own apartment buildings, there are REITs that specialize in apartment buildings. If you want to own nursing homes, there are REITs that specialize in nursing homes. These are typically publicly traded companies that you can buy and sell using the same brokerage where you would buy shares of Google or Facebook.

What Is So Special About REITs?

If you go on E-Trade and start researching REITs, on the surface they will look similar to all of the other stocks. And they do trade with the ease of regular stocks. But there are a few key differences that make REITs especially appealing for income investors.

First is corporate structure. Most large corporations that you would purchase through your brokerage are C corporations. C corporations are almost treated like people by the law, so they pay their own taxes. A C corporation pays dividends to you (or buys stock back) with whatever money is left over after taxes. A REIT is a different legal structure than a C corporation. A REIT is considered a "pass through entity." This means that REITs pay no taxes at the corporate level. To be considered a REIT, the entity must pay out 90% of its profit in the form of dividends. Then the individual shareholders are responsible for the taxes. A C corporation, such as Dow Chemical, must pay taxes at the corporate level, but then can pay out, or not pay out, whatever amount of cash the board of directors decides upon. In order to be classified as a REIT by Uncle Sam, the real estate-owning entity is legally required to pay out 90% of profits. This requirement tends to make REITs lean, mean, dividend-paying machines.

This small difference in corporate structure has some big implications for investors. One aspect is that many investors feel that REITs are more transparent in their accounting and reporting structure. If you were around in the 90s, you may remember Enron, a high flying "technology" company that turned out to be a total fraud. In fact, it's one of the largest corporate frauds in history. Because Enron was considered by the market to be a growth stock, no one expected Enron to pay dividends. This means that Enron could easily embellish, and then outright invent, paper profits, because they never needed to pay out cold hard cash. At some point, they realized their accounting was barely scrutinized, because they were playing with all theoretical values anyhow.

The corporate management of large REITs is the exact opposite. They live under a microscope, because their cash payout must be constant and regular. It's easy to invent profits on the accrual system of accounting, but if your business is secretly flailing, it would be almost impossible to churn out the regular dividends that REIT investors demand. It's easy to fake accounting profits; willing cold hard cash flow into existence is a little tougher.

Along those lines, the accounting terms utilized in the REIT world are slightly different from the Generally Accepted Accounting Principles (GAAP) that are the language of the C corporation. I can already picture you banging your head against the wall. More accounting! Different accounting! First he asked me to learn one language, now I need an additional language?

Yes, and no. The accounting vocabulary around REITs is actually easier than GAAP. The actual vocabulary might seem intimidating at first, but with just a little practice, it's easy. The reason for this is the simplified structure of the REIT entity.

You may recall from earlier chapters that in the world of C corporations—big, well-known concerns such as Microsoft or General Motors—a standard financial report consists of three parts, the profit and loss (P&L), the cash flow, and the balance sheet. You may remember that the P&L is a largely theoretical form of accounting that aims to quantify ethereal costs such as stock options and depreciation, while the cash flow sheet accounts for a business operation as if your kid was running a lemonade stand (cash in, cash out, etc). Furthermore, the balance sheet of a typical C corporation can get complicated, because much of the value of today's C corporations is intangible. If you were running a lemonade stand, it would be easy for you to assign a hard value to your inventory of lemons, sugar, and ice. But

148

if you're running a biotechnology firm that has been developing intellectual property for years with no revenue to show (yet), that asset and liability accounting can get tricky.

You might be surprised, but running a multi-billion dollar real estate business is a lot like running a giant lemonade stand. Because your investors are almost exclusively interested in cash flow, the accounting is much more simple. What the investor really wants to know is; how much cash does the operation throw off? What is the market value of the property that the company owns, versus how much mortgage debt is owed against the properties? Accounting concepts in the world of REITs are very tangible and concrete. If you are accounting phobic, REITs may actually suit you better than other forms of income investing.

If you would like to learn about accounting for Real Estate Investment Trusts, here are a few reliable sources with glossaries and in depth explanations:

-REIT.COM
-REITINSTITUTE.COM
-DIVIDEND.COM

You can also find in-depth yet simple explanations of REIT accounting at fool.com and investopedia.com.

Other Benefits of REITs

One big benefit of real estate investment that is often touted is the very light taxation for investors. This has become a polemic theme over the last few years, as it was revealed that a certain real estate mogul turned United States President has barely ever paid taxes over his long and supposedly lucrative career. The fairness of the system is extremely questionable, but as I write this text, real estate investors still pay very low tax. The reason is the difference between theoretical accounting and actual cash flows.

As we discussed before, GAAP accounting factors in theoretical costs and benefits. This is actually the kind of accounting that our tax system works on. In the world of real estate, the biggest theoretical cost is asset depreciation. In theory, a hard asset loses value over time because it decays and needs to be maintained. These theoretical costs, which are often substantial if you buy a twenty-year-old apartment building, are recorded against real revenue, such as rents. This leads to a situation whereby many real estate projects can show an annual accounting loss (or at least minimal profits) when, in reality, cash flow greatly exceeds hard costs. This means cash flow is positive, even if a loss is recorded on the P&L statement.

Of course, there are many variations on this theme, and big, sophisticated investors who directly own hard real estate utilize an endless playbook of tax minimization plays. Most exploit that difference between "real world" cash flow accounting and "theoretical" GAAP accounting. When you own a stock in a REIT, you get many of those same tax benefits, except you get none of the complexity and headaches. As a shareholder, you have a skilled management team in place who does all of the work for you.

REITs file tax reports to the Federal Government on a GAAP basis. However, the amount of cash that flows to you is determined on a real world basis. This often leads to a situation whereby your REIT dividend theoretically represents more than the profit the company made that quarter. In that case, the REIT is theoretically implementing what is termed a "return of capital"" This means that they are theoretically returning some of your own capital to you, thus, that portion of the dividend isn't taxed. This can mean, for example, that if you received $10 in dividends, only $7 are taxed. In reality, all $10 are profits that the company generated. Through magical accounting pixie dust, you just got a huge discount on your taxes.

The term return of capital is something that we will discuss in several chapters in this part of the book. This is a commonly misunderstood phrase, because it means different things in different circumstances. We will discuss each circumstance as we get to it, but suffice it to say, in the context of equity REITs, return of capital is a good thing. It means lower taxes for you.

Another big benefit of REIT investing is that you can get more than just steady cash flow. Many REITs also appreciate in value over time. Remember, when you own a REIT, it's very similar to you and three partners owning a ten-unit apartment building. In the case of the REIT, there are just a lot more partners. The owners of the apartment building hope to reap regular income from the investment, but they also hope the apartment building will be worth more in ten years than it is now. According to Investopedia.com, the average REIT earned a 10.5% return in the twenty-five years between 1984 and 2019. During that same time period, REITs have yielded an average between 4 and 6%.

You may remember the "Rule of 72." This rule states that you can take the number 72, divide it by a rate of growth or dividend payout, and the resulting number will represent the amount of years to double your capital. In this example, your average REIT returns 10.5% annually, of which 5% is dividend and 5.5% is capital appreciation. So, if we take the 72, and we divided it by 5.5, we find that you would still have doubled your money every 13 years, even if you spent your dividends every quarter. All of that without ever fixing a toilet or chasing a deadbeat tenant for rent. Not bad!

Different Strokes For Different Folks

So, if there are dozens of different kinds of REITs, how do you choose the right ones for yourself?

There are a few different methods; you will use a lot of the same skills that were described in earlier chapters. Remember, REITs trade like any other publicly traded stock; the main difference is the underlying corporate structure. So, you would still pick REITs the way you would pick most stocks.

The first method is to focus on a sector that you know a lot about, or want to know about. In my own case, I am very concentrated in healthcare REITs. These are companies like Ventas, Medical Properties Trust, and Welltower that own broad portfolios of healthcare properties including retirement communities, doctors' offices, clinics, and even scientific laboratories. Before I became an author and professional investor, I was an award-winning medical salesperson for two decades. Healthcare is near and dear to my heart, so it was only logical for me to feel comfortable researching and choosing REITs in this field.

You might like hospitality, or rental apartments. There are many REITs that focus just on those fields. If you think about it, you can probably recall a time when you drove by a certain kind of property and said to yourself, "That looks like a goldmine. I wish I owned that." You can. You can own almost any sub niche of real estate by purchasing shares of a REIT.

Another method would be the fallen angel method described earlier in the book. One example of a fallen angel purchase that has worked out very well for me is SABRA Healthcare REIT, Inc. A few years ago, mainstream healthcare REITs decided that they wanted to get out of the nursing home business. They decided that they wanted to own senior living properties that enjoyed revenue from wealthy old people, or private pay, in industry parlance. These are considered "active senior living communities" for healthy elderly folks who only need a little help to get by. Nursing homes are different. Nursing homes are heavily dependent on Mcdicaid payments and various state aid schemes; they are not built for active senior living. Nursing homes are built for very sick people who are mostly paid for by the government. The thinking was that depending on the vagaries of our quasi socialistic medical system was bad business. In addition, frankly, true nursing homes are seen as dirty and disreputable. A lot of the more mainstream medical REITs didn't want to be linked with the bad feelings associated with nursing homes, and they didn't want to depend on the government for payment.

A few REITs decided that they were happy to do the dirty work. SABRA Healthcare was one of them. I've had a few personal experiences in my life that have convinced me that, as distasteful as they are, nursing homes aren't going away. In fact, with 10,000 Baby Boomers per day turning 65, the need for extensive end-of-life care will only increase. The fact that nursing homes were shunned by the major healthcare REITs meant I could buy Sabra shares with a yield anywhere from 7 to 10% annually. This was almost double the yield of healthcare REITs that focused on more prestigious businesses, like life science laboratories. I have collected that handsome yield, every quarter like clockwork, for years now. Sabra turned out to be a classic "fallen angel. Great properties sold cheap because they were misunderstood.

As I write this text, the COVID crisis has caused many formerly premium REIT names to sell for very cheap. Simon Mall REIT currently yields over 6%, double what it yielded just a few years ago. Many of the hotel REITs can be had for a song. Sifting through REITs that have been damaged by the pandemic is risky business. Many of these properties are cheap for a reason. But there are some diamonds in with the coals if you care to put on your research glasses and carefully survey the wreckage.

You can also go in the opposite direction. Just as certain stocks can be termed high dividend growth companies, so can REITs. Some REITs may offer relatively low yields today, but giant growth prospects. One example of a growth REIT is Alexandria Real Estate equities. This is a REIT that focuses on developing and acquiring highly specialized laboratories in the life science business. Because the life science business tends to be clustered in several crowded, expensive cities, creating and owning these kinds of properties is challenging to say the least. The big REITs in this space don't have much competition. Alexandria currently yields a paltry 2.58%, but they are anticipating decades of double digit growth as the American biotechnology industry grows and grows. Another example of a REIT planning some big growth is Digital Realty Trust. This is a REIT that owns highly customized properties that house data centers. Today, the REIT yields just 3.1%, but management promises years of stellar growth, as society grows to depend more and more on Big Data, with special storage requirements.

Many investors are excited and motivated when they find out that they can choose from thousands of different kinds of REITs. However, some feel overwhelmed. The many choices can feel like a burden; inexperienced real estate investors may fear an unwise purchase. If that is how you feel, you can always just buy an exchange traded fund (ETF) that offers you a broad diversification of REITs. Any major investment firm offers ETFs that will represent a broad range of real estate investments. You get the same yield that you would get from individual investments, but the chance of your investment going to $0 is miniscule. Look on the websites of companies like Vanguard, iShares, and Proshares to find these ETFs. They should each charge an annual fee substantially less than 1% of the total assets.

Ownership of real estate is a tried and true method of generating income in your sleep. With your REIT dividends showing up every quarter, you should sleep well indeed.

Chapter 9: Mortgage REITs - Solid Paper

L et's jump back in our imaginary car for a moment, and go for that imaginary ride. This time we are going to cruise through some residential neighborhoods filled with single family homes. What do you see? Green lawns and children playing? Neatly arranged stacks of bricks with immaculate paint and sturdy roofs? When I look at a residential neighborhood, all I see is dividends. Every time these folks make a mortgage payment, I get a piece of it. That is because I own mortgage REITs, (mREITs). Long story short, the mortgage debt of the average American family is one of my best paying investments. You can also benefit from America's obsession with home ownership.

This chapter is not a repetition of the last chapter. In the last chapter we discussed regular REITs, which are technically referred to as equity REITs. Equity REITs are corporate entities with special rules that own real estate. Traditional equity REITs own the actual bricks and mortar. Mortgage REITs own the debt associated with real estate. Equity REITs own physical assets, whereas mREITs just own piles of paper.

For many people, the lack of physical assets is off putting. Your typical equity REIT pays between 3 and 6% dividends quarterly, while your typical mREIT pays between 8 and 12% dividends monthly. Mortgage REITs are like financial rocket fuel that can help your retirement soar. However, to the novice investor, they feel risky. If the returns are so high, and the assets aren't even tangible, is it really safe to count on these vehicles for steady retirement income?

If history is any guide, mREITs are a lot safer than they seem on the surface. Annaly Capital Management, the largest mREIT that invests in single family mortgages, has paid a steady dividend every month since 1997. This means that the company weathered at least three stock crashes and the mother of all real estate crashes in 2008 and still never skipped a dividend. Annaly's principal rival, AGNC Investment Corp, can say almost the same. They have been paying steady monthly income for twelve consecutive years. In our latest coronavirus crisis, no major mortgage REIT went bankrupt; a few did trim their dividends, but now those dividends are quickly rebounding.

How can a security pay out 10% month after month with so little risk? To understand the risk profile of the mREIT sector, you need to understand how these companies work, and why they exist.

Simply Complex

Did you know that the American system of home ownership is utterly unique in the world? In most countries, there is no such thing as a thirty-year mortgage. Additionally, in many countries, you need a much larger down payment to buy a house. 50% down, up front, is not uncommon. The idea that an average Joe could buy a house with just 20% down, or 10% down, or even 5% down is uniquely American. In fact, it's not just an unusual system. It's an unnatural system.

When I say unnatural, all I mean is that the American homeownership system is the direct result of massive government intervention. No private lender would ever lend $400,000 to a middle class family where both partners have to work to pay the mortgage, and the family is only one job loss away from default. Even if a private lender would make such a risky loan, they certainly wouldn't do it at today's absurdly low interest rates.

The reason why an average American family can get a mortgage, even with just 5% down and a shaky income situation, is because the Federal Government removes the risk for lenders. That's right, in the vast majority of American mortgages, the lender can't lose because the Federal Government has guaranteed the loan. You wouldn't want to lend large amounts of money at low interest rates to barely solvent families if you bore the true risk. But if you could lend the money with virtually no risk, then you might do it.

I say "might," because even with federal guarantees, lending large amounts of money at low rates over long periods of time is not very sexy. Your risk would be low, but so would your reward. It's asking a lot of a bank to tie up billions upon billions of dollars at 4% interest for decades. So our system has evolved into a situation where most banks simply originate loans. Meaning they go through the time and trouble of building a sales, marketing, and mortgage processing machine, but they don't actually hold the loans at those low interest rates. After they originate the loan, they take the fees, and then sell the loan to someone else. This allows the entire mortgage business to become a fee generation machine for big lenders. They collect fat fees, collect a little interest, sell the loan, and then use the same money all over again to repeat the process. Even with no risk, the interest rates still suck; it's the constant fees and the recycling of money that makes mortgage origination a good business. If the originators could not sell the loans they make, the entire system would ground to a halt.

Which is why mortgage REITs have had such a steady track record. Mortgage REITs buy loans from originators. They don't buy the loans directly. They buy what are called Mortgage Backed Securities, or MBS. Each MBS represents hundreds or thousands of loans that were originated by banks, then packaged and sold to investors as bonds. Mortgage REITs are some of the largest buyers of MBS in the United States. These MBS are fully guaranteed by the Federal Government. The largest, most brand name Mortgage REITs focus on buying

Mortgage Backed Securities that are explicitly guaranteed by the Federal Government. The magic of the mortgage REIT is that, when you are the largest buyer of government backed securities, you also have the implicit backing of the Federal Government. Remember, the entire Frankenstein's Monster of a system only works if someone keeps buying the Mortgage Backed Securities that originators create.

Banks and other large lenders originate loans and then sell them, because the characteristics of the loans aren't too sexy. So how can mREITs take a lame 3% interest 30-year loan and transform it into an attractive 10% monthly yield?

The magic that turns lead into gold is leverage. Mortgage REITs borrow money on a short term basis at very low interest and invest that money on a long term basis in the form of mortgage backed securities. The difference between the interest they receive on the mortgage backed securities and the interest they must pay on the short term borrowings is called the Net Interest Margin.

The fact that mortgage backed securities are explicitly backed by the Federal Government means that they are great collateral. You can borrow heavily against them. mREITs use large amounts of leverage, and that is how they wind up squeezing so much juice from a rather unappetizing fruit.

While mREITs are a crucial pillar of American housing, there is still some risk for an investor. The main risk comes in the form of interest rates. The amount of money that an mREIT makes is dependent on that net interest margin, or the difference between long-term and short-term interest rates. The movement of interest rates can be arcane, and at times hard to predict. That is why mREITs are less common than fast food or drycleaning businesses. However, an experienced management team does have a large toolkit to manage these interest rate risks.

Be aware, not all mortgages are guaranteed by the Federal Government, and not all mREITs exclusively buy loans guaranteed by the feds. There are a few extra risky mREITs that specialize in non-guaranteed loans. These are called non agency REITs. But most of the largest names in the business focus exclusively on the conforming FHA loans; the bread and butter of middle class housing. REITs that exclusively buy mortgages backed by the Federal Government are referred to as agency REITs. If you are a conservative investor, I would stick to large, long-established agency REITs such as Annaly Capital, AGNC, or an exchange traded fund that specializes in mortgage REITs, such as iSHARES Mortgage REIT Real Estate fund (REM) or VanEck Vectors REIT Income ETF (MORT).

Never Fear, mREIT Is Here

For the longest time, I couldn't get over the fact that a mortgage REIT was just a pile of paper. It just didn't feel solid to me. But history tells us something different.

If you lived through the Great Recession, you know that it seemed like the entire house of cards was about to tumble down. There had been all kinds of excesses related to mortgage backed securities. It seemed like everyone was getting foreclosed upon, and American housing would never be the same. Everyone said that there had to be reforms; surely big changes were in the works.

That prognostication turned out to be totally incorrect. Twelve years after the real estate crisis to end all real estate crises, what has changed is… nothing. Well, almost nothing. For a long time after the crisis, it was tougher to get a mortgage. Down payment requirements increased. Credit score requirements increased. But now it's almost like the whole thing never happened. I recently had a friend who bought a house with just 5% down. I even know people who went into foreclosure in 2009 who have now bought houses all over again, once again with just 5 or 10% down.

During the worst of the mortgage crisis, few mREITs went bankrupt. In fact, most never even stopped paying a dividend. The fundamentals of our housing system today remain unchanged from 2008. And mortgage REITs are a critical element of those fundamentals. Without the liquidity created by mREITs, millions of middle class people would be unable to own a home. The Federal Government has demonstrated an absolutely ruthless resolve to keep the home ownership contraption alive, even if it remains dependent on government life support. When you bet on a mortgage REIT, you are betting that American society will continue to prize homeownership, and that politicians will do just about anything to keep voters happy.

mREITs have transformed my financial plan. They pay a steady dividend every month, allowing me to plan my life around my monthly "paycheck." I am not particularly risk averse, so most of my mREITs invest in government-guaranteed mortgages, but I do own a few smaller mREITs that invest in non-conforming loans or more specialized niches.

On average, mortgage REITs yield double what most dividend stocks yield. However, be aware that most of the value of mREITs is in the dividend yield. So, for example, a regular equity REIT may yield 4%, but return a total of 11% with share price appreciation over the years. A mortgage REIT may pay out 10% every month, but the share price may not increase much. So, even though the equity REIT pays out less, it may offer larger total returns over the long run. Thus, a well diversified portfolio of income producing equities remains recommendable.

The math and the concepts behind mortgage REITs may seem complicated at first. If you choose to study the industry, you will learn your way, just like any other business. But you only need a simple understanding in order to dramatically increase the yield on your equity portfolio, and dramatically decrease how much you need saved for retirement.

mREITs invest in mortgage debt, and American society is highly dependent upon these entities to continue the tradition of homeownership. mREITs pay monthly, and the payouts can vary depending on trends in interest rates. With that little bit of information, you can increase your monthly income a lot.

Chapter 10: BDCs - Small Loans, Big Dividends

Once you have become comfortable navigating the world of mortgage REITs, your next logical step is to learn about business development companies (BDCs). BDCs are a cousin of the mortgage REIT, both in corporate structure and business concept. If you can understand one, you can understand the other. Business development companies are somewhat more risky than mortgage REITs, but they offer stellar monthly cash flow. A few select BDCs can go a long way toward providing durable income diversification to fuel your retirement.

Much like a REIT, a BDC is a special corporate structure, authorized by Congress, that pays out 90% of its profits in the form of dividends. This means that, much like mREITs, the primary function of the entity is to kick off the maximum cash flow on a regular basis. Investors are only taxed once, at the personal level. It also means that, despite the complicated sounding jargon, the accounting is actually quite easy to understand. The cash flow sheet is what matters by far the most, so the vagaries of the profit and loss statement are less important.

BDCs are also like mREITs in the basic mechanism used to generate cash flow. Business development companies borrow money at very low interest rates and for short time periods, and they invest that money at very high interest rates for longer periods of time. In this case, however, they don't buy mortgages. Business development companies make high interest rate loans to specialized businesses. The result for investors can be monthly income that can equal 10, 11 or even 12% of their total investment.

Why and How

When I first learned about BDCs, my first question was, "why do these entities even exist?" If I wanted a loan for my business, why wouldn't I just go to a bank? Why do BDCs exist when established, big name banks also give out loans?

The answer is related to risk, reward, and regulation. Most banks use the funds of depositors to make loans. This means the hard earned savings of grandmas and average working stiffs. These regular folks deposit their savings with a bank because they believe the savings are safe. This means that banks, by law, have very strict guidelines about how and when they are allowed to utilize depositors money to make loans. Banks are interested in low-risk, low-reward, long-term loans in businesses that are easy to understand.

These restrictions mean that there is a whole world of mid-market firms that would have trouble securing a loan from a bank. An example of a mid-market firm would be a family dry cleaner that had, over time, grown to a chain of one hundred dry cleaners. Or a firm owned by private equity investors that has hundreds of millions of dollars in revenue, but is not generally known on Wall Street or by the general public. For every big name, publicly traded firm like Apple out there, there are tens of thousands of mid-market firms; businesses that are growing rapidly, but not necessarily on any bankers short list of desirable credits.

In particular, BDCs tend to thrive by servicing niche markets. One example of a niche BDC that does very nicely is Horizon Technology Financial Corporation (HRZN). Horizon specializes in loans to mid-market companies in the biotech and IT sectors. Horizon makes secured loans, which can utilize intellectual property as collateral for a loan. Can you imagine your average loan officer at Bank of America trying to figure out the collateral value of a new molecule? This is why dozens of companies have turned to Horizon. They need a lender that understands their particular niche.

A lot of BDCs specialize in short-term, high-interest rate loans. One could use the term bridge loan. An example would be a biotech that is planning to go public in the next year. The time between the company filing its paperwork to go public and the day of the actual IPO could be 12 months or more. This would mean that the biotech is expecting a big influx of cash soon. In fact, they may actually be working with an underwriter on the IPO that has guaranteed a big influx of cash. But in the meantime, the biotech may actually need more cash to ramp up operations in expectation of this IPO. They wouldn't want to sell stock, because they have this big liquidity event coming up, and they don't want to dilute the ownership stake of the existing shareholders. Enter the BDC. The BDC provides a high interest loan, secured against intellectual property, that only lasts for a year. When the biotech client goes public, they immediately turn around and pay off the high interest loan. Meanwhile, the BDC has made great interest, and can now turn around and recycle the same money. If you repeat this same process while minimizing any loan losses, the situation gets lucrative very quickly. That high rate of income and the recycling of capital is why many BDCs can pay an investor double-digit dividend yields month after month.

Risks

So, BDCs share a lot of factors in common with mortgage REITs. One thing that BDCs do not share in common with agency mortgage REITs is that they are not investing in loans that are guaranteed. Which means BDC management teams are borrowing money to turn around and lend that money to smallish corporations that can default. In theory, this makes BDCs risky. But many BDCs have done a thorough job of managing risk.

If you want to see an example of how a sharp BDC management team can navigate risky waters, check out New Mountain Financial Corporation (NMFC). New

Mountain focuses on what they call defensive sectors, i.e. business sectors that are resistant to economic downturns. This theory was put to a radical test during the worst of the coronavirus crisis. With America closing down, and businesses failing left and right, these were scary times for business development companies.

NMFC responded by providing extensive transparency to investors. They furnished frequent reports quantifying and explaining the financial situations of each of the loans that they had outstanding. They made some swift moves to limit their exposure to the worst hit sectors of the economy, and maximize exposure to sectors that "won" the coronavirus crisis.

The result? Not only did NMFC not go bankrupt during this time of national crisis, but investors would have barely noticed any crisis at all if they hadn't been paying careful attention. The company did temporarily trim their dividend by less than 20%. But other than that, the cash flow kept rolling, month after month.

Not every BDC did this well, but a surprising number of lending corporations came through the entire ordeal unscathed. This means that BDCs have earned a place in the income portfolio of any investor who lives off of passive income.

How To Invest

There are dozens of different business development companies out there. Not all are created equal. How do you choose the right ones for your portfolio?

One approach is simply to go with the largest companies. Larger companies have deeper pockets, better connections on Wall Street, and larger stakeholders that make it hard for them to go bankrupt. According to theblalance.com, here are the ten largest business development companies by assets under management as of Spring 2021.

1. Ares Capital Corp (ARCC): $6.96 billion
2. Owl Rock Capital (ORCC): $5.70 billion
3. Prospect Capital Corporation (PSEC): $3.20 billion
4. FS KKR Capital Corp (FSK): $3.03 billion
5. Golub Capital BDC, Inc (GBDC): $2.35 billion
6. Goldman Sachs BDC Inc (GSBD): $1.57 billion
7. Main Street Capital Corp (MAIN): $1.43 billion
8. New Mountain Finance Corp (NMFC): $1.19 billion
9. Hercules Capital (HTGC): $1.18 billion
10. TPG Specialty Lending Inc. (TSLX): $1.14 billion

If you stick with the top half of this list, you gain a degree of safety due to sheer size.

Another way of selecting some good BDCs for your income portfolio is to choose companies that specialize in a niche that you know. For example, I know a lot about biotech (I actually wrote a book on the subject, Your First Biotech Million). That is why I chose Horizon Technology (HRZN). They make loans to a lot of biotech concerns. I feel that I am in a unique position to understand the quarterly reports they send me, and take action if necessary. (That would be rare, by the way. I almost always buy and hold).

There are dozens of BDCs that serve specialized niches. If you feel that you know a lot about construction, you can find a fund that specializes in construction lending. If you feel that you know a lot about IT, you can find a firm that focuses on information technology. Everybody knows about something. Leverage your knowledge to pick some winners.

Lastly, if you just want a taste of the sector, but don't want to spend time and energy researching something that is not your core competency, you can always buy an exchange traded fund that represents the sector. This way, you will gain broad exposure to the asset class, without betting too much on any one sector. Because the BDC sector is itself considered to be a niche investment, one of the few pure play ETFs is BIZD (Van Eck Vectors ETF BDC INCOME ETF). This exchange traded fund is currently paying a meaty 9.4% yield, delivered to your inbox monthly. Many other alternative income exchange traded funds offer some amount of BDC exposure. One example would be the Global X Superdividend Alternative ETF (ALTY). Although this exchange traded fund does not focus purely on BDCs, it offers a broad range of high dividend, niche companies that favor big cash flow. ALTY pays slightly north of 8% dividend yield at the moment.

If you think of your retirement income portfolio as a savory gumbo, with many tasty ingredients all boiling together in a pot, you can consider the BDC sector as a dash of cayenne pepper to give the gumbo some kick. You would never want your portfolio to have more than 5 or 10% exposure to business development companies. But just a dash of these high dividend yield corporations can spice up your retirement income in a flash.

Chapter 11: Preferred Stocks - For Those Who Prefer Safe Income

O ne of the big reasons why I wrote this book was because traditional retirement planning has changed radically in just a few short years. I wanted to help people navigate those changes. You'll remember the big change that we discussed earlier is that bonds, the cornerstone of retirement income for most of the 20th century, have been rendered all but useless due to ultra low interest rates.

Why exactly is it that bonds were so popular to begin with? In the world of finance, where complicated events often have complicated explanations, this explanation is easy. It boils down to just one word. Safety. Bonds were very popular for decades on end because they were an extremely safe investment for retirees who just wanted modest, regular income to pay their rent.

The Federal Reserve has all but taken away that option for most retirees. Today, most decent bonds pay 3% interest or less. Many bonds have had protective covenants reduced or removed entirely so they are no longer the safe harbor they once were.

With inflation taken into account, most bond investors lose money every quarter. But, as the saying goes, "where there is a will, there is a way." If you long for bond-like safety, but need decent income, there is still a way that you can achieve this goal. Preferred stocks are a separate class of securities that offer the best of both worlds: the security of a bond with the beneficial tax treatment of a stock. Even in this era of micro interest rates, preferred stocks may be a great answer for investors who prefer safe income.

Half and Half

Preferred stocks are often referred to as hybrid securities. They offer a mix of bond-like and stock-like features. Sort of the financial equivalent of a platypus. The different features, grafted together, may seem unnatural at first, but this odd mix has actually survived for a very long time, and fends for itself quite nicely in the financial jungle.

Preferred stocks have existed as a class of securities for many decades. There are some records of preferred shares existing even hundreds of years ago. Simply put, preferred shares are a kind of stock that prioritizes income over appreciation and control. Many of the world's biggest, best-known companies offer preferred shares; they offer more income and more safety for your average investor, even if they offer less total upside than common shares.

First, let's talk about safety. When a company goes bankrupt, the courts may decide to liquidate the company's assets. In these cases, bond holders and other debt holders get first right of repayment from the liquidated assets of the deceased company. If there are any assets left after that debt repayment, then preferred shareholders get repaid. Common shareholders always come last in a bankruptcy; they typically get nothing. So, while preferred shares are less safe than bonds, they are still more safe than common stock. And remember, many of the world's largest, most established companies offer preferred shares, so bankruptcy is unlikely to begin with.

Preferred shares also offer a more secure and regular stream of income for shareholders. Although most large, established companies prioritize paying a regular dividend every quarter, they don't have to. Each quarter, the board of directors reviews financial results, and decides how much dividend to pay based on a wide variety of factors. In times of trouble, a dividend can be slashed or eliminated altogether. Not so with preferred shares.

Preferred shares are sold with a pre-determined, fixed rate of yield, that must be paid every quarter. So, while the board can slash a common stock dividend for any reason, at any time, the preferred shareholders must be paid a fixed amount. If the company hits desperate times and is teetering on bankruptcy, the board of directors may halt the dividend for everyone. But this is only in the most extreme and rare situations. Many preferred shares offer a feature known as cumulative dividends. This means that, if an emergency occurs and the board suspends dividends for everyone, then a debt accrues to the company, and all preferred shareholders must be paid back dividends before common shareholders get a penny. These features wind up delivering a high level of safety to income dependent investors.

Preferred shares typically yield about double what common stocks pay. As I write this, the average S&P 500 stock pays just over 2% dividend yield. Many of those very same mega corporations also offer preferred shares that pay 4 or 5%.

It should be noted that although preferreds are often called hybrid securities, they still qualify as stock in the eyes of your Uncle Sam. This means that they receive a beneficial level of taxation next to bonds. Details can vary based on your particular tax bracket and situation, but many investors would pay much lower taxes on income derived from preferred shares as opposed to bonds. Consult with your CPA.

Of course, nothing in life is free. In exchange for great income and superior safety, investors in preferred shares give up a few things. First, preferred shares do not have voting rights. So, a preferred investor has the best claim on a corporation's income, but no claim on governance when proxy vote time comes. Second, a preferred shareholder will rarely see price appreciation on her shares the way a common shareholder might. Preferred share prices are more likely to be governed by fluctuations in interest rates than the supply and demand dynamics that govern common share pricing. A lot of retirees have enjoyed steady, soothing income from preferred shares, but few have gotten rich this way.

Risks

While preferred shares are low risk investments, they are not risk free. Like any investment, there are a few risks that an investor should understand. In this case, there are some unique risks that relate to the hybrid structure of the securities.

The two biggest risks have to do with interest rates. If rates are rising, this may hurt the market value of your preferred shares. For example, let's say that you purchase some preferred shares in Bank of America today at 5% yield. Right now, that is an amazing yield at fairly low risk, because a ten-year treasury bond, the gold standard of credit quality, yields something in the range of 1%. But let's say interest rates rise dramatically over the next five years. Now you can buy a ten-year treasury bond for 4%. That would hurt the market value of your preferred shares. That is because risk averse investors will now flock to the treasury bonds. The closer the treasury yield gets to the yield on your preferred shares, the less valuable your preferred shares may be. The scenario I am describing here hasn't happened in decades, because rates have only moved in one way (down) for a long, long time. However, if rates were to rise substantially, you could get hurt.

It's important to note that in the "bad" scenario above, nothing about your income even changes. If you are happily living your retired life, and you use the steady income from your preferred shares to pay for your lifestyle, you may not even care if the market price of the security goes down. The cash flow coming from the shares stays the same. But it is a risk you should be aware of.

The other big risk also has to do with interest rates, but it's actually the opposite of the prior scenario. If you own a preferred security at 5%, and market interest rates fall precipitously, the issuing company may have the right to call the shares. This means that they can redeem the shares at their par value, without any regard to what you actually paid for the shares. They would do this because, now that interest rates have fallen, they can redeem your 5% shares and offer new 4% shares to the public. Since prevailing interest rates have fallen, they can pay less yield and still be competitive.

Calls have happened a lot over the last few decades, as interest rates have fallen and fallen. There was a time when many preferred shares paid 10% yield! Obviously, those have mostly been called and replaced with lower yielding securities. This phenomena can be damaging for a retiree. If you are happily receiving 5% yield, and your shares get called, then you may have to replace those old shares with new, lower yielding shares. That can hurt your cash flow on a practical level. The good news is that, as I write this text, interest rates are at an absolute rock bottom. They have fallen so far, for so long, that calls now seem unlikely. If interest rates rise from 2021 levels (a huge "if") then this risk may be something you need to factor in.

The last risk is simple liquidation risk. Although bankruptcies are rare with major corporations, it does occasionally happen. If you were a bond holder of Lehman Brothers when they went bankrupt back in 2009, you did better than if you were a holder of preferred shares. (Remember, debt holders are first in the repayment line, preferred shareholders are next). This is why you shouldn't just buy any preferred share from any company without investigating. Do your research, buy names you know, and scour the media landscape to make sure that you avoid media red flags on any particular company.

Looking For Safety

You can buy preferred shares through whatever stock brokerage you typically use. If you opt to own individual preferred shares, the biggest issuers are often banks and utilities. You can often buy from big names such as Bank of America, Citibank, Duke Energy, or NextEra Energy. The fact that these titans of business are household names means that you can easily find research reports on the companies and you can easily access their financial statements to make your own assessment of their financial strength.

Another great way to go with preferred shares is to buy the preferred shares of equity REITs and mortgage REITs. A lot of investors feel that this is a very safe investment, for the following reason: REITs only exist to pay dividends. They are specifically set up as cash flow machines, with stock appreciation a distant second priority. This means that the management is very, very unlikely to cut the dividend of a REIT. As a counter example, Disney recently cut their dividend simply because management thought they could invest that money in building up their streaming service, and the market value of the shares would rise. Disney management is more focused on share price and less on the dividend. REIT managers are famous for obsessing over the cash flow necessary to grow the dividend; they know that the dividend is what keeps their shareholders around. Thus, preferred shares offered by real estate companies are often considered among the safest.

Another way to manage your risk is to simply buy exchange traded funds that represent a basket of preferred shares. This move may not eliminate your interest rate risk, but it brings the risk of bankruptcy almost down to zero. One company can go bankrupt, bringing your investment down to zero. A basket of fifty companies, many of which are big, well known banks and utilities, is very unlikely to lose all of your investment. The Invesco Preferred fund (PGX) and the Global X Preferred ETF (PFFD) are two great options that pump out steady, tax-favored dividends, quarter after quarter, year after year.

Sadly, no one can wave a magic wand to bring back the days when ultra safe bonds paid 5, 6, or 7% per year. But preferred stocks can still fill that fixed income gap in your portfolio. Remember the platypus; it may display a weird mix of features for a living creature, but apparently the design works. The animal has thrived for long periods of time. So have preferred stocks.

Chapter 12: Closed End Funds - Open the Door to Income

You may have noticed by now that as we have moved through part II of this book, we have spent a lot of time discussing interest rates and the borrowing of money. That is because our current ultra low interest rate environment is a classic double-edged sword. On one hand, the only reason why this book is necessary at all is because interest rates are so low that a retiree would struggle to live off the interest from traditional investments. But on the other hand, interest rates are so microscopic that now is a great time to borrow money. As you may remember, both mortgage REITs and business development companies exist almost exclusively because of borrowed money, or leverage in industry parlance.

Does this mean that you should start borrowing lots of money yourself to invest? Probably not (although we will discuss a specific tactic in the next chapter). Borrowing money at any interest rate comes with outsized risks, and is best managed by a team of professionals.

But what if I told you that you can hire such a team of professionals for a modest fee? What if I told you that there is a kind of investment security created specifically to benefit from borrowed money, but at the same time designed to limit your risk?

These securities are known as closed-end funds. Closed end funds (CEFs) are a world unto their own. There are many different kinds, all of which target different investment objectives. But they all have a few things in common. They utilize leverage to create more income than is commonly available on the market. They contain the risks of leverage and leave those risks to professionals. They trade like a regular stock that you can buy and sell on E-Trade, Charles Schwab, or whatever brokerage you use.

On the Highway to Income

You really can visualize a CEF as a financial vehicle. That is because a CEF itself is a kind of entity that carries other securities inside of it. For example, the Tekla World Healthcare Fund (Ticker: THW) is a closed-end fund that carries within it shares of major publicly traded healthcare companies. Also within the fund is a certain amount of borrowed money. This means that the fund yields 8.2% monthly; if you had bought the healthcare shares outright, they might only yield 3% quarterly. In this example, the CEF is the vehicle and the securities and leverage inside are the passengers.

You can think of the CEF world as a highway. At any moment when you are driving down a crowded highway, you might see hundreds of different kinds of vehicles; some large like a bus, others small like a Fiat. Each vehicle might have different passengers. But they all have a few key things in common; they all have wheels, they all have a steering wheel, and they are all trying to get somewhere. Same thing with closed-end funds.

On the highway to income, you might see Tekla World Healthcare, which borrows a lot of money and specializes in brand name healthcare stocks. But you might also see a fund that invests in municipal bonds, a different one that carries utility stocks, and finally a third one loaded with preferred shares. Each one may carry different quantities of borrowed money, and each one may have a management (or driver) who drives more or less aggressively. But almost everything on this highway pays better dividends than regular stocks.

Why are these vehicles called closed-end funds? What does that even mean? Well, an open-end fund is a typical mutual fund or exchange traded fund, where the fund's managers can create just as many shares as the market demands. So the share price of the mutual fund or exchange traded fund typically very closely tracks the value of the underlying assets (also known as NAV, net asset value). In a closed end fund, the entity only has so many fixed shares. So the shares themselves trade based on supply and demand, and may exceed the NAV in value, or lag the NAV. This can create mismatches that can be exploited by astute investors. It's not uncommon for a closed end fund to trade below the value of the fund's assets. So, a closed end fund consisting of utility stocks could trade at $10 per share on the open market, but the NAV is currently $11. In this case, you can buy shares in the fund for less than the current value of the underlying assets. As you might guess, this is called buying at a discount. You could literally get a $1 worth of value for $0.90!

Typically, open-ended mutual funds and exchange traded funds don't employ leverage. So, whatever yield the underlying securities produce is what you get. For example, the Select Spider Healthcare ETF (Ticker: XLV), one of the most widely held open-ended healthcare funds, currently yields about 1.6%. The Tekla World Healthcare fund pays around 8% every month! Leverage is the magic fuel that has turbo charged the Tekla vehicle. That sucker is now flying down the highway.

Some Words About Leverage

If leverage can boost your dividends from 1.6% to 8%, it must be the greatest thing ever, right? Does that mean that everyone should be borrowing?

No. There are a few times when I might recommend that regular investors borrow at today's crazy low interest rates, but generally it's too risky for most people.

Investing borrowed money is the only way that you can actually lose more than you own. If you have $100 to invest, and you make a poorly advised bet, you can lose all of the $100 (although this is very rare). Then you have $0. That outcome hurts, but may not be the end of the world.

If you have $100 to invest, and you borrow another $100 to invest, then you can potentially lose $200. At the end of this bad bet, you are actually $100 in the hole! Investing with borrowed money is often a "live by the sword, die by the sword" proposition, and typically not suitable for your standard retiree. (There is one big exception that we will discuss in the next chapter).

When you choose to invest in a closed-end fund, there are a few protections that moderate your risk. First and foremost is the law. CEFs can only take on a certain amount of debt as per the law. According to the Investment Company Act of 1940, the maximum amount of debt that a CEF can carry is $1 for every $3 in assets (33.3% of assets). To put things in vehicle terms, this means that each car on the highway must have, at a minimum, a seat belt, good breaks, and a reasonable speed limit.

Another reason why leverage is best left to a CEF is because the sponsors of these companies have deep Wall Street connections and can borrow money on very good terms. At this point, many of the larger CEFs are literally borrowing money at interest rates of less than 1%, with very flexible repayments terms. It's highly unlikely that you, as an individual amateur investor, could borrow money on these fabulous terms.

Lastly, most CEF managers have decades of experience in very specific niches. The fact that the industry is regulated by a law that was promulgated in 1940 demonstrates that these managers potentially bring a lot of experience to the table. They are not necessarily any smarter than you, but they are more experienced. They may know when to hit the gas and when to hit the breaks in terms of leverage, and they may utilize sophisticated derivative strategies (calls and puts) to protect against sudden movements in interest rates. Oftentimes, they also have very deep expertise in the particular securities that their fund invests in. For example, the Double Line Income Solutions Fund (Ticker: DSL) boasts a team of managers that specializes in mortgage bonds and foreign sovereign bonds. They don't do pharma stocks or utility stocks; they just offer dozens of years worth of experience in certain kinds of bonds. Can you say the same for yourself?

Red Light, Yellow Light, Green Light

As you are cruising down the CEF highway, there are some key factors that need to be considered as you select the right funds for you.

The first thing that you need to check when a fund grabs your eye is if the fund can cover its monthly dividend distributions through organic earnings. If a fund meets its monthly obligations through return of capital, that is a yellow or a red light.

You may remember that we used the term return of capital earlier in our discussion of REITs. While in the REIT world, return of capital can be a good thing, in the CEF world, the same term means something very different. Closed-end funds are famous for steady, generous monthly distributions. But it's important for you to understand just a little bit about the engine that makes your vehicle function.

Most CEFs follow what is referred to as a managed dividend policy. This means that every fiscal year, the board of directors decides on a fixed amount of dividend and pays that amount out every month. The idea is to provide certainty and regularity to retirees like yourself who live off those dividends.

There are four ways that a CEF can generate those payments every month. The first way is through net investment income. This means that, in any given month, the securities inside the fund threw off enough cash to meet the monthly distribution goal. Because up to 33% of the securities were purchased with debt, they should throw off more income than a normal portfolio with no leverage would throw off. Strong, consistent net investment income is a big green light for you.

The second way that a fund could generate cash for monthly distribution would be through net realized short-term capital gains. This would mean that the share price of the passenger securities within your vehicle have appreciated lately. So management choses to sell some of those shares, reaping the capital gains, and funnel some of the profits your way. This is a good enough way to generate income for investors, but it's the reason why CEFs don't appreciate over time the way a plain exchange traded fund would. Most of the benefit you will receive as a shareholder in a CEF will come from your monthly income; that is because some or all of the capital gains are liquidated on a regular basis and paid out to you.

The third way that a fund could generate that monthly cash payout would be net realized long-term capital gains." This is exactly the same concept as method number two, except it's selling some passenger securities that have been inside the fund for a long time. The only difference between method #2 and method #3 is taxation. Long-term capital gains are taxed at a lower rate than short-term, so that makes method #3 somewhat preferable.

Your yellow light or red light occurs when you see "return of capital." In this context, this means that your fund did not generate enough money this month to make the payout, so the fund is just taking a portion of your own invested capital and handing it right back to you. This can be a useful and beneficial tool to some fund managers in some cases, but it's often widely abused.

Return of capital is a beneficial tool in some cases because it allows management to maintain the managed distribution policy without disturbing the regularity of your income. So, for example, if a certain fund pays you $100 every month, for years on end, and one month the fund doesn't generate that much cash organically, the fund managers might employ the return of capital. That way, your monthly income is not interrupted, and your lifestyle is not disturbed. They might send you $50 from profits, and $50 from return of capital. Or $90 from profits and $10 from return of capital. Or, on some really bad months, 90% return of capital.

You might remember from our chapter on REITs that in that world, return of capital is merely an accounting term with little relation to reality. In the CEF world, return of capital has real consequences. Whatever amount is sent to you that is not profit, (i.e. return of capital) gets deducted from your fund's net asset value (NAV). In other words, in the CEF world, return of capital literally means return of capital, so the value of the assets of your fund is reduced. If we go back to our vehicle analogy, when a CEF returns your capital, they are throwing things out the window. First they throw out a passenger's sunglasses. Then they throw out a passenger's iPhone. If management isn't careful, they wind up throwing whole passengers out of the vehicle. You left your destination with ten passengers loaded with belongings and arrived at your destination with just seven passengers stripped of their sundry possessions. Not good. Not good at all

Unfortunately, the apparent complexity of this situation scares away too many investors from what is really a superior asset class. If this all sounds too complicated for you, stay calm! I am about to make it very easy.

It's very easy to check on the health of any closed-end fund. Simply look for a document entitled 19(a). "19a" stands for Section 19(a) of the 1940 Investment Company Act. That's right, CEFs have been compelled to follow more or less the same rules of the road for more than 80 years. If millions of Americans have figured these rules out over several generations, you can, too.

You can typically find these 19(a) forms on the website of any closed-end fund. The 19(a) form is a simple form that the fund must file, every month, that explains the source of it's distributions for that month. For example, if you go to the website for the Cohen & Steers Infrastructure Fund (ticker: UTF), you can easily find monthly 19(a) forms going back for years.

This form is a very basic grid that will show you, each month, where your payment came from. If your payment was 90% net investment income and 10% return of capital, the form will show that clearly. And vice versa.

The Cohen & Steers Infrastructure Fund is an example of a CEF that has used return of capital responsibly. After clicking on a few of the 19(a) forms from 2020 and 2019, it's plain to see that most months, their payment comes from net investment income and long-term capital gains. Occasionally, when they have a bad month, they use return of capital to fill in that gap. That way, I can count on my steady payments no matter what. That small amount is deducted from the underlying net asset value. But in good months, they replace what they took out, and in fact, over the last decade, the fund's net asset value grew by about 10% a year, despite the occasional returns of capital. This is a status green light.

Other funds are not as responsible. They over promise on their monthly distributions in a bid to attract as many investors as possible. They know they can abuse return of capital, slowly depleting the NAV, because they are counting on an investor base that is not educated, does not ask questions, and does not supervise management. As long as you check those 19(a) forms a couple times of year, that group of chumps will not include you.

Navigating NAV

The concept of net asset value ("NAV") in regards to CEF share price is also a critical bit of mechanics to understand. A solid understanding of this idea will power your portfolio to profit.

To review, the CEF is the vehicle, and the NAV are the passengers within the vehicle (the assets). Sometimes, the passengers within the vehicle are worth more than the vehicle itself, and sometimes the vehicle fetches more on the open market than the passengers alone would. When the shares of a CEF trade for less than the value of the NAV, then they are said to be trading at a discount. When the CEF shares trade for more than the NAV, then they are trading at a premium. The discrepancies between these two prices can turbo charge your profits.

Sometimes, there is a good reason why shares of a CEF might trade for less than the NAV. Maybe the whole sector is depressed and has attracted negative media attention (2020 was the annus horribilis for oil, for an example). Maybe the fund in particular has problems (accounting scandal, corporate takeover drama, etc). But very often, whole sectors simply fall out of fashion for very little reason. As we've discussed, this is like the Z-Cavarricis lurking in the back of your closet. There is nothing wrong with them; they were fine garments when you originally bought them, and in fact, you could wear them today, if you could stand being mocked by your colleagues. ("Hey, the 90s called, they want their pants back!"). People that enjoy bargain hunting can find some real value in the CEF space by looking to buy funds that are trading at a discount to their NAV.

Let's look at my investment in the Tekla World Healthcare Fund (Ticker: THW). When I bought this fund, it was trading at a discount to NAV of about 10%. The thinking was that Donald Trump was going to take a wrecking ball to the American pharmaceutical industry and that long threatened pricing reforms would greatly limit Big Pharma's profits moving forward. I never believed in that theory, and I'm just a nerd for healthcare stocks, so I bought THW. At the time, the CEF was yielding in the range of 9%. So, for every $1,000 I invested, I could get an annual payout of $90 while I waited for the world to come to its senses on healthcare.

Guess what? They did. Big Pharma weathered the storm of hot air about pricing reform (as they always have) and then COVID-19 happened. All of a sudden, instead of being the boogieman of American capitalism, Big Pharma was viewed as the hero. In America's time of need, they came running for help, and Big Pharma produced massive quantities of highly efficacious vaccines in record time. To return to the fashion analogy, suddenly those Z-Cavarrichis came roaring back into fashion, and you were the first guy at the party to rock that style. After all, you never threw them out to begin with. Today, Tekla World Healthcare Fund actually trades at a premium of about 10% to the NAV. So, not only have I collected a juicy 9% dividend every month for years, I have also enjoyed substantial price appreciation on my shares.

Am I some kind of investing genius? Not really. I just learned the rules of the road and learned to drive astutely. You can do the same.

Vehicle Shopping

Armed with knowledge, you are ready to hit the CEF highway. These funds typically pay between 4 and 10% monthly dividends, often on a tax advantaged basis. These strong, steady payouts can make a huge difference in your retirement income.

As we said earlier, there are thousands of different CEFs with as much variety as that crowded highway we have been talking about. There are few different ways that you can shop.

The first way is to choose a sector and work backwards. In my example, I have a particular interest in healthcare stocks; this led me to Tekla World Healthcare Fund. Maybe you like municipal bonds, or utility stocks, or even preferred shares. All of these are different kinds of passengers that can be stuffed into a CEF vehicle. The reason why you would buy them through a CEF as opposed to an exchange traded fund or directly would be because the CEF will provide higher yield. As stated earlier, Tekla World Healthcare often yields 8% or more, while the underlying stocks, if bought directly, would only yield between 2 and 4%.

Another example would be CEFs that invest in municipal bond funds. My elderly aunt loves to invest in municipal bonds. These are ultra safe bonds issued by state and local governments to pay for municipal projects, such as water and sewer. These bonds have been a staple of retirement planning for decades because they are very safe and offer tax free yield. However, in the last decade or so, "muni bonds," as they are called, have offered less and less yield to the point that you would be lucky to collect 2% on your money. Now my aunt buys muni bonds through closed-end funds and she can collect 4% or more, tax free (note: taxation treatment of CEFs is related to the taxation treatment of the underlying securities. Consult your CPA).

The risk profile of the CEF is somewhat more than if you bought the securities directly. That is because the funds employ leverage. However, much of this risk is simply volatility, meaning that the price of the fund may fluctuate somewhat more than the underlying securities would if held directly. So, when choosing how much of your portfolio to allot to CEFs, be aware that they are somewhat more volatile than lower yielding options. However, the chances of your CEF value going to $0 are very remote. Remember, each CEF has dozens of investments inside of it. It would take a cataclysmic event for that many names to fail all at once.

So, you can shop for closed-end funds by first choosing a sector, then finding funds that cater to that sector. If you are a value shopper, like myself, a different method may appeal to you.

You can run a screen to help you focus only on funds that are currently trading at discount to NAV. This is like going to the Goodwill and hunting for treasure among the trash. If you find ten CEFs where the NAV is worth more than the open market share prices, there will be a reason for eight of those funds. For two out of ten, the shares will just be on sale for no apparent reason. The CEF market is very inefficient, and a determined shopper can find some real deals and steals.

It might seem intimidating at first to sift through hundreds of coals to find a few glittery CEF diamonds. But there is a whole community out there that can help you. Closed-end funds investors are the Trekkies of the investment world. They have a cult-like devotion to their niche, and they often gather online, or sometimes in person, to exchange tips and tricks. People really geek out over closed-end funds ("Set your phasers to 'profit!')

There are dozens of newsletters you can subscribe to where they have done a lot of the research for you in terms of identifying undervalued CEFs. These newsletters can range from $9 per month to $99 per month; a great deal compared to the cost of an MBA. There are also countless analysts on Seeking Alpha who specialize in closed-end funds. For a very modest subscription fee, you can browse a wide variety of CEF research.

You can also just do the research yourself. Like anything else, it seems hard at first, but becomes exceedingly easy with practice. In both of the examples that we have discussed in this chapter (Cohen & Steers and Tekla), all of the information you would ever need is posted directly on their websites. You can compare NAV to share price, you can compare NAV to share price over time, you can check out those all-important 19(a) notifications, and you can read detailed biographies of the fund's management.

When you are working a job for a living, you have no residual. Even though I was an award-winning salesperson, I was only as good as my last sale. I worked, I got results, I got paid. The very next week, it was back to work, hoping to get results, hoping to get paid.

When you teach yourself how to shop for closed-end funds, you only need to do the work one time. It might take you a few months to learn the basics, and a few years to get really good. But once you have learned how to do it, then you know how to do it. You do the research once, you buy the securities once, and then you put up your feet and enjoy the fruit of your hard work for decades to come. Does this sound like a good "job" to you?

Closed-end funds have been popular high yield investments since at least 1940. This is because they use leverage in a controlled, focused way without burdening the investor with the risks that come with directly borrowing money. For most retirees, this indirect borrowing is all the leverage they would ever need. But there are a few cases when it pays to borrow directly. We will conclude the special vehicles section of this book by examining some special scenarios where borrowing directly is the smartest move.

Chapter 13: Borrow Your Income

H ere is a quick historical quiz for you. Complete the following aphorism: "The only sure things in life are death and…"

Even if you don't like history, you may very well know the phrase. If you have made some money in business you certainly know the phrase.

"The only sure things in life are death and taxes." -Benjamin Franklin.

No one really likes taxes. They are a necessary part of society, and the law should be followed at all times. But most people are always happy to hear about ways that taxes can be minimized while still following the law. When interest rates are this low, one great way to minimize your taxes is to borrow against your stocks for your spending money. This works especially well with dividend stocks.

Income from stock dividends and stocks sales is categorized as capital gains and often taxed at rates between 0% and 23%. (If you only hold stocks for a short period of time, the tax structure is worse. The rates discussed here are for long-term capital gains.) What determines whether you pay 0, 15, or 23% on your capital gains? Your income level. The higher your income, the higher taxes you pay. This rate can be even more if you are a high income earner in a state like New York or California. In those states, you could easily be paying 30% or more of your capital gains to tax. So borrowing for income rather than selling shares makes more sense the richer you get.

As I write this text, our proud nation has fallen on desperate economic times, whether it feels that way on the street or not. Every single month our Federal Government spends much more than it takes in; the current fiscal situation is unsustainable due to ever growing mountains of national debt. Thus, we can reason that taxes are likely to go up sooner or later. People who pay 23% on capital gains income today could easily wind up paying 37% or more. Just to put that percentage in perspective, if you invest $100,000 and over time the value of your shares rises to $200,0000, then you will have to pay $37,000 in taxes when you sell.

Or you can just borrow against your shares and never sell them. In that case, you would pay 0% capital gains tax, because borrowed money is not considered income (since you will have to pay it back eventually).

This is not a solution for everyone. As the saying goes, it only works "when the stars align." There are two basic constellations that must be right. The macroeconomic situation of society must be right, and your personal situation must be right.

What Condition Your Condition Is In

The first element that must be right is the ratio of interest rates to the rates of return on your investments. In the 1980s, when interest rates were at 9 and 10%, and your stocks might return 8% or less, then this strategy would have made no sense. Today, qualified borrowers can get loans for 3% or less, and a conservative stock portfolio could return 7% or more. Under those circumstances, borrowing against stocks, rather than selling against stocks and triggering big taxes, starts to make sense.

This is especially true for dividend stocks. As we discussed earlier in the book, most people just earn 2 or 3% dividends on their stocks. By now, you should feel confident that you can earn 5 or 6% without breaking a sweat. If you borrow money at 3% interest against stocks paying a 6% dividend, the stocks pay the interest for you and the loan is basically free.

I say basically free because the money might still need to be repaid at some point. So this technique might not be right for everyone. It's only right for certain kinds of people in very specific circumstances.

The first circumstance might be if you are a traditional retiree advancing in age, or if you are generally in poor health. If, for whatever reason, you think you have less than ten years to live, you might be able to take the loan and never need to worry about paying it off while you're still above ground. If you are a high income person, that means you could be unlocking 37% more value to be used and enjoyed while you're still alive, because you can use more of your money without paying taxes on it. Upon your death, your estate will have to pay off the loan, but at that point you'll be beyond those kinds of earthly worries.

Another less grim scenario might be if you have many years left to live, but your income is lumpy. For example, I know several real estate brokers who happily live off borrowed money. They borrow against their assets to unlock tax free income, living off that money for months or even years. The whole time, they know they have large commissions coming to them, but they can't predict quite when. When the commissions do come in, the money is used to pay down the loan. If their operational bank account runs short, they then borrow against their assets to tide them over until their next big commission comes in. This approach allows them to be more patient in business, focusing on doing the right deals the right ways instead of worrying if they can pay their rent every month.

This approach can work for anyone who has an income that is large, but somewhat erratic or unpredictable. Some people receive unpredictable income from hedge funds, venture capital funds, or real estate projects. This lifestyle could even work for an actor or script writer who makes big, but irregular income from her creative work.

The other category of people where this might make sense are people with a borderline taxation status. Sometimes liquidation of securities can boost you into a higher tax bracket.

Let's say your regular income from your daily activities is $150,000. You have a paper profit of $250,000 in your stocks. Your daughter is getting married and you want to throw her a big party. But if you liquidate that large profit, you are going to trigger large taxes because the one-time, irregular profit will accidentally catapult you into a higher tax bracket. In these kinds of cases you might prefer to just borrow the money against your stock, and defer the big tax bill to another day.

Good Credit vrs Bad Credit

Credit and loans got a bad name in personal finance circles because most people have abused the privilege of credit and thus wound up with disastrous results. So-called "professionals" have also abused credit, for different reasons, and unleashed some infamously bad consequences. Credit is like fire; if you use it right, it will keep your shivering village warm throughout the cold night. If you use it wrong, you'll burn down the village. If your guts tell you that you could fall into the second group, then don't borrow anything at all. I built up my wealth for two decades before I began to explore this space.

The typical credit disaster involves credit cards. Credit cards are a terrible idea for two reasons. First, they charge absurd interest rates that actually would have been illegal throughout most of history. There is no such thing as a "good" loan at 19% interest. Second, they require regular payments that must be made on a dictated schedule. Any deviation from the dictated schedule triggers ruinous fees that bury consumers alive. All of these bad elements of credit cards stem from the fact that credit cards make unsecured loans. This means that huge corporations are making dubious loans to strangers with no assets to hold for collateral. Collateral is an asset that the lender holds as security to make sure they will be repaid. Would you make loans to a stranger with little legal recourse if they defaulted? Probably not, but if you did, you would demand outrageous interest rates and fees, because random lending is risky business.

What we were discussing above is secured lending, whereby you offer your stock as collateral. This dramatically changes the price of the loan and the terms of the loan. Currently I am able to borrow at less than 3% annual interest and I can pay back the loan whenever I feel like it. Compare that to 21% on your credit card with required payments every month. The cruel truth is: the richer you get, the easier it is to borrow money on great terms. If you get an asset based loan from your brokerage house, your interest rate will typically be determined by the size of your account. I know people with smaller brokerage accounts who are paying 5% for loans, and I know a few very rich people who have massive stock holdings who are paying as little as 1% to borrow money. When you have assets, you are the one with the advantage; don't be afraid to shop around and negotiate on price and terms.

That being said, there are still plenty of ways to set yourself up for disaster, even with asset based lending. That is typically where professional investors have gone terribly wrong in the past. They simply borrow too much. It's very possible to enjoy too much of a good thing. Remember the last time you had five glasses of champagne instead of just one or two? How did you feel the next morning?

Financial history is replete with cautionary tales of financial managers who borrowed too much, leaving their finances very fragile. You must remember that your relationship with your lender is very dependent on the condition of your collateral (in this case, your stock). Although we have already discussed many strategies to mitigate stock market risk, there will always be volatility, and even occasional stock market crashes. If you borrow $100,000 against $300,000 in collateral, and your portfolio crashes 30%, your collateral is still worth $210,000, which easily secures your $100,000 loan. However, if you borrow too much, say $250,000 against $300,000 in collateral, and your portfolio experiences the same stock market crash, suddenly the collateral will not secure the value of the loan anymore. Then your brokerage may automatically sell the underlying stock, paying off the loan and protecting themselves. Some version of this scenario is typically what causes financial empires to fall apart. The term is over leveraged. Basically, five glasses of champagne instead of just one. Don't borrow too much.

But how do you know what too much is? Everyone's situation is different and needs individual consideration. But a good general rule of thumb would be to follow the guidelines that closed-end fund managers must follow. Remember the Investment Company Act of 1940 that governs leverage and closed-end funds? That rule limits certain money managers to 33.3% leverage. In other words, if they have $3 in assets, $2 must be their own, and $1 can be borrowed. Remember, that is the maximum amount of leverage. Closed-end funds that use 33.3% are considered to be the most aggressive, most risky funds. Use that as your own personal benchmark. 33.3% is the maximum amount you could borrow against your stocks, but you should probably borrow less.

A Word About Margin

When discussing borrowing and stocks, terminology is important. What I have been discussing is asset based lending, i.e. using your stock as collateral so that you can take money out of your account, tax free, and spend a little.

The other kind of stock related borrowing is called margin. This is when you borrow money against your existing shares to buy more shares. This is a very common tactic in the high risk world of Wall Street, but I wouldn't recommend it for most regular retirees.

Why? Because margin investing can get complicated and risky fast. Most importantly, it doesn't necessarily help you build a stable, long term portfolio that yields passive income. Typically, people who buy stocks on margin are risk junkies who are trying to maximize short term price appreciation of their assets. It's a legitimate way to make money, with its own risks and rewards, but it's not necessarily going to help you create the steady passive income that a retiree should crave.

There is a reason why I put asset based lending at the end of this section of the book. It isn't for everyone. In fact, anyone considering this should consult with her own CPA or financial advisor about her own particular situation. However, if you think you'll live less than ten years, or you're a high income individual, or you are nervously waiting for that next commission check, it might make sense to borrow your income. Elon Musk famously lived off borrowed money for years because he didn't want to sell a single share of Tesla. While you may, or may not, achieve similarly electrifying results, ownership of assets is generally a good thing, and the techniques described above may help you unlock income without reducing ownership.

If you've made it this far in our book, you've now read 13 chapters, each one about a different way of generating growing passive income for yourself. You could think of this as 13 different pieces to a puzzle. We've taken each puzzle piece out of the box, looked it over carefully, and now we understand conceptually how the pieces might fit together.

But if you've ever worked with a puzzle before, you know that you don't really know anything until the hands-on fun begins. There is a big difference between studying the puzzle pieces and actually putting the thing together.

In the last part of this book, we will attempt to leave the theoretical and enter the practical. We will explore some real world case studies where you can meet people who are either building or reaping a retirement portfolio rich in passive income.

Who knows, maybe you will even recognize yourself! Whether you recognize yourself or merely recognize who you want to be, visualization is a powerful exercise.

As Walt Disney used to say, "If you can dream it, you can do it."

Part 3: The Real World

*All Characters represented in this section are fictional; for illustration purposes only.

Chapter 14: Sample Portfolio - The Kid

That perfect day in early June is still one of Meredith Johnson's favorite memories. She remembers the pins and needles she felt as she sat there in her black gown and scholar's cap. She held a little framed picture of her grandmother, which she intended to take on the stage with her when she accepted her diploma from her dean. Even though her grandma had recently passed away, just missing this great day in Meredith's life, she knew her grandma would be proud. After four years of hard work, her granddaughter would be graduating with a degree in computer science. It had amazed the matriarch that her grandbaby would have a college degree, and, of all things, was studying computers. Grandma had three children by age 22, and computers barely existed back then. Meredith's father operated a small plumbing business; after he and her mother divorced, her mother went to community college and got enough education to begin a career as an accounting assistant. Both her mother and father beamed up at her from the multitude of parents attending the graduation. Even though the two had barely spoken in a decade, on that day it almost felt like her family was back together again.

A number of prestigious corporations had come to campus to recruit promising graduates. Meredith had created her first resume with the guidance of the career office, and, despite trembling on the inside, had done well in her interviews. The result was an entry level job as an Information Technology Analyst at a well-known consulting firm. Although she had needed some loans to attend that four-year college, it seemed like all the hard work and risk was paying off. She and a college friend moved to Washington, D.C. together, sharing an apartment. The company that hired Meredith had an excellent training program, and she found that she was able to handle her new responsibilities without too much trouble. She even found a few colleagues at work that she could go to happy hour with. Everything was going to plan.

Well, almost everything, except for a nagging feeling. She tried pushing it down, but the feeling always came back. A stubborn voice in her head that whispered, "This isn't for you."

She liked computers. Her colleagues weren't too bad, and there were even a few that she liked. Her boss seemed reasonable, most of the time. But she just woke up every morning with that wind whistling through the back of her mind. The wind said, "What are you doing here?"

She tried to be a team player, and fit in, but she hated the endless conference calls and training sessions that seemed to just go in circles. She often had to work in teams, whether she actually needed the help or not. This was very annoying to her. While her boss never yelled at her outright, this boss was fond of spouting all kinds of sayings that made no sense, and it rankled Meredith to realize that her well being was so dependent on the whims of someone she really couldn't respect.

So, work was work. It wasn't the exciting world she had imagined on that perfect summer day when she walked across the stage to receive her diploma. But it wasn't terrible, either.

What was exciting was her dating life. When she first arrived in D.C., she went out with friends almost every weekend, and went to plenty of happy hours too. There were a few handsome guys in her life. Some she liked a lot more than others. But in the last year, she had been dating a guy she really liked, and things were getting serious. He was talking about them moving in together. But at 26, she wasn't a baby anymore, and she let him know that having a family was important to her. Even though the whole idea of moving in with him left her tingling with excitement, nothing was quite decided yet. Only time would tell.

For a Rainy Day

Meredith's mom and dad weren't financial geniuses, but they had done well enough after all. Dad still owned his plumbing business and Mom had worked her way up the accounting department and now reported to her company's VP of finance. Both of her parents had suffered through some rough financial years after the divorce. So, while they were kind of baffled by their daughter's new life as a young professional in the big city, they did both have the same piece of advice, "Honey, save some money now; it doesn't get any easier as you get older."

Meredith could see the wisdom of that advice. Afterall, she remembered going over to her newly divorced mother's house and finding an almost barren fridge. Also, there was that nagging feeling about her career. It really wasn't clear to her if she would move ahead in her company, or if she even wanted to move ahead in her company. Everything was going well enough, but it was hard for her to see herself attending Zoom meetings and corporate trainings for the rest of her life.

Additionally, she wasn't quite sure what would happen when she got married. Sometimes she needed to stay at the office until 7 or 8PM to get an important project done. Sometimes she needed to work most of Sunday to be ready for a meeting on Monday morning. How would she do that if she had two or three children? On one hand, she saw how her mother struggled for years after the divorce, so financial independence was important to her. But on the other hand, her older sister living in Northern Virginia married a partner in a law firm, and was able to quit her job to raise her two children. Although Meredith's sister sometimes complained about lack of stimulation, it seemed like a pretty nice life to Meredith.

The bottom line was, she just wasn't sure exactly what her path would be. Was her current boyfriend "the one?" Would she work in Corporate America, or something more entrepreneurial? Or maybe her most important work would be raising a family? She felt torn and unsure about these questions. What was clear was what her dad told her, "More money saved means more options, honey."

So Meredith had resolved to build herself up financially and let the other questions work themselves out. That is why she split a two-bedroom apartment instead of renting her own apartment. Some people in D.C. had cars, but since she rarely left the city, it wasn't totally necessary. So she just took the Metro or Uber. She had seen friends spend thousands of dollars on clothes and handbags, but she mostly stayed away from that stuff. Otherwise she would have no income to save. Just living a modest existence in D.C. was expensive enough.

At age 26, Meredith made $70,000 before taxes. After taxes, health insurance and monthly contribution into her company's 401(k) program, she took home about $4,000 per month.

Of that $4,000 that she took home, $1,400 went to rent. Another $300 went to student loans. Roughly another $1,000 went to her food (Sunday brunch was a weekly social ritual with friends). Another $500 just disappeared somehow, going to expenses that just popped up. This left her with about $800 a month to invest (in addition to her 401(k) contribution).

What would be the smartest way for Meredith to invest if she wanted to maximize her financial security and flexibility in the decades to come?

Forging ahead with the 401(k)

Meredith had already taken the critical initial steps to establish a solid financial base for herself. She had limited her expenses, made progress towards paying off her educational debt, and not incurred any high interest rate credit card debt. During her first few years as a working adult, she saved up almost $20,000 in cash as an emergency fund. This way, if she got laid off for no fault of her own, she wouldn't have to go running back to her parents.

Even without fully understanding her future path, she was now in a position to begin building real wealth. If she ever wanted to quit her job and try something other than the corporate world, she would probably need several hundred thousand dollars in investments, if not even more. That may seem like a distant goal, but we'll soon see that some amount of financial independence would be achievable if Meredith invested wisely.

Let's start with her 401(k). This is a special investment account offered by her employer that offers some unique advantages. First, contributions to the 401(k) come directly from the top line of her paycheck; any amount that gets diverted from her paycheck does not get taxed. Furthermore, the money compounds inside of the account, tax free. Eventually, when Meredith withdraws the savings when she hits retirement age, the income will be taxed. But in the meantime, she could benefit from decades of powerful tax-free compounding. This means that the investments inside of the 401(k) could yield 2% dividends, or 12% dividends, but the income will just compound untaxed. For a dividend lover, this is a mouth-watering proposition.

Another huge benefit of the 401(k) account is that many employers match their employees contributions up to a certain limit. For example, some employers will pay $0.50 for every dollar you put in. Some match less, some match more. Really good employers will match your contribution $1 to $1 up to a certain limit.

Between the tax savings and the employer match, the 401(k) is a no brainer. However, there are three major pitfalls to avoid. First and foremost is fees.

In some circles, 401(k) plans have suffered from bad publicity, because sometimes employers don't do a good job of looking out for their workers. This has led to heart-breaking stories about unsophisticated employees being taken advantage of through high fees. While the match may come from your employer, the investments are often offered by a third party. The abuse happens when your employer neglects to negotiate a good deal regarding the management fees that the third party will charge. Good market rate fees should be 1% or less. However there are stories out there of unwitting employees paying fees of 2, 3 or even 4%, which would seriously harm their long-term returns. Since these embarrassing abuses have been revealed, many employers have gotten a lot tougher on negotiating fees for the third party investments that they offer. However, the person who will do the best job of looking out for you will always be you, so make sure to research the fees in your 401(k) before investing.

The second common pitfall can be over investment in company stock. The typical 401(k) will offer investment options such as the S&P 500 index, a growth index, or a bond index. It's also not uncommon for them to offer their own company stock, usually at preferential terms. This is often a popular option for 401(k) savers. They like the preferential terms on the stock purchase, and they feel comfortable buying company stock. They figure that, since they work at the company, they know a lot about the company and they believe in it's long-term prospects.

Sometimes this approach does work out great, but there are some tragic stories out there about workers who invested everything in their company stock, only to be totally wiped out decades after they ceased to work at the company. Remember Sears, RadioShack, and Kodak? They were all great companies that employees loved in the 80s and 90s. But if you had worked there from 1980 to 2000 and subsequently retired, you might well be living in

190

poverty now. Additionally, some retirees have fallen victim to fraud; hundreds of thousands of Enron employees lost everything when it was revealed that the company was one of the largest frauds in American history.

It makes sense for you to want some ownership in the company you work in. It makes sense to believe in your company's mission. The problem is the lack of diversification. If you rely on your paycheck to support your family, and you also depend on that same company's stock to finance your old age, you just have a lot of exposure in one place. Consider a plan for financial diversification before you choose to put all of your 401(k) savings in your company's stock.

The last potential pitfall of a 401(k) is that it is really a traditional retirement vehicle. This means that once you put money in, it's hard to take money out until you hit age 59 ½. It's not impossible to take money out, but it's complicated and can trigger taxes and fees if done wrong. So, if you think you want to retire early, or you just want some funds that you can access easily, you might want to limit your 401(k) contribution to just the company match. For example, in many companies, your employer will match you $1 for $1 up to 3% of your salary. While you can still save tax free with additional amounts of your salary, your company won't match more than 3%. If you don't at least put in 3% of your salary, you are leaving your employer's free money on the table. But past that, how much more you put in depends on your goals.

Since the 401(k) would be the first investment that Meredith had ever made in her young life, she was a bit nervous. She converted this nervous energy into action, and she thoroughly researched her options. Since her future goals were somewhat unclear, she decided to put just 3% of her salary into her 401(k), so she could get her company's 100% match. This would mean that, before she earned $1 on her investments, she would be getting an automatic 100% return from her company.

But what investment to choose within the 401(k)? The plan didn't offer individual stocks; rather, most plan choices were different kinds of mutual funds. She could have chosen a fund that represented the S&P 500, the 500 largest stocks in the USA, she could have chosen a technology fund that specializes in high flying technology stocks, or she could have chosen an international fund, a fund that gains exposure to international stocks.

All three of the above would be fine choices, but she remembered that tax-free compounding. That means that every penny of dividend produced inside the fund just goes to buy more stock, growing the whole pie. Hard to get that kind of growth without special tax protection. So, she chose a dividend fund with less than a 1% fee. The fund yielded 4% and had delivered total returns of about 10% over decades.

Congratulations, Meredith! You just made your first simple step into the world of equity ownership. After she made her election, every biweekly paycheck saw a deduction of 3% of her gross pay. That 3% was matched by her employer. Remember, Meredith made $70,000 annually, pre-tax. So about $2,100 of this goes into the fund, and is promptly matched by another $2,100 from the company. With very little effort, Meredith was now saving $4,200 a year.

$4,200 a year in savings. Not bad at all for a young woman just starting out her life, but certainly a far cry from the quantities that she would eventually need to quit her job. With her future path uncertain, let's just see how these savings would add up over the next ten years.

We can use an investment calculator from www.smartasset.com. Other such calculators are easy to find on the internet, such as those offered by www.nerdwallet.com and even www.investor.gov.

If we assume that Meredith averages a 10% annual return on her 401(k) stock investment, and she keeps her contribution steady at $4,200 per year, then in ten years she will have amassed $77,831. Not bad at all, considering that she barely even notices the 3% taken out of her paycheck every two weeks. This projection also assumes that she will never get a raise, and never get promoted, which is unlikely for a bright young achiever like Meredith. If she gets promoted, and she makes more money, the 3% she puts in will automatically grow, and so will the match.

Meredith doesn't really love her job. But she does love her 401(k), and well she should. For as long as she chooses to stay on the corporate path, it's a great benefit.

To Roth, or Not to Roth? That Is The Question

That fact that she was doing nicely with her 401(k) did not deter Meredith from wanting to invest that extra $800 a month. In fact, once she jumped into the investment game with her 401(k), it only increased her confidence to take the next step.

The next question for her would be whether or not she should utilize a Roth IRA. A Roth IRA is a kind of retirement savings account that you can open up even if you already have a 401(k). You won't get all the same benefits as a 401(k), but the Roth still offers some neat tricks.

First off, the Roth IRA is an independent savings vehicle. You can put money in there, or not, but what you do is of your own initiative and your employer will probably not match that contribution.

You also won't get an immediate tax benefit. You may remember that the 401(k) contribution is made with *pre-tax* dollars. Unfortunately, that is not the case with the Roth

IRA. Any funds that Meredith contributed to the Roth would have to come from the earnings she took home after her income taxes were paid.

But the Roth does offer one very special benefit. Whatever amount of money you amass over the years in your Roth will be *tax free* when you take it out in your old age. So, if you amass $100,000 in a Roth, and you take out $10,000 per year at age 60, that income will be untaxed. If you amass $1,000,000 in a Roth, and you take out $100,000 a year at age 60, then even that large amount will be untaxed. Not bad, not bad at all!

Additionally, the Roth provides the all-important tax-free compounding. Like the 401IK, any dividends you earn on money in the account just keep compounding. This makes the Roth a very friendly vehicle for dividend aficionados.

So then, obviously, Meredith should put all $800 per month into the Roth, right? Maybe. There are two caveats.

First, much like the 401(k), what goes in, can't come out. Well, it can come out, but not easily. If Meredith were dead set on a corporate career for the next forty years, with a standard retirement at age 67, then I would say that the Roth was a no brainer. But she doesn't have a crystal ball. What if she needed the money sooner?

Second, the Roth has some pretty low contribution limits. For 2021, the most you could legally put in there would be $6,000 per year. Since Meredith was projecting that she can put $800 per month into investments, even with her current modest financial situation she would max out quickly. If she got promoted over the years, she would quickly outgrow her Roth.

Her problem was her answer. Since she couldn't put the full $800 per month into the Roth anyhow, she might as well just put in half. So, each month, $400 went into the Roth IRA, and $400 went into a simple investment account that she opened on E-Trade.

This hybrid investment structure would also help diversify her investments somewhat. Since the regular account offered no tax protection, a young person such as herself could focus on pure growth. Remember, currently an investor pays no taxes on paper gains; she only pays on dividends or the sale of shares.

So, if Meredith developed a portfolio of high-flying tech stocks, she could double, triple, or quadruple her money without ever paying a dime of tax. She would only pay when she liquidates. She looked at a few different exchange traded funds that offered exposure to tech stocks, and ultimately she chose the QQQ. The QQQ is an exchange traded fund with a very low fee structure that offers exposure to the whole NASDAQ stock index. If you invested in the QQQ anytime over the last twenty years, it meant you rode the wave of unprecedented growth provided by companies such as Apple, Netflix, and Tesla. Nobody knows what the tech giants of tomorrow will be, but it's very likely that they will be listed on the NASDAQ.

When Meredith chose the QQQ for her simple, taxable E-trade account, she chose maximum long-term growth prospects with minimum costs and taxes.

With her Roth account, she knew she had a better opportunity to leverage tax-free compounding of dividends. She hung out with some pretty motivated friends, many of whom have MBAs, and she asked around a bit. Some of her older friends pointed out to her that, since she was still somewhat young, she didn't need to find the stocks with the highest dividends. Instead, they thought that she needed to find the stocks with the highest *dividend growth.* Since she wasn't spending the dividends anytime soon (they were just going to pile up in her Roth), growth was the name of the game. (As we reviewed in Chapter 4).

Meredith explored her options. Remembering that she chose funds for her 401(k) and her regular account, she looked up some dividend growth funds. She found many offerings in this category, such as the iShares Core Dividend Growth (Ticker: DGRO) and the Vanguard Dividend Appreciation ETF (Ticker: VIG). These funds all have very low fees and offer broad exposure to a list of stocks that have grown dividends like clockwork for years, if not decades.

But now that she had success with her 401(k) and her E-Trade account, Meredith was feeling a little more gutsy. She was ready to pick a few individual stocks to buy and hold. Afterall, she was still young, so if she screwed up, she would have learned a lesson and would still have time to recover.

She took a few weeks and thought it over. What was a business that was always growing? She asked her dad. Now in his 50s, he said, "For some reason, my damn medicines always just cost more and more. They must be making money."

A light went on in Meredith's head. If pharma prices go up every year, they must make more and more money every year. After some research, she found that they do. Meredith came to realize that big pharmaceutical companies have been churning out ever higher dividends for decades. She bought shares in Pfizer (Ticker: PFE), Eli Lilly (Ticker: LLY) and Bristol Myers Squibb (Ticker: BMS).

After adding the Big Pharma stocks to her young portfolio, she waited a while before inspiration struck again. One day at happy hour with friends, she got into a conversation about what they missed from the suburbs. Most of her friends were crammed into apartments like her, and many didn't have cars, like her, and they only saw the suburbs when they went home to visit their parents.

One of her friends said, "I miss the $1.50 hotdog at Costco." Costco! It had been a while since she'd been to one of those, but then she remembered going with her mom in their SUV, and loading that thing to the brim with groceries, and not needing to go again for a month. Very different from how Meredith survived in D.C.

This recollection made Meredith curious, and she did some research. Turns out that Costco is well known for raising their dividend, and in fact, in recent years they'd raised their dividend by as much as 12% per year, essentially doubling their dividend every few years. So, Meredith added some Costco shares to her portfolio.

Lastly, her gut told her that she should buy some kind of "green" stock, something related to renewable energy. Her few friends who were interested in cars only wanted a Tesla or another electric car. At her job, she constantly received memos and newsletters celebrating the company's commitment to sustainable energy. Even her father, never the most progressive guy around, had mentioned that he was thinking about getting solar panels on the roof. She did some research and stumbled upon a company called Next Era Energy. This company owned a traditional utility business, and was also one of the biggest players in wind and solar energy nationwide. The name turned up on several internet lists she found of "fastest growing dividends." Soon, NextEra (Ticker: NEE) had a place in her portfolio as well.

So Meredith had begun her investing journey. Every month she put $400 in the QQQ exchange traded fund in the regular E-Trade Account. Every month she put $400 in the Roth IRA, dividing the $400 amongst the five stocks named above. When cash dividends entered her Roth account, which happened every three months, she simply reinvested those dividends in more shares. Sometimes the share values went up; sometimes the share values went down. She barely noticed. She didn't know where the future would take her, but she was committed to investing for the long haul.

What would Meredith's picture look like if we took the same view that we took of her 401(k)? Let's say she achieved a 10% annual return on both her E-Trade account and her Roth account. Remember, this could mean that one account only hit 8%, while the other hit 12%. It could also mean that some years were way down, while other years were way up. But, after 10 years, let's say she achieved an annualized return of 10%. That would be fairly in line with what the stock market has produced over long periods of time.

If Meredith put in $800 a month, after just ten years, she would have $177,899!

For a young woman under forty, who had started with almost nothing, Meredith would have a net worth approaching $250,000 by age 36.

For someone who isn't quite sure what the future holds, $250,000 means a lot of options. If she decides to take some time off from work to raise a family, she can do so without being penniless and helpless. If she wants to take a shot at something entrepreneurial, she can try that without risking total financial disaster.

For a 26-year-old woman with an active love life and a promising career, the sky's the limit. A successful marriage may reinforce her growing wealth, or she may be unlucky in love, and take the financial stress that comes with that setback. She may start a small business that becomes a large business, or she may fail again and again at entrepreneurship. Anything could happen. But at age 26, she certainly has set herself up to take control of her own future.

Let's just explore one possibility for fun. Let's say that Meredith marries, has children, and maintains her employment exactly as it is today. She never really moves up the corporate ladder, but she doesn't get pushed off, either. She gets only marginal raises to keep up with inflation. Her husband contributes financially, but only modestly so. She remains frugal, so she keeps up the very same investment regime described in this chapter. Except, in this theoretical word, she keeps it up for 30 years, from age 26 to age 56.

In that case, her 401(k) would be worth $764,162. Her Roth and regular E-Trade account would be worth $1,746,657. At age 56, Meredith would be looking at a robust and early retirement, even if her husband contributed little and she never made any progress in Corporate America. That's the astounding power of dividends and compounding. The secret is not being a great stock picker, or the smartest girl on the block. The secret is simple consistency and time.

If you, or someone you love, has an opportunity to start investing early, please encourage that possibility. It made all the difference in the world for our fictional Meredith; it can make a very real difference for you as well.

TABLE 1: MEREDITH JOHNSON'S FINANCES (ANNUAL)

Pre-Tax Income	$70,000
Take Home Pay	$48,000
Rent	-$16,800
Student Loan	-$3,600
Food/Entertainment	-$12,000
Miscellaneous	-$6,000
Remainder to Save	$9,600
Total Savings Including 401(k)	$13,800

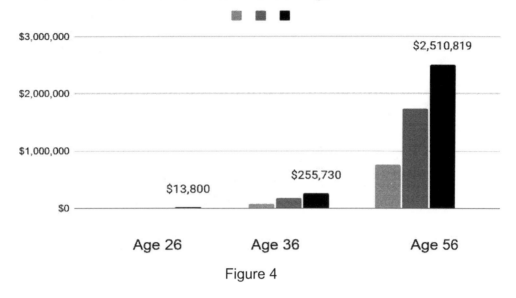

Growth of Meredith Johnson's Savings

$3,000,000

$2,510,819

$2,000,000

$1,000,000

$255,730

$13,800

$0

Age 26   Age 36   Age 56

Figure 4

The chart above shows the growth in Meredith's savings, assuming she contributes at a steady rate, earns a 10% compounded total return, and never saves any more than what she started saving at age 26. The three bars represent her 401(k), her Roth and regular E-Trade account, and her total savings. (Total savings are the black bar; light grey is the 401K and dark grey is the Roth IRA+regular savings).

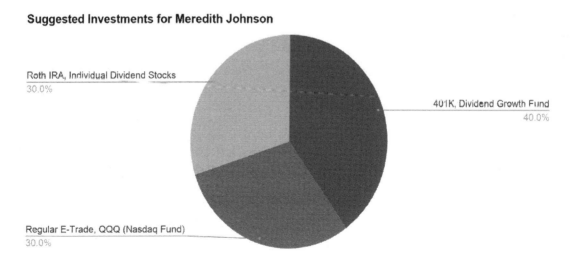

Suggested Investments for Meredith Johnson

Roth IRA, Individual Dividend Stocks
30.0%

401K, Dividend Growth Fund
40.0%

Regular E-Trade, QQQ (Nasdaq Fund)
30.0%

Figure 5

Chapter 15: Model Portfolio - The Professional

If you asked Marcus Jackson to describe his family in just one word, he would say "hardworking." For as long as he could remember, everyone in his family had at least two jobs. His dad worked construction during the week, which was good, steady work as the Atlanta metro area just kept growing, and then worked as a handyman on nights and weekends. His mom worked as an aide at a nursing home during the week, and then on weekends would work as a private helper for rich older folks. His grandma lived in his house growing up and kept an eye on the kids while Mom and Dad were working. He could just barely remember his grandfather; he died young from a heart attack, and Marcus's mother always used to say that working too much killed him.

No matter how hard everyone was working, the family always made time to go to church. That was Grandma's favorite day. Marcus can still remember her carefully pressing and ironing her Sunday best. In some ways, church was awfully boring for a little kid, but Marcus remembers loving those times because it was one of the few times when the whole family was together. He also remembers the feeling of dread on Sunday night; he knew that soon his mom and dad would go back to work and he wouldn't see them much during the week.

His absolute favorite time as a kid was Sunday afternoon, after church. The family would sit around the supper table with hot steaming food piled high. This was Marcus's time to shine. His parents wanted to know everything about school. Which teachers did he like? Did he learn anything interesting this week? How did the other kids treat him? School was alright, but mostly Marcus loved all the attention. After discussing his latest report card, his mother would take him in her arms, and rock him just like she had when he was a baby; she talked about a place called "college." She said it would all be worth it when her baby grew up and went to college. Young Marcus didn't quite understand what that place was, but if it made Mom happy, then he was going.

Marcus did go to college. He was the first person in his family to attend college and graduate with a degree. Due to his parents' many years of hard labor, the family was able to pool their resources to make just enough for Marcus to graduate with no loans. He had been a top student in his high school, which also helped him score some partial scholarships.

His mom cried at graduation and she said that she knew her father, who had worked himself to death as a janitor, was smiling down from heaven.

Marcus got a degree in accounting and began his career as a junior accountant at one of the big firms downtown. Although he had just barely made it out of college with no debt, he didn't have much other than a used suit he bought at Goodwill and a beat up old Honda that his uncle had given him. So, Marcus decided to get ahead the only way he knew how: hard work.

That first decade in Atlanta, Marcus took any assignment he could get his hands on. Did a vice president need someone to prepare a report on a Sunday? Call Marcus. Did some urgent firm business come up on Christmas Eve? Call Marcus. Did something critical come up during Marcus's scheduled vacation? That's fine, Marcus would just cut the vacation short and get back to work.

His hard work and dedication started to pay off as he slowly but surely got promotions at the accounting firm. But Marcus had bigger ambitions. Somehow, some way, he just knew he wanted to work for himself. Sometime around his 35th birthday, he had finally amassed the capital and the guts to make the big leap. With just a couple of his own clients lined up, Marcus resigned from the big firm downtown and put up his own shingle: "Marcus Jackson, CPA."

Around the same time, something else very special happened. He met Monique. After some old college friends twisted his arm, he took some rare time off of work to attend a concert with a group. And Monique was there, looking fine. His heart skipped a beat.

Not only was Monique beautiful, but she was also a hard worker. Just like Marcus. She was also the first college graduate in her family, and she worked as a nurse in a well known local hospital. In fact, Monique had started out as a nursing assistant, and eventually put herself through college at night while working full time. Monique attracted Marcus like a magnet; not only was she beautiful, but she was a hustler!

Soon, they were married, and Marcus not only had a new firm of his own, but soon two babies of his own as well.

Those first few years were some of the toughest of his life. Not only was he in charge of business development and marketing, but now he was also his own chief financial officer and secretary. Oh, yeah, at some point someone had to do the actual accounting work as well. Monique's income and benefits as a nurse were critical for his family's survival those first few years. Even though their families helped out with child care, between babies crying all night and adult clients crying like babies, from age 35 to 40, Marcus only slept five hours a night.

Once again, hard work and courage started to pay off for Marcus. By his early 40s, his life started to stabilize. His fledgling firm started to attract richer clients. Richer clients meant more complex accounting needs, with more in depth consulting needs. Now Marcus wasn't just some guy who prepared taxes once a year. Marcus was starting to work himself into a position where wealthy people in the Atlanta area looked at him as a trusted counselor and advisor on accounting and taxation matters.

It was around this time, in his early 40s, that a revelation came to Marcus that rocked his world. He noticed it with his first few wealthy clients, but the pattern became more and more pronounced. Eventually, the pattern became so obvious that the realization was undeniable.

His clients did not work hard. In fact, many barely did anything at all. One client had to take a year off from work altogether for cancer treatment, and during that year of not working, his income was the largest it had ever been due to stock and real estate investments. Many of his clients were widows or ex-wives who had lived off investments for decades without ever doing anything more than volunteer work.

At first, he paid no mind; he just did the taxes, and collected the fees. But as he grew closer and closer with some big clients, the realization was inescapable. His richest clients did very little work, because they had *everyone else working for them.*

It was a bitter pill to swallow at first. He thought of his grandfather, falling over dead one day while mopping a floor. He thought of the tears in his mother's eyes when she explained why she had to miss an event at Marcus's school. Marcus was good at math; he knew darn well that a lot of these rich folk made more in a month doing nothing than his mom had made in a year working her fingers to the bone.

But his second epiphany was even more important than the first. It took some soul searching and some consideration, but once the idea crept into his brain, there was no going back. If his rich clients could set themselves up for a life of leisure, so could he. They possessed no magic abilities that set them apart from Marcus. They had just been born into different circumstances, or had made a few very good moves in business. A few had just gotten lucky.

But Marcus was smart. Marcus had been born into modest circumstances, but positioned himself with a clear view into how the other half lived. And he could be just as lucky as the next guy if he made his own luck.

What Marcus and Monique needed was a plan. A plan by which they could start working less and making more. A plan by which they could sleep more than five hours a night. A plan by which they could take control of their own lives without falling over dead from a heart attack in a conference room somewhere.

Marcus and Monique started talking, and started planning. Soon, they decided to make some big changes.

A Plan is Born

When Marcus and Monique started to plot out their future in earnest, Marcus was 42 and Monique was 36. They had two children, ages 5 and 3. The couple had both been pretty good savers before they met each other and after, so they had around $200,000 in 401(k) accounts. As we have discussed previously, both Marcus and Monique had taken advantage of generous corporate matching contributions when they could. They also had about $75,000 in home equity, and a few thousand dollars saved for the children's future college education. Marcus was proud of his family's savings. Not bad at all for a guy who had nothing but lint in his pockets at age 22!

As happy as he was with his progress, he knew he still had a long way to go if he wanted his investments to pay him a monthly passive income that could replace his working income. Part of the challenge was simply that, between his growing accounting practice and Monique's income from nursing, his family had a pretty good income. High current income meant he would need a lot of assets to replace that income.

Marcus was making roughly $160,000 from his accounting business. If Monique worked full time at the local hospital, she could make $65,000 plus healthcare benefits for the whole family. This would give his family a pre-tax income of $225,000. After taxes, the family took home roughly $180,000.

The couple spent roughly $4,500 per month on housing. That was mortgage, taxes, and insurance. If you factored in maintenance as well, that was at least another $500 per month. With both he and Monique working full time, nobody had time to fix things around the house, or to mow the lawn. They just hired people to do those jobs.

The second biggest family expense was day care. That cost about $1200 a month for the two kids. Even though Marcus and Monique had a loving family that could help out with the kids one or two days a week, Marcus didn't expect his mother to raise his kids the way his grandmother had raised him. His mom had diabetes, arthritis, and high blood pressure; she barely scraped by every month with a part-time job and her social security check. Marcus wouldn't feel comfortable with the family's elder generation caring for his kids full time.

The third biggest expense was the two family cars. Safety was important to Marcus, and no one really knew how to fix a car, so he didn't want anyone driving used up old beaters (he had enough stories about his uncle's old Honda to entertain friends for hours). But they didn't need luxury either. So, Marcus drove a new Toyota while Monique drove the family minivan. Monthly cost? About $1200 including insurance and gas.

This meant that his family had about $7400 per month in "hard" expenses. These were expenses that were pretty much fixed and were predictable every month. Or about $88,800 per year against their post tax income of $180,000.

Food costs about $1,000 a month. Another $1,000 went towards entertainment, vacation, or whatever. So the family spent about $112,000 a year of the $180,000 that came in post-tax. As long as everyone kept working hard, they were in a good financial position.

But the work came with a price. One weekend, after working all day from Monday to Saturday, he was awakened at 6AM on Sunday by his kids toddling into his room and jumping on his bed with cries of "Daddy, aren't you awake?" Of course this was irritating given that Sunday was, theoretically, his one day to sleep in. But mostly, he was just baffled. Weren't these two just babies in their cribs? Now they were walking and talking and getting into trouble just like little people. What happened? Where did the time go? Marcus had been working six days a week as long as he could remember. Why was he spending six days a week taking care of someone else's family?

After talking it through, and working out the numbers together, the couple decided on the following. Starting immediately, Monique would cut back her hours and work part time. She would work just enough so that she could still get those valuable healthcare benefits from her job. But she would keep working; in case she got bored, or if the family wound up with unexpected financial problems, she could always go back full time. Marcus would continue working as much as needed to build up his firm, but the family would make a commitment to cultivate passive income through rigorous saving and investing. Marcus figured that, if he did things right, the passive income would supplement his family's active income, and he could cut back to working just four days a week by age 50. This way, he would never have to explain to his kids why he was missing their baseball games.

An Active Plan for Passive Income

When Monique slashed her hours at the hospital, the following changes occurred in the family's finances. The total post tax income was reduced from $180,000 to $160,000, but the daycare expense was also cut in half to $7,200. So now the family spent around $105,000 a year against income of $160,000 of take home pay.

This left a meaty $55,000 a year to invest. Since Marcus wanted to enjoy the passive income from these investments sooner rather than later, the money went into regular, taxable accounts. They calculated that they could leave the $200,000 in their 401(k)s untouched and it would eventually grow into a substantial retirement fund all on its own. The funds they were aiming to build up now were to help pay for a "semi-retirement."

Where to invest? How to invest? The money in the 401(k) had just gone into a S&P 500 index fund; it was the most simple answer. But now the couple specifically needed income. Even though Marcus had already spent two decades moving numbers around for those rich clients, he was still a bit intimidated at first. Although he considered himself an expert on other people's finances, he had never really thought so much about his own.

One clear pattern that had emerged from his exposure to the affluent set was that many had done very well with real estate. Some owned apartment buildings, others had owned shopping centers. More often than not, they did quite well over time. However, as a consultant and counselor, he also knew more than a few clients who had gotten sucked into hairy situations related to maintenance and management of their properties. The whole concept of the couple's new plan was to work *less,* not more. So, direct ownership of real estate was out.

This led Marcus to investigate REITs (which we covered in Chapter 8). The more he read, and the more he broke down the accounting statements of these publicly traded companies, the more he felt he could get a lot of the same benefits of direct ownership, without the hassles. So, he and Monique agreed to put 30% of their annual investment money into REITs. In this allotment, they chose the Vanguard Real Estate ETF (Ticker: VNQ) and a few individual REITs based on their particular interests. Monique had spent many years working in hospitals, so they felt comfortable investing in a REIT that owns hospitals, Medical Properties Trust (Ticker: MPW). Marcus had known many clients who got rich renting simple, affordable apartments, so they bought AIMCO (Ticker: AIV) and AvalonBay Communities (Ticker: AVB). As an accountant, Marcus was also very attuned to the need for storage of records, both paper and digital. So he chose Iron Mountain, a company that specializes in document storage and digitization, (Ticker: IRM).

Using information that was readily available on his E-Trade account, Marcus could calculate that this part of his portfolio would yield an average of around 5% annually. But while he was doing his research, there were other REITs that stood out because they paid more, *much* more. In fact, it seemed like they paid too much. If most REITs paid 4 or 5%, how could these other REITs be paying 10%?

This discrepancy awakened the beancounter in him, and he decided to comb through a few of the companies' annual reports. This is when he discovered that the higher paying REITs were actually a different kind of REIT. They were mortgage REITs. (We explored mortgage REITS in chapter 9). They paid a higher income because they were a different kind of business. Although both businesses were classified as REITs, it was apples to oranges, really.

He talked it over with Monique, and no matter how he made the argument, it just smelled wrong to her. They paid too much. It must be too risky. After a few heated conversations, the couple settled on the following compromise. They would put 10% of their monthly investment money in mortgage REITs, and then only the largest, most established company. If it went OK, then they would try more over time. The next day, Marcus went onto his E-Trade account and bought shares in Annaly Capital Management (Ticker: NLY), the largest mortgage REIT. This investment was yielding around 9%.

As a nurse, Monique felt comfortable with the idea of investing in pharmaceutical stocks. That whole world was foreign to Marcus, so he completely let her control this portion of their investments. He let her do the research, and then she told him which companies she preferred. It was honestly a relief to hand some of the hard work off to someone else on his "team." On Monique's recommendation, they bought shares in Pfizer (Ticker: PFE), Abbvie (Ticker, ABBV), Novo Nordisk (Ticker: NVO) and Johnson&Johnson (Ticker: JNJ). Although some of these companies paid lower dividends than the REITs, Marcus could see that they had a stellar track record of growing their dividends. In fact, they had often doubled the dividend every ten years or so. This would mean that, if his family came to rely on the dividend income, he could also count on a pay "raise" every year. Not a bad deal; he certainly couldn't say the same for his own business. The Big Pharma component would be 30% of their monthly investments.

70% of their monthly investments were now allotted. When he thought of the very richest clients who had walked into his accounting firm, Marcus thought of borrowed money. Not the bad kind. Not the kind to buy bigger houses and fancier cars. Rather, the kind to buy more apartment buildings or double the size of a small business. He recalled a feeling of amazement when looking over the books and records of these particular clients. They made a lot of money, fast, by using other people's money.

However, he had been doing it long enough that he had also seen a few high rollers crap out in the leverage game. He saw a few real estate developers lose everything after years of work. It was tempting to go for it anyway, but Monique reminded him that the point of the whole portfolio was to *reduce* stress, not ramp it up.

There had to be a middle way, a way of taking advantage of the astounding power of leverage while still sleeping at night. That was when Marcus discovered closed-end funds.

He read about the concept in Kipplinger's Magazine, a finance publication that he had subscribed to years ago. (We learned about closed end funds in Chapter 12). For the longest time, he got weekly newsletters from them in his email, which he never made the time to read. When he forced himself to start reading, amazing things started to happen. One of those amazing things was his realization that closed end funds fit the description of what he was looking for.

He wound up starting out with a shotgun approach. He bought a few different closed-end funds, each one with a different specialty. He figured that this bought him some protection in diversification, and it also allowed him to maximize his learning. He bought a fund that specialized in infrastructure, the Cohen & Steers Infrastructure Fund (Ticker: UTF). He bought another fund that specialized in high yielding international dividend stocks, the Aberdeen Global Dynamic Dividend Fund (Ticker: AGD). He even bought a fund that specialized in bonds (The Double Line Income Solutions Fund, Ticker: DSL). He figured this was one area where he could benefit from professional management, since he knew little about fixed income. All and all, he calculated that this part of his portfolio should throw off a monthly income of around 8% of the initial purchase price.

Sowing and Harvesting

Within a year of beginning their plan, the Jackson family had a diversified portfolio of high yielding stocks. The average yearly yield was about 6%. So, on that first $55,000 invested, they earned about $3,300 of passive income. It wasn't much, but Marcus's heart raced the first few months when dividends appeared in his brokerage account, as if by magic. After all those years of busting his rear for every penny, here was money that just fell from the sky. Astounding.

Marcus and Monique went into their plan understanding that anything could happen. At age 42, Marcus had taken enough hard knocks in life to know that no one has a crystal ball. But his mathematical nature just couldn't resist making some calculations on what his life *could* look like on his 50th birthday.

His assumption would be that all dividends would be reinvested until his 50th birthday. If the dividends had been in a tax-sheltered retirement account, he might have used a compounding rate of 10%. But that would have meant that he could not access the funds until age 59 ½. So, he planned to "Render Unto Caesar," which would reduce his effective compounding rate to 8%. Even at that rate, if he continued to salt away $55,000 a year between age 42 and age 50, he would have amassed $686,000.

At age 50, that $686,000 could provide $41,160 if he continued to receive a 6% yield. Remember, based on the costs that Marcus analyzed earlier, that passive income could easily cover the cost of his family's cars and their annual vacation.

It's possible that, after eight years of experience, Marcus and Monique would feel comfortable investing in more high yielding securities, like mortgage REITs or more aggressive closed-end funds. So, perhaps they could receive income of 8% on their $686,000 instead of 6%. At that rate, their investments would throw off $54,880 of pure passive income. In that scenario, Monique could quit her nursing career altogether if she wanted, or Marcus could simply stop taking phone calls on Saturday.

If the Jacksons start to enjoy that passive income at age 50, does that mean that they are sacrificing tomorrow in order to work less today? Not necessarily.

Remember, the Jacksons already had $200,000 in 401(k)s plus home equity. The whole time, that money is growing untouched. What financial position would the couple be in at age 67?

If they had $200,000 in their 401(k) at age 42, and it achieved a 10% compounded return (tax-sheltered) in the 401(k), then they would have $2,166,000 in the accounts when Marcus hits traditional retirement age. At the same time, they would have their additional $686,000 portfolio that they began tapping at age 50. Except, in this case, the dividend income has grown at an annual rate of 6%, meaning that the cash flow has *tripled* between Marcus's 50th birthday and his 67th birthday. The portfolio that paid $41,160 in passive income on Marcus's 50th birthday would pay roughly $123,000 on his 67th birthday.

Even as companies have been raising the dividends, the share prices have slowly been increasing as well. If we assume that the share prices grow at just 3% per year, the securities themselves would be worth roughly $1,133,000 on his 67th birthday, *even though Marcus has been spending the dividends for years.*

Even if the Jacksons begin to tap their passive dividend income when Marcus turns 50, it's quite possible that they will be looking at a retirement income in excess of $200,000 in their old age.

The Jackson family has traveled a long, long way from the days when Marcus's grandfather worked two jobs until his heart stopped beating. They've gone from working for income to having others work to provide income for them. They may not have direct contact with their employees, but each stock they own represents a dedicated management team and thousands of employees working to make the Jackson family rich every day. If you hold corporate shares, then these same managers and employees can work to make your family rich, too.

TABLE 2: Jackson Family Finances (In Annual Numbers)

Old Plan	New Plan
Total Family Income: $225,000	$205,000
Post Tax: $180,000	$160,000
Housing costs -60,000	Housing costs -$60,000
Daycare -$14,400	Daycare -$7,200
2 Cars -$14,400	2 Cars -$14,400
Food -$12,000	Food -$12,000
Entertainment -$12,000	Entertainment $-12,000
Total spent: $112,800	Total spent: 105,600
Total left to invest: 67,200	Total left to invest: $54,000

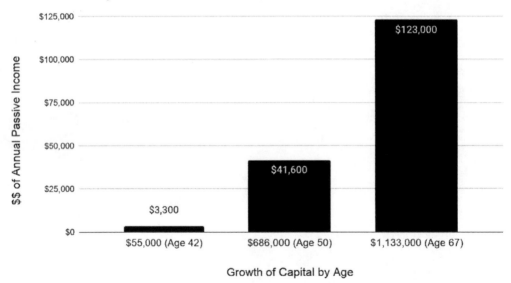

Jackson Family Passive Income Growth

Figure 6

This chart assumes that the Jackson family invests $55,000 per year starting at age 42 with a compounded annual rate of return of 8%. At age 50, Marcus starts to withdraw and spend the dividends and contributes no more money. Between age 50 and age 67, the portfolio produces a 6% dividend, which Marcus spends. By age 67, with no further contributions, the portfolio has grown to $1,133,000 and throws off about $123,000 in annual income.

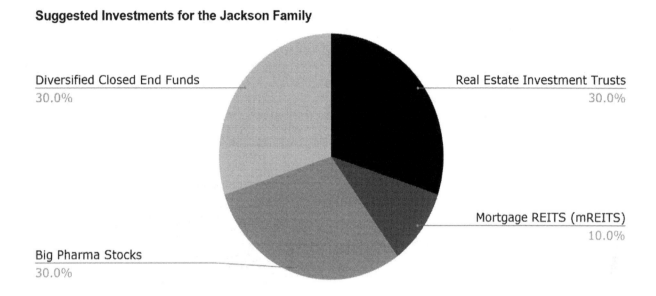

Figure 7

Chapter 16: Model Portfolio - The Pre-Retiree

Early April meant spring in Charlotte, North Carolina, and spring meant barbecues for the Smith family. And why not? Afterall, Mitchell J. Smith and his wife Gracie had worked hard to afford their luxurious, six bedroom, 5,500 square foot home on a golf course. He had put in thirty years working for some of the more prestigious companies in America, eventually becoming a regional sales manager for a medical device company. Gracie had tackled the tough task of raising two beautiful daughters while also working as a pharmaceutical representative. She had never moved up, but she had always been happy and well paid as an individual sales contributor for her employer.

Because they had spent so long in the medical sales world, a lot of their social acquaintances were also from that world. In fact, Mitchell and Gracie's best friends, the Smeads, were also long term medical sales pros. Barney Smead was a sales manager just like Mitchell, and Raquel was an accomplished pharma rep just like Gracie. The two couples had a lot of fun over the years comparing "war stories" from their days in the corporate trenches.

But today was all about fun. After being bundled away all winter, the industrial size, stainless steel grill was fired up with some prime meats from the local boutique butcher. The aroma of sizzling beef tickled Mitchell's nose as he poured his first drink of the day for himself and Barney.

A few families stood around and chattered blithely as they enjoyed the direct view from the home's teak wood deck onto the golf course. Nothing today but blue skies and balmy breezes; it felt like winter had ended a million years ago.

But somehow, Barney just wasn't himself. One reason why Barney had done so well as a sales manager was his gift of gab. Normally, Barney would be the life of the party, always getting the conversation going with some kind of jovial story. But today he wandered around the deck silent and ashen, just barely following whatever conversations were percolating.

Mitchell put his arm around Barney and walked him to the edge of the deck, away from the others. "How ya feelin' today, Barn?" Mitchell inquired.

"Not great. Not great at all, to tell you the truth. They shitcanned me, Mitch. Twenty five years and they shitcanned me like some punk."

Mitchell recoiled as if he had seen a snake hissing in the bushes.

"Seriously? Didn't you just win manager of the year last year?" Mitchell asked.

"Yup, manager of the year, 2019. You know how many of those awards I won over the years? And now, three months severance and 'good luck'. Shit, my kids aren't even done with college yet. And all they tell me is 'good luck.'"

The shocking news reverberated around Mitchell's head like an errant bullet, damaging every point that it hit. It really wasn't surprising news. He had seen dozens of good reps and managers laid off over the years, seemingly at random. But it had never hit this close to home. Shit, Barney lived in a house just like his right in the next development down the road.

"Awww. Screw 'em, Barn. You've got a string of awards a mile long, I'm sure you'll find something new in no time. Maybe even something better," Mitch threw his arm around Barney's shoulders as the pair gazed out onto the endless manicured green of the golf course. "This will just mean the beginning of something new for you, Barn."

The words tasted like acid before they even came out of Mitchell's mouth. The beginning of something new, for sure. But of what? Barney had some big bills to pay. Between his $2,000,000 mortgage, his two kids in private college, and the fact that he supported his elderly in-laws, Barney had confessed to him in the past that he and Raquel didn't have much in the bank. It was true that Barney had a long track record of success as a sales manager, but at age 56, Mitchell wasn't really sure if that would work for Barney or against him. At age 58, Mitchell was usually the oldest sales manager in the room when he attended corporate meetings. Even he would admit, strictly in confidence, that he typically did not like to hire or manage reps who were older than 40-something. They just didn't seem to have the drive of the younger reps.

And of course, in the deep dark recesses of Mitchell's mind, well out of sight of his everyday thoughts, a nasty little voice scoffed, "If Barney is screwed at age 56, then what about you at age 58?" He tried to banish the voice before his appetite was ruined by a wave of nausea. Well, maybe Barney hadn't done a good job of saving, but the Smith family would be A-OK. Mitch and Gracie had about $500,000 in 401(k) plans, and about another $500,000 in this $2,000,000 home. They would probably be just fine whenever their careers ended.

Still, Mitchell had to admit that things were changing around him. The youngest of his two daughters was finally graduating from college; that would free up a substantial chunk of change. The culture of the medical sales business was rapidly changing; going way downhill in Mitchell's opinion. In the old days, it was all about building relationships with doctors and administrators. Luxurious golf rounds, fishing trips, and concerts with clients were the norm. Now, if you gave the wrong person a free pen, HR would be up your ass. Mitchell was getting pretty darn tired of the whole thing.

His daughter was finishing college, and with this thunderbolt from Barney, maybe it was time to meet with a financial advisor. He felt sure that half a million in 401(k)s meant his family was on track, but you never could be too sure. As he patted a palid Barney on the back, he resolved to make an appointment with that advisor who had been recommended to him.

In the meantime, it was time for that next scotch. Better make it a double.

An Inconvenient Truth

A month later, the Smiths sat down with Bill Anderson, a financial advisor that had been recommended by Mitchell's cousin. They hadn't had a meeting like this in a long time.

Bill proposed the following method. First, to discuss just the raw numbers behind their financial life, and then to discuss the "why?" behind some of their investment concepts and spending. That seemed logical to Mitch; he ran annual reviews with his sales employees in a similar manner.

For starters, Mitchell earned about $230,000 annually in his job as a regional sales manager. As about 30% of his pay was variable incentive that depended on his team's performance, that number could fluctuate up or down. But the average was around $230,000. He had earned that average, adjusted for inflation, for many years.

Gracie earned roughly $110,000 as a pharmaceutical representative. She also could see some variation, but $110,000 was typically her target number.

Together, the couple earned $340,000 pre-tax. They also got two brand new, if utilitarian, company vehicles to drive. Additionally, both got great health insurance as part of their jobs. Although there was a monthly cost deducted from Mitch's paycheck, that cost was much lower than if he were self-employed, and his deductibles and copays were reasonable during the rare occasions when he needed medical attention.

Boy, that seemed like a lot of money. Mitchell's own father had been a school teacher. If he were still alive today, he would have considered Mitchell to be rich.

But then taxes happened. Between federal, state, and social security taxes, the Smith's actually took home much less than they earned on the top line of their paychecks. Additionally, Mitch's two daughters, age 21 and 26, were also on his corporate insurance. While Mitch was grateful for this benefit, it still meant a chunk of money came out of his check every month. All and all, the Smith family only took home around $220,000 of the $340,000 that they earned every year.

Next Bill and the Smiths went over expenses. Mitch's home was his castle, and castles don't come cheap. His monthly mortgage payments, plus taxes and insurance, could add up to $90,000 a year. After Bill gently twisted his arm, Mitch had to admit that maintenance cost at least another $10,000 a year.

This winter, and most winters, the Smith's spent time in their ski cabin in the mountains. That cost about $30,000 a year after mortgage payments and everything else were factored in.

The couple had driven to the appointment in a convertible Porsche. Even though the company provided two new vehicles for the couple to drive, no one was going to get a thrill out of a Buick SUV with a basic trim package. The truth was, most corporate fleet cars were makes or models that the manufacturers had tried and failed to sell to the general public. Not very fun to drive. So Mitch and Gracie had decided to live a little and leased the Porche for $1,000 a month.

Next were their daughters. Even though the two hadn't lived in the 5,500 square foot Smith home for quite a while, they still got plenty of support. Jennifer, the youngest daughter, went to a private college that cost around $40,000 a year. The elder daughter, Samantha, had graduated from a similar private college.

The Smiths were very loving, giving parents. Some of Mitchell's very favorite memories were his little daughters running around the big house. He would shake his head in amazement, "where did all the time go?" He knew he wanted the best for his daughters. And that meant the best education. Mitchell himself had barely gotten into any college at all, and that was mostly just because he had been a football player. If his daughters did well enough in school to go to a private college, then it was Mitch's responsibility to pay for it.

He was very proud to have been able to put his daughters through good schools without them taking on a penny of debt. His own situation was different. He went through a rough patch about midway through Samantha's schooling, and the commissions just didn't come in the way they were supposed to. What was he going to do, suddenly ask his 20-year-old daughter to drop out of school, leaving behind the only world she had ever known? Ask her to take on loans before she was even old enough to buy a beer? No, instead Mitch and Gracie had taken out a modest educational loan, to be paid back over ten years. They had never even told Samantha. Now that loan payment was about $7,000 a year.

Mitch would never regret paying for his daughters' education. But that didn't mean he was happy with Samantha. After majoring in anthropology, she had never really been able to secure a good job after graduation. She had worked at an independent book store, worked as a docent in a museum, and now she was a barista at an independent, organic, fair trade coffee shop. It seemed like every time she came by the house to ask for more money, she had more and more tattoos. The last time she had stopped by she introduced someone named "Yor" as her partner. Mitch and Gracie struggled to figure out if Yor was a man, a woman, or something else. They were afraid to ask. Apparently there were more than two options on that front, these days.

At any rate, no one wanted to talk about it, but in the comforting space of Bill Anderson's office, Gracie admitted that she gave around $1,000 a month to Samantha, her 26-year-old daughter.

After that, their family spent about $10,000 per year on food, and $10,000 on entertainment and miscellaneous expenses.

The numbers were pretty plain as Bill wrote them up on a white eraser board. Mitch knew it already, but to see the numbers just hovering there in naked defiance of his wishful thinking was galling. The Smith family made more than 98% of all American families, but spent every penny, every month.

Reality Bites

Bill said that the next part of the discussion was to review assets and retirement expectations. Well, that was easy. The Smiths had $500,000 stashed in a few 401(k) accounts, mostly invested in plain vanilla stock index funds. They had about $500,000 in equity in their $2,000,000 house. They had maybe $50,000 in equity in their ski cabin.

Mitchell told Bill that he felt fit and energized enough to keep working until his mid 60s; Gracie could do the same. But they had to admit that they just didn't know how long they would be invited to stay at the corporate party.

After thirty years in sales, Mitch knew how to gauge the energy in a room. He could tell that both he and his wife were feeling comfortable with their advisor Bill. Bill was clearly listening to what they were saying, and had broken the ice enough to earn their trust. Perhaps this is why Bill felt comfortable dropping this bomb:

"Guys, based on what we are discussing here, I am professionally obligated to warn you that your retirement is in great jeopardy. I know $500,000 sounds like a lot, but you're not even close to being able to replace your current income with that. And if, God forbid, someone were to get laid off tomorrow, through no fault of your own, you would run through that $500,000 very quickly."

The words hung weighted in the air. Gracie looked like someone had just slapped her in the face.

"How...how could that be?" she muttered. "Half a million dollars. Half a million! My parents never had that much in their dreams."

Bill remained cool as cucumber. Apparently, this was not his first rodeo. He calmly went over the math.

If they assumed that they both could work until age 67, a *big* "if", then they would earn social security income of about $50,000 combined. By that time, *with good luck*, their $500,000 in the 401(k) would have grown to $800,000. That $800,000 would throw off around $40,000 in passive income if traditional methods were used. So, if they both could make it in the corporate world to 67, then they would still only have around $90,000 in retirement income. They were currently spending $220,000 per year.

Yes, they were looking at a big reduction in expenses because they're youngest daughter was finally finishing college. But even if they saved every penny of that $40,000 for the next 8 years, it just couldn't add up. The Smith family had some tough decisions to make.

They drove home in their shiny Porsche in a state of shock. No one said a word, until they did. Mitch spoke first. "Goddammit, enough with Samantha, enough! Didn't we pay for the best school? Didn't we kill ourselves for her? What are we, a bank?"

"Well, she has to live somewhere safe, Mitch. I'm not going to have my daughter living in a shack. I'm not! And what about this stupid Porsche, who's idea was this?" retorted Gracie.

The fight went from there. An eruption of bitterness, resentment and fear that had been bubbling just under the surface for years. That night, the Smith house got a workout; it seemed like the pair argued in every one of their six bedrooms. Who's fault was this situation? What did they do wrong? What should they do now? Obviously, there had to be big cuts, but it felt like asking the patient to choose which limb she would want amputated first. After a few days of nastiness, what they did was: nothing.

Samantha showed up with her partner Yor, and like clockwork, Gracie wrote her daughter a check. As a balmy Charlotte spring became a scorching southern summer, the air conditioning went out in the house, and Mitch had to pay $5,000 to replace it. It would cost thousands of dollars to break the lease on his Porsche, so he continued to enjoy it with the added pleasure of defiance. Turns out, ignoring problems was easier than Mitch ever would have imagined.

The Winds of Change

They kept it up this way for a number of months. They barely even mentioned that meeting with the financial advisor, and summer was filled with lavish pool parties and vacations. Then Gracie ran into Raquel one day at Whole Foods.

Halfway through customary greetings and salutations, Raquel burst out in tears. She tried to cover her face, but soon her loud sobbing in the produce section was enough to draw attention from the organic, cruelty-free kale and directly to the two women. Gracie had to drag Raquel into the bathroom for some privacy.

Everything was going wrong. Six months had gone by and Barney couldn't find a new job. He had gotten one or two offers from friends to work as a rep, but the pay would be much less than what he was earning before. Raquel continued to work as a pharma rep, but her income just wasn't enough to make ends meet. They hadn't made their mortgage payment last month; they had no idea how they were going to pay their daughter's fall tuition, and now, she had even heard rumors of layoffs at her own company.

It tore Gracie up to see her old gal pal in such a state. Her hair and makeup, typically immaculate for the last several decades, now looked like she had been sprayed by a fire hose. And, other than platitudes, what could Gracie really say? She did her very best to offer compassionate words, but in reality, she wasn't thinking about the Smead family at all. In fact, except for her body, she was barely in that Whole Foods bathroom at all. Her mind was in that office with Bill Anderson and her husband. This was it. No more denial. No more faking it. She wasn't going to let the Smiths wind up like the Smeads. Mitch and Gracie Smith were back in Bill's office within a week. This time, they weren't walking out of there without a plan.

Bill suggested that they break the conversation down into three parts. First, they had to determine which expenses would be cut, and how they would be cut. Second, they had to determine what cash flow that would free up. Lastly, they had to decide how that cash flow would be invested, and what results could be hoped for.

The couple already knew that the big house on the golf course had to go. They could agree on two things: one was that it made no sense for an aging pair of empty nesters to continue living in a six bedroom behemoth, and two was that it would really hurt to sell their dream home. This was the sacred space where they had raised their children and hosted countless warm and cheery barbeques and Christmases. But at a cost of $100,000 a year, the house was undeniably the largest expense that drained them every month.

The next thing that had to go was the Porsche. That stung. There was just no joy in tooling around town in a Hyundai SUV. But it was impossible for Mitchell to ask Gracie to give up the house where she had raised her children without him also giving up his "baby."

The most controversial issue was Samantha. Gracie could not be moved off the idea that her daughter would be in danger if she didn't receive regular financial support. Mitchell loved his daughter dearly, and more than a little part of him wished she was still that playful seven year old running all over their big, sunlit house. But she wasn't seven, rather she was turning twenty-seven and now she seemed to be running wild with money that was needed elsewhere. The couple agreed on the following compromise. Monthly support would be cut from $1,000 to $500, and that $500 would be on a credit card that the elder Smiths controlled. Mitch and Gracie wanted to see exactly where that money was going. It had certainly occurred to Mitch that his ever more tattooed daughter could have a drug problem. At least with this compromise he wouldn't be fueling any bad habits.

Establishing and committing to a concrete cost-cutting plan made Mitchell nauseous. At times he felt like his head was swimming and he had to grip onto the arms of his chair to keep himself from floating away. However, the next part made him happier. Much happier.

They would keep the ski cabin, and continue to build equity in it with an eye on living there in retirement. By selling the main house, they could achieve two main goals. First, they would be freeing up an extra $500,000 in capital that could be invested to create retirement income. Second, they would be cutting their monthly housing expense from $9000 to just $3500 (They aimed to move into a luxurious two bedroom rental in a similar golf community to where they were currently living). When combined with the savings achieved by returning the Porsche and cutting back on Samantha, they could now look forward to saving $7000 per month, or about $84,000 a year.

Because the couple enjoyed fabulous 401(k) matches from their work, Bill suggested that about half of that money go directly from their paycheck into their 401(k). This way they could count on a generous company matching contribution, and reduce the temptation to spend the money. A juicy $42,000 would never pass through their hands; rather, it would go straight to retirement.

With the company match, the Smiths could plan on socking away as much as $62,000 per year into their 401(k). Bill suggested that the couple select a high dividend exchange traded fund for that money. They chose to divide the money between the Spdr S&P Global Dividend ETF (Ticker: WDIV) and the iShares Core High Dividend ETF (Ticker: HDV). That way, the dividends would compound tax free over the next nine years, and the couple would be able to build confidence in their passive income stream. They would be able to check their quarterly statements four times a year and watch the dividends come in. This should help with that queasy feeling every time there was a rumor of layoffs.

For the other $42,000, Bill suggested a diversified portfolio of closed-end funds. (Reviewed in Chapter 12 of this book). The plain truth was that they were currently so far behind in their retirement savings that the simple 2% dividend yield of typical stocks wasn't going to do it. Bill illustrated how the couple could hope to generate 6% monthly income, tax preferred, by investing in a range of CEFs. Ultimately, they chose a suite of established CEFs like Cohen & Steers Infrastructure Fund (Ticker: UTF), Doubleline Income Solutions (Ticker: DSL), The Black Rock Enhanced Global Dividend Trust (Ticker: BOE), and the Pimco High Income Fund (Ticker: PHK).

Lastly, there was the matter of the $500,000 that would become available after the sale of the house. For this pot of money, Bill suggested a "high low" strategy. Since the couple had been in the medical business their whole lives, they felt very comfortable investing half in constant dividend growers such as Big Pharma and medical device stocks. They would expect a quarterly dividend in the 3% range with these stocks, and that payout would likely grow dramatically as they aged. For the other half of the money, they could purchase mortgage REITs. Although these were more *high beta* (high volatility) than their other investments, they would need the high income. A monthly 9% paycheck would help to cushion the blow in case they couldn't work until age 67.

For the Big Pharma portion of the portfolio, Bill and the Smiths chose names that they knew and trusted: Pfizer (Ticker: PFE), Eli Lilly (Ticker: LLY), Bristol Myers Squibb (Ticker: BMS), Abbot (Ticker: ABT), Medtronic (Ticker: MDT) and Stryker (Ticker: SYK). You may remember that we discussed Big Pharma stocks in Chapter 6.

For the mortgage REIT half of this portfolio, Bill steered them to three of the biggest names in the business, Annaly Capital Management (Ticker: NLY), AGNC Investment Corp (Ticker: AGNC), and Blackstone Mortgage Trust (Ticker: BXMT).

Bill ran the following simulation. If they continued to grow their current 401(k) savings at a steady rate of 8% and could grow the $500,000 from their house at a rate of 7%, then they could have almost $1,800,000 by the time Mitchell turned 67 and could collect social security.

But the big reductions in lifestyle really made the difference. If the couple saved $135,000 a year over the next nine years (the money saved from lifestyle cuts, plus their second daughter finishing college, plus 401(k) match), and they earned an average return of 8%, then they could expect to add $1,686,000. If everything went to plan, Mitch and Gracie could be looking at a 3,800,000 nest egg by age 67.

If their investments threw off 6% in yearly income, they could look forward to a tax preferred income of $228,000 plus around $50,000 in social security. That would easily pay for their more modest lifestyle and still enable them to put some gold in their golden years.

Bill was careful to caution that those projections were only if everything went just right. The Smiths absolutely had to follow through on their lifestyle cuts. They both needed to put in every possible effort to remain employed until age 67. And of course, they needed some luck in the market. Bill chose a projected return of 8%, lower than the market's average return, to take into account taxes and the ups and downs of the market. But in reality, they could experience a market crash during the following nine years. No one has a crystal ball. Luckily, by dramatically cutting their expenses and ramping up saving, their retirement would likely survive all but the most dire scenarios.

What an emotional rollercoaster ride had just occurred in Bill Anderson's office. The dejection and disgust at having to sell the house, the fear when going through the numerical scenarios, and the sheer elation when Bill announced that, not only could the couple's retirement be salvaged, but could actually look quite rosey!

After decades of success in the cut throat world of corporate sales, the Smith family knew what it meant to strive towards a goal. They had thrived under pressure for many years, and rarely failed to meet quota. This challenge would be no different. They left that office with a strong feeling of purpose; they knew what they needed to do. As Mitch and Gracie jumped in the Porsche for the last time, they put down the top and enjoyed an exhilarating ride. Somehow it just seemed so much more fun to drive when you finally knew where you were going.

TABLE 3: The Smith Family Finances (All numbers are Annualized)

	Old Expenses	New Expenses
His Income	$230,000	
Her Income	$110,000	
Total Pre Tax	$340,000	
Total Take Home Pay	$220,000	
	Old Expenses	New Expenses
House	$100,000	$42,000
Food & Entertainment	$20,000	$20,000
Porsche	$12,000	$0
Mountain Cabin	$30,000	$30,000
College Expense	$40,000	$0
Educational Loan	$7,000	$7,000
Daughter Support	$12,000	$6,000
Total Expenses	$221,000	$105,000
Available to Invest	$0	$115,000
401 K Match	$0	$20,000
Total To Invest, yearly	$0	$135,000

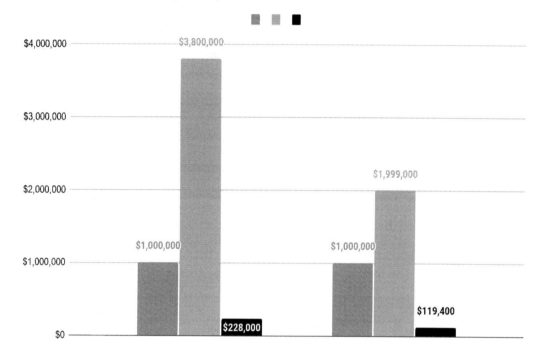

Figure 8

The far left column is the family's current assets. The middle column assumes the assets grow at 8% rate over the next 9 years. (Remember that the new Smith Family Plan includes $135,000 a year in extra savings.) The last column on the right represents the annual income the family can expect from their assets at age 67.

Suggested Assets for New Smith Retirement Plan

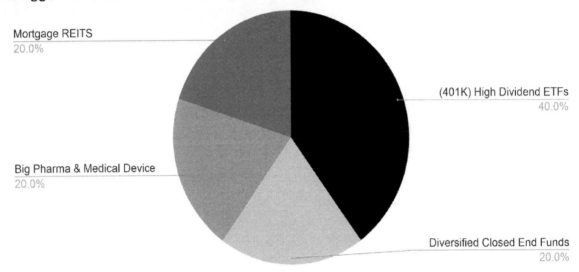

Mortgage REITS
20.0%

(401K) High Dividend ETFs
40.0%

Big Pharma & Medical Device
20.0%

Diversified Closed End Funds
20.0%

Figure 9

Chapter 17: Model Portfolio - The Retiree "Forever Young"

It just wasn't fair. Dolores struggled with the thought day and night. She knew that only the Lord got to determine matters of life and death, but the bitterness still felt like a leaden weight she carried around with her all day. When her ever more frail husband needed help in the middle of the night to crawl to the toilet. When her lousy, good-for-nothing daughter looked right past her dying father and asked how much money would be left when he passed. Even when Dolores escorted her failing husband to the transfusion center for his chemotherapy, she wanted to scream at the doctor, at the nurses, at the world, "It's not fair!"

Her husband Gonzalo had done nothing but care for this family since age 19 when he and Dolores had left everything and everyone they had ever known in Nicaragua and came to America on a wing and a prayer. He was 19 and she was 17; they spoke no English. Soon, Gonzalo wasn't even old enough to order a beer in his new country and he had one baby and another on the way.

She tried to be happy and upbeat, but it was tough. Sometimes when he was sitting in the infusion chair, reading a magazine in the cold, sterile light of the clinic, she would stare at the living skeleton who had once been Gonzalo Rodriguez. Was this really the young man who had come to America at 19 and worked tirelessly, six days a week, decade after decade to provide for his three children and his wife? Was this the same man who displayed endless patience when his eldest daughter showed up at their house, constantly pregnant with no partner to speak of? This was supposed to be *their* time together. Their golden years. Finally, Gonzalo had paid off the house, finally there were no more children or grandchildren living with them. Finally, she convinced Gonzalo to hand off the air conditioning business to their son and retire at age 72. They were supposed to travel, to go out to dinner with friends, to finally live a little before dying. And now this. Cancer. Not fair.

It was also more than a little upsetting to hear that people just seemed to want to talk about money. With doctors trying treatment after treatment, sometimes with limited success, sometimes not, and Gonzalo looking worse by the week, people wanted to know how they were going to be living when Papa was gone. Her son wanted Gonzalo to sign some paperwork so that he officially owned the AC business. It wasn't much, just a few guys and a truck, but that little AC business had helped the Rodriguez family make a life in a strange new land. Her good-for-nothing daughter just wanted to grub for whatever handout she could get; no surprise there. Only her youngest daughter, Jennifer, seemed genuinely concerned about Dolores. Jennifer had been on her own since age 18. Gonzalo and Dolores had given her what they could to afford college, but mostly she made her own way with a combination of loans and scholarships. Today, she was a married mother of two and had some kind of job in finance. No matter how many times Jennifer had tried to explain the job, Dolores didn't really understand what her *hija* did every day. Oh well. When she drove to Jennifer's house, which would have looked like some kind of dream palace to her cousins back in Nicaragua, with her all American kids playing football in the yard and her gringo husband grilling something up by the sparkling suburban pool, it was just pure joy for Dolores. "All worth it," she thought to herself. At least here she and Gonzalo had done something right.

She assumed that her daughter could afford the nice suburban house. Just like her daughter assumed the elder Rodriguezes could afford to retire. Dolores assumed that whatever amount of money they had, it was enough. The bills were always paid. She knew Gonzalo had finally paid off the mortgage. But other than that, no one ever really talked about money. Not that it was some kind of big secret, but it just felt like a private subject. Asking Jennifer about money would have felt like asking about her sex life. Just sort of weird and icky.

Dolores had always been the family caregiver. She was pregnant for the first time by age 17; caring for three rambunctious children in her mid-20s was no easy feat. Caring for three rebellious teens in her 30s wasn't much easier. In her 40s, when life was supposed to get easier, her own elderly mother arrived from Nicaragua to live in their house, and the middle daughter seemed to show up every few years with a new baby that she didn't really feel like caring for. Between caring for her own demented mother in her 40s and 50s, and trying to raise unwanted grandchildren for her constantly troubled middle daughter, the time just went by. Gonzalo went to work, they lived simply, bills got paid. Money wasn't really her department.

When he was initially diagnosed, Gonzalo remained upbeat and vigorous. But with each passing month, and each failed chemo treatment, the life seemed to leak out of him bit by bit. Soon he told her he was satisfied with his time here on Earth, and ready to come face to face with the Lord when he was called home. This seemed to comfort Gonzalo, but Dolores was inconsolable. She had met him in her village in Nicaragua when she was 16. Could there even be a life without him?

Gonzalo was the one who called Jennifer for a private family meeting. The other two Rodriguez children were not invited. "I've got bad news, and I've got good news," was the first thing he said.

The bad news was that the doctor had told him to get his affairs in order. The other bad news was that the last three years of cancer therapy had been very expensive. Even though they had Medicare, there were still a lot of big expenses that Medicare didn't cover, and he had been forced to spend most of the couple's retirement savings.

The good news, he said, was that "he was worth more dead than alive." Years ago, he had purchased life insurance that would take care of Dolores in her old age. He tried to laugh as he said it, but it just came out as a wheezing cough. Dolores didn't think any of it was "good" news. She ran out of the room crying and didn't hear any more of the details. She didn't care about any details. She would have given every last penny to keep Gonzalo alive. But it wasn't to be.

A Life for Dolores

The rest went by in a flash. Years later, she could just remember bits and pieces. The stench of bleach in the hospital, the flickering lights in the church, phone calls from cousins she hadn't spoken to in years. The first few awful nights of being in her house alone. In fifty years, she couldn't remember spending a night alone in that *casa*. Now it was her new reality.

Soon, a new feeling crept in. Something that had never even occurred to her during Gonzalo's long, slow decline. Fear. Sure, she had money coming to her. But what if she screwed up? She barely knew how to write a check. She had very rarely looked at the charges on their credit card. She would get one big payout, just one big chance. What if she screwed up and lost everything? Would she wind up the old crazy *abuela* living in Jennifer's house? Or worse?

Just a few weeks after the funeral, the check came in the mail. So strange. Just a simple piece of mail; on the outside no different than a bank statement, or an ad from a mortgage company. Except this one held a check for $500,000 with her name on it. When she took the check out of the envelope, she must have stared at it for half an hour. Her hands were trembling when she deposited the check at her local bank.

Soon, she had another sit down with Jennifer, and her youngest daughter went over the current situation with her.

Dolores owned her house outright. It was no mansion, but it was a well kept, clean home in a nice, safe neighborhood. Jennifer, who by her late 40s had already owned several homes, estimated that the maintenance and taxes on the house would be about $1,000 a month.

Dolores also owned her own car, free and clear. Sure, it was a ten-year-old Honda, but it worked. Since Dolores actually drove very little, the car had low mileage on it. Even so, an old car was an old car, and it could need some maintenance. Jennifer figured that cost at $5,000 per year.

If there was one thing that Dolores had learned to do while raising three kids, several grandkids, and taking care of friends and neighbors, it was cook. Everyone wanted a taste of her famous *pupusas* and other Nicaraguan dishes. It was tasty, but not expensive. So Jennifer estimated Dolores's food costs at about $4,000 per year.

At age 70, Dolores was in pretty good shape. Other than the standard pills for cholesterol and blood pressure, she had really only been in the hospital as a visitor. Still, the whole ordeal with Gonzalo had taught the Rodriguez family that old age could be expensive. So Jennifer estimated $4,000 per year in medical costs.

All of this added up meant that Dolores needed about $25,000 a year just to keep the lights on. In other words, since she already owned a home and car, $25,000 would be enough for her to maintain basic independence, although she would have almost no money left over for hobbies or fun. As a surviving spouse, she could count on $25,000 a year in social security money, guaranteed from the government (although some of that would be taxed, leading to less spendable income). So how should she invest the $500,000 in life insurance money to meet her needs?

Jennifer presented three different options. Dolores could earn about 3% annually by depositing her money in very safe, very secure, traditional options like municipal bonds, long term treasuries, and a few blue chip stocks. This would yield $15,000 annually. All of Dolores's basic bills would be paid, but she had better adopt some cheap hobbies, and forget giving anything to her church or her grandchildren. Also, if she were unlucky enough to live into really old age, and inflation ever surpassed 3% annually, she could suffer a dotage of real poverty.

The next option was to invest somewhat more aggressively, aiming for a 5% annual return. This would provide Dolores with roughly $25,000 in annual income. This would be a mix of traditional, ultra safe investments like municipal bonds, and a few higher dividend paying stocks and REITs. This portfolio could see its total value fluctuate more than the ultra conservative portfolio, but it would mean that Dolores could take one trip per year, and eat out once or twice a week.

The last option was a more aggressive portfolio aiming to yield about 7% annually. This would give Dolores $35,0000 a year in passive income, for a total pre-tax income of $60,0000. Since she already owned her house and car, this would mean that Dolores would have as much as $19,0000 a year to travel, go to dinner with friends, and even spoil her grandchildren. The 7% portfolio would consist mostly of closed end funds, preferred shares, and REITs. While the principal balance could fluctuate significantly, the income would be robust and reliable.

It all made Dolores's head hurt. There was a lot to think about. A lot of different considerations. When she asked Jennifer which option she thought was best, Jennifer simply replied, "They're all just fine choices. I guess it really depends on how active you want to be, and how much up and down you can stand with your money." Dolores took a month to think it all over.

Dolores's Choice

It was a lot to consider. But she felt less scared with Jennifer lending support. She also had the strangest feeling; it was like Gonzalo had never died at all, like he was right there with her to help her decide. Of course, he wasn't there to speak physically, but it was his money too; his hard work to take care of his family, even in the afterlife. She pretty much knew what he would say.

When speaking of their eldest daughter, she of the random children, she of the brushes with the law, she of the "occasional mother" act, Dolores knew that Gonzalo had finally just had enough. They had practically raised two of her four children, and who even knew where the other two were now? In fact, the grandchildren themselves were just arriving at the age where they could conceivably show up on Dolores' doorstep with a little bundle of joy, expecting that *abuela's* now empty house could be a daycare center, or an orphanage altogether. She could picture her late husband turning purple with rage, but struggling not to speak ill of his own kin; "It's not for us to judge, it's for the Lord to judge, but Lord help her, because I've just had enough of this *mierda!*" He would say. If Dolores stuck around the house too much due to low income, then that no-good daughter of hers might see she had nothing to do, and *find* something for her to do.

Her middle child, her son, had his father's business now. He seemed content enough. So, the first child deserved no inheritance, and the second child had already got an inheritance. Anything left over when Dolores went to reunite with Gonzalo could go to Jennifer, although she really didn't need it. All of which meant that Dolores only needed enough money to live out the rest of her life.

Once again, she could feel Gonzalo advising her from heaven, "So live! Live while you are still living, *mi querida!* Take those trips!" Before the diagnosis, they had both been excited about the prospect of traveling the world in retirement. Truthfully, it had been her idea. She knew that her church ran all kinds of trips to special places, like the Vatican and Israel, and even special pilgrimage sites around Europe. He had wanted to go on these trips, but he just couldn't see himself not having to work anymore. After fifty years of labor with his hands, the splendor of the Vatican just didn't seem like it could be for the Rodriguez family. But now it was. The money was there. Jennifer had done the math twice. With Gonzalo, or with Gonzalo in spirit, Dolores Rodriguez could realistically set foot in the Holy Land. Imagine that! A trip to Israel. The poor girl from a Nicaraguan village living long enough to see the very spot where her Lord and Savior had walked the Earth and preached his Gospel. She felt something growing inside of her that she hadn't felt in years. Joy. Joy!

So, clearly, the idea of seeing the world in her old age was exciting to her. But what were the risks? Well, Jennifer had warned her that the higher yielding portfolio could fluctuate up and down in value. Maybe she could even lose some money. But she owned her house, free and clear. That wouldn't fluctuate much. Her Social Security check was as much of a sure thing as there is in this life. At some point, keeping the house would be impossible anyhow. As a fit, youngish retiree she could continue to maintain a single family home. But she would probably have to sell it in her 80s anyhow, if she actually made it that far. And by that time, her major traveling days would probably be done, so how much money would she really need, anyhow? At any rate, Jennifer emphasized that the 7% portfolio would very likely throw off great income for years to come; it was just a little more volatile than the other options. Something could go wrong, but probably not. Dolores has survived coming to a new country with no language skills and little education, and somehow raised three kids in her new country. She could probably survive a few ups and downs in the stock market in exchange for the ability to finally have some "me time" at the end of her life. 7% it was.

Jennifer and Dolores began a process of exploration, and after a couple of months of deliberation, chose the following investments.

They chose Iron Mountain (Ticker: IRM), Kinder Morgan (Ticker: KMI), and Lumen Technologies (Ticker, LUMN) as three fallen angel stocks. (We learned about this technique in Chapter 3).

They chose the exchange traded fund iShares Preferred and Income Securities (Ticker: PFF) as their core investment in preferred shares. They also chose some preferred shares from Bank of America, NextEra Energy, and AmTrust Financial Services. (See Chapter 11 to review preferred shares).

In the closed-end fund sector, they chose to focus on utility funds and municipal bond funds. Jennifer felt that these were the safest sectors. They bought Reaves Utility Income (Ticker: UTG), BlackRock Muniyield Quality Fund II (Ticker: MQT), and the Gabelli Utility Trust (Ticker: GUT). (Check Chapter 12 to review CEFs).

Finally, they sprinkled in some REITs and mortgage REITs, purchasing Sabra Healthcare REIT (Ticker: SBRA), W.P. Carey (Ticker: WPC), and Annaly Capital Management (Ticker: NLY).

Soon, all of the investment arrangements were made. In no time, investment income started showing up in her brokerage account like clockwork. Dolores went out to dinner with friends. She made a donation to a charity. She bought some nice Christmas gifts for her grandchildren.

Finally, the day came when she felt comfortable booking that church trip to Israel. She blinked back tears when the salesperson asked her how many tickets she needed to buy. "Just one," she said. Even though he wouldn't be needing a ticket, she knew Gonzalo would be with her.

TABLE 4: Dolores Rodriguez's Finances

PreTax Income	$60,000
Post Tax	$48,000
Home Maintenance & Taxes	$12,000
Car Maintenance	$5,000
Food	$4,000
Medical	$4,000
Grandkids & Miscellaneous	$4,000
Travel & Entertainment	$19,000

3 Portfolio Options and Resulting Cash Flow

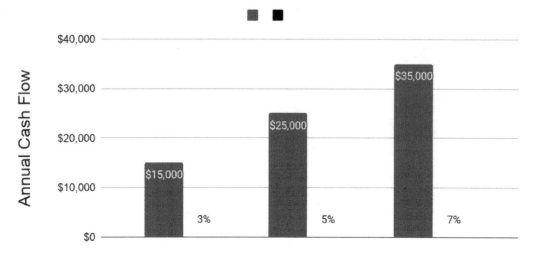

Figure 10

This illustration assumes that Dolores is investing $500,000. These cash flows do not factor in her social security income.

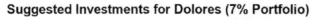

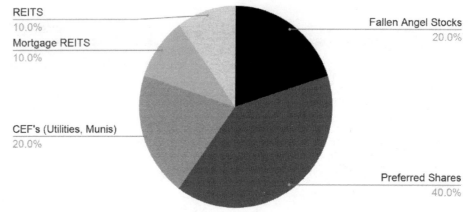

Figure 11

Chapter 18: The Knowledge Dividend

"An investment in knowledge pays the best interest."
-Benjamin Franklin

With this chapter, we come to the end of our book. My fervent hope is that the end of this book is only the beginning of your journey into knowledge.

In today's world, you can't avoid constant discussion about the growing gap between the "haves" and the "have nots." Let me tell you, if you have the intelligence, drive, and determination to have finished this book, you already have a whole lot more than a lot of people. There is no reason in the world why you can't position yourself firmly in the "have" column of our rapidly bifurcating society.

To have money, it really helps to have knowledge first. Even though knowledge is more valuable than ever, amazingly, you can access most of the knowledge you need for cheap or even free. The information that you can get for free on your E-Trade account with the stroke of a few keys used to take numerous trips to the library for your parents or grandparents. You can do a lot of the same reading that a Harvard MBA would do for the simple price of a subscription to the Wall Street Journal or Barron's magazine. In that spirit, please find a list of recommended resources at the end of this chapter. Many are free.

As I write this, I am sitting in a park, sipping a cup of coffee. Today, I woke up when I felt like it. After I finish this chapter, I may go have a beer in the middle of the day to celebrate the successful completion of another book. One beer on a hot afternoon is a terrific celebration of my freedom.

I say this not to arouse jealousy or to boast. I say this because I am not any better than you. I don't have any special formal education (I have an undergraduate history degree). I am not smarter or even luckier than anyone else (I suffered plenty of painful failures along the way). I just had a burning desire to release myself from the corporate chains that bound me. If you have selected, purchased, and read this book, you probably have a similar desire. If I made it happen through passive income investing, then you can too.

The Takeaway

When I think of business books that I have read in the past, what seems to separate the excellent books from standard books is that the excellent books made just a few key, memorable points. I can tell you a few books that I read decades ago where a few key points still stand out in my mind.

Have I written an excellent book? I don't know; I hope so. But here are three key points that you should take with you long after this book starts gathering dust in your library:

1. Rich people don't work hard. Rich people have everyone else working hard for them. This is not a nice statement. This is not a fair statement. But it reflects reality. The reason why I can sit here in the park and write this text today is because I know that, on the first of the month, I have payment coming to me from the companies that I own. Those companies employ thousands of people who work hard every day so that I don't have to.

And I am still an amateur! Just this week, I read a headline that Bill Gates got a quarterly dividend check from Microsoft for $57,000,000. He hasn't worked there in at least a decade. Walmart, one of the largest companies in the world, is still controlled by the Walton family. They haven't shown up to do a day of work at their own company in multiple decades.

When faced with this reality, we can sit around and complain about how unfair it is, or we can figure out what these people all have in common, and try to emulate their ways. What the Waltons and Gates and even myself all have in common is: ownership. We own companies. The Waltons own 50% of Walmart, while I own 0.00005%. But the general principles are the same. Use the tactics and techniques in this book to put yourself in the same position.

2. Don't be afraid to shop for equity securities that pay higher dividends than average. As we reviewed in this book, many of the largest companies that you are familiar with are obscene money machines. They churn out indecent cash flows year after year, decade after decade. They only pay 1 or 2% dividends because they feel like it. They could easily pay higher dividends, but for a variety of reasons that we covered in chapter 2, they prefer to use the cash in other ways. Stocks that pay double or even triple the norm are not necessarily suspicious or suspect. They simply choose to pay out their cash instead of buyback stock or buy other companies. The simple difference between a portfolio that yields 2% and a portfolio that yields 6% can be life changing.

3. You may have noticed from our case studies that, surprisingly, the highest income people did not always have the easiest path to retirement. To use the old adage, "It ain't what you make, it's what you keep." This book is chock full of methods of maximizing income from your savings, but if you don't have much savings, you will have a very hard time generating passive income, no matter how much you make from your job.

Trust me when I tell you that I have known people who earn millions, *millions,* but also somehow spend millions. They wind up just as stressed out and depressed as someone working at Target and living in a trailer park. "It ain't what you make, it's what you keep." In just a page or two, you will find a list of cheap or free resources that will provide you all the knowledge you will ever need to turn your savings into a passive income machine. But only you know how to monitor or control your own spending. Too much spending means too little savings, and that means little freedom in your life.

I'll close with one last saying: "Freedom ain't free." Sadly, it ain't. Even though in America we are all born free on paper, every day millions of people spend their precious time on this Earth doing things they don't want to do because they are locked in the invisible cage of poverty. Very often, they are not just poor in money; they are also poor in knowledge. Your newfound financial knowledge is the key that will set you free.

When will your day of liberation come? It may not be tomorrow, or even the next day. But if you use the principals you have learned in this book, trust me, it's just a matter of time until you break free. Financial freedom, viewed by millions of people as an impossibility, will become your inevitable reality.

Your First Biotech Million

How To Earn Your Fortune In Biotech Stocks

Introduction

Let's start out with the most essential, core concept.
I am not any smarter than you are.

It's true that I had access to a good education as a kid, and I did fairly well in school. But I am not an MBA, MD, or PhD. I am not some kind of rocket scientist that won awards and accolades, and you have never seen me on the cover of Forbes magazine. In fact, I never was particularly strong in the math department. Anything more advanced than basic arithmetic and algebra tormented me in school. Any Wall Street analyst would take one look at my pitiful attempts to build spreadsheets and laugh.

So then I must be more hardworking than you. After all, I found the time to write this book. It must be a lot of hard work getting rich in the stock market.

Not really. Again, I have at least average work ethic, but I would be lying if I told you that I routinely put in twelve-hour days. In my career I have typically preferred to work roughly 9 to 5. Vacations are important to me, and when I am on vacation, I don't answer the phone for work. So, frankly, I don't work any harder than you do.

Then I must be tougher than you are. If there is one thing we have learned from watching Hollywood movies, it's that the big stock market profits go to the brave, the bold, and the brash. You never saw a tear coming out of Gordon Gekko's eye.

But you did see plenty of tears coming out of my eyes. I have suffered some jumbo-sized losses in business, and I was not capable of just laughing off the losses and moving on. Throughout my adult life I have fallen into deep depressions related to money problems. One particular time, when I experienced a pretty serious reverse in my business, I suffered a total mental breakdown, and I lost a promising young marriage. I was a 30 something man wearing a bathrobe for days at a time and living in my mother's spare bedroom. I was so depressed, in fact, that many of the small children in the family did not want to be around me.

Eventually I pulled myself back together, and carried on to fight another day. But certainly, I am a human who can feel beaten down, anxious, or hopeless, just like anybody else. I am not any tougher than you.

Then I must just be plain lucky. What else could explain how I became a biotech millionaire by age 40? I wouldn't need to be smarter than you, or more hardworking than you, or tougher than you, if I were just plain luckier than you, right?

Not really. While I have enjoyed good luck in the cosmic sense (good childhood, good health, solid financial background), I have endured plenty of bad luck in the financial sense. I lost a six-figure inheritance trying to be an entrepreneur. I failed again and again while watching my friends rocket to multi-million-dollar career success. I saw my fledgling net worth crushed when the Dot-com Boom of the 90's ended badly. So, while I certainly can't complain about my luck in life, I didn't just snap my fingers and wake up a biotech millionaire. I got my ass whipped many, many times along the way.

So that may be the real answer. I am not smarter than you. I am not more hardworking than you. I am certainly not tougher than you. But I am probably more experienced than you. Simply put, I've been to hell and back so that you don't have to go through the same odyssey. I've made enough mistakes that I learned a few things the hard way. The distilled product of this life experience is what follows in these pages.

I hope that you are both entertained and informed by this work. I know for sure that you can become a millionaire biotech investor, because I have done it. You may not know it, but you are already, "The right person, in the right place, at the right time." What I offer you is not a "get rich quick scheme."

Rather, this book is a "become wealthy plan." And you're going to become wealthy by helping others. If you choose to follow the path laid out in this book, you will wind up rich in every sense of the word.

Now let's get down to work.

Chapter 1: Why Biotech Investing?

The wealth building program that I am going to teach you will be tough at times. It won't be tough intellectually; I will teach you methods that would work for anybody with a basic education. It will be tough *emotionally*. The world's most famous investor, Warren Buffet, once said, "We don't have to be smarter than everybody else. We have to be more disciplined than everyone else." In order to maintain the necessary discipline, you will need to understand exactly why biotech is a great way to get rich. You will need more than understanding; you will have to feel the opportunity in your bones. It's that feeling that will keep you going through the tough moments when others foolishly bailed out.

There are a lot of ways to get rich...or attempt to get rich. Real Estate, gold coins, that Amway franchise your cousin keeps trying to sell you on. So what is so special about biotech investing? Why on earth would I recommend biotech investing to someone who is not a doctor or scientist?

Let's go over some of the ideal qualities of a business. If you were going to employ time, energy, and hard-won capital in a business, would you want to be in a business where demand almost always exceeds supply? Would you want to be in a business with high perceived barriers to entry, so that you don't face lots of competition? Lastly, would you want to be in a business that grows and thrives exclusively by helping people?

If the above stated qualities describe your ideal business, then biotech is right for you. Let's explore.

DEMAND ALWAYS EXCEEDS SUPPLY

Think quick. How many people do you know over 80 years of age? That's probably an easy question for you; your grandma, the lady who bags groceries at the local Walmart, even several presidential candidates are approaching 80 years of age. No big deal, right?

Wrong. For millions and millions of years of human history, the average age of death hovered around 40. A childhood without antibiotics (or really any understanding of human biology) was risky indeed. Wolfgang Amadeus Mozart was originally one of six children. Only two of the six survived to adulthood. Mozart in turn fathered six children, and only two of his six children ever grew up.

Even if you did survive to reasonable old age, the slightest infection would kill you.

Millions upon millions of people died from diseases that don't even exist today in the developed world. The point is: surviving well into your 80's is not a natural phenomena. Sky rocketing human longevity is a direct result of ever improving medical technology.

And it's a self-fulfilling prophecy that only creates more and more demand for medical services. Think about it. You are mowing your lawn in your 50's and you cut yourself, eventually resulting in a nasty infection. Instead of a slow death from infection, you're given antibiotics and live to see another day. In your 60's, your doctor discovers that your arteries are blocked and lifesaving stents are implanted into you. In your 70's, you are diagnosed with throat cancer, but chemotherapy saves the day. In your 80's, you have a stroke, but they get you to the hospital in time and they are able to unclog the clot in your brain. Finally, at age 90 you fall, break your hip, and die after three agonizing months in the hospital.

At each step along the way, you would have died without medical intervention, but due to an ever-expanding array of available medical services, you survived to grow even older. And as you grew older, you leaned on those medical services more and more. The supply of medical services only staves off death, therefore creating more and more demand for medical services. Does this sound like something you would want to own?

The supply of effective medical services is creating so much demand, that many experts fret about the developed world being overwhelmed by what they are calling, "The Grey Tsunami." Remember the 60's rock band The Who, singing, "hope I die before I get old." Well, they didn't. In fact, 10,000 Americans per day now turn 65, after which they will be legally entitled to almost unlimited medical care until they finally expire, which won't be anytime soon, by the way. According to the Organization for Economic Cooperation and Development (OECD) a 65-year-old American woman today should expect to live to age 85. In Japan, another advanced economy where biotech products are commonly sold, that same 65-year-old woman would expect to live to 90! In most developed nations, these legions of geezers are legally entitled to extensive medical services for at least twenty years at the end of their prodigious life spans.

At the same time, modern technology still leaves so very much to be desired. The Pharmaceutical Giant Merck has made some dramatic headway in recent years with it's introduction of Keytruda, the first widely used cancer immunotherapy. Recently, Merck proudly circulated a press release pointing out that lung cancer patients on Keytruda can expect a 23.5% survival rate after five years. This compares to just a 5% survival rate in the pre-Keytruda era. This is step represents great progress, but it still means that 75% of Keytruda patients will not survive 5 years. Do you think that there could be good business opportunities in trying to improve upon that dreadful survival rate? And, if rival pharmaceutical companies can improve on that survival rate, are elderly lung cancer survivors more likely to use more biotechnology down the road, or less? Every patient that Merk saves today, will just consume more Merck products as they age. How is that for the perfect circle?

So, we can verify that we have at least one half of a great business. Unlimited demand. What about supply?

Well, let's think about what it takes to get into the Biotech business, and what it takes to effectively market and sell finished products.

To get into the business of drug discovery, you would need at least a few PhD's and/or MD's working for you. These people are not cheap, if you can even find them!

According to a press release by the American Association of Medical Colleges, America could face a shortage of 130,000 primary care providers by 2030. Simply put, while the demand for medical services grows more rapidly than a California wildfire, requirements to become a licensed medical practitioner have not shrunk. The learning process remains grueling and long, taking, on average, at least 10 years of education and many hundreds of thousands of dollars of investment. The PhD process may be even more demanding in some ways; academic scientists face a similar tortuous path to acquire prized knowledge, but may well be discouraged because the financial payoff of a PhD is not as assured as an MD. At any rate, if you want to recruit a good staff of biologists and physicians to help your company pry open nature's secrets, you had better have at least a few million dollars laying around…

Even if you do have enough seed capital to make those critical early hires, you had better have a team member who is highly skilled in raising capital. Exactly how much it costs to develop a new drug is a matter of intense debate. According to Forbes magazine, respectable estimates range from $650 Million to $2.7 Billion to get an innovation from the petri dish to the pharmacy shelf. Even if that enormous investment eventually gets whacked up between several different companies in the business ecosystem, that is pretty massive barrier that will stop your next store neighbors or your cousin from attempting to start a biotech business. Got a $1,000,000 to invest? Great, buy a Subway franchise. You would need at least $50,000,000 to even contemplate starting a biotech innovation company. If you've got that laying around, say in a swimming pool filled with hundred-dollar bills and gold bars, call me.

So, we don't have to investigate too much to realize that the ratio between supply and demand is both favorable for the investor, and only likely to get even better with time.

But doesn't that mean that, as an investor, you will face overwhelming competition to purchase the best biotech shares?

THE MOAT: PERCEPTION IS EVERYTHING

It is really hard to start a biotech company. You need a lot of capital, someone really good at raising capital, and all-star team of highly educated professionals. But *investing in* a biotech is not hard at all. It is simply perceived as hard.

Why would biotech investing seem so daunting to most people? Well, let's look at the matter from the point of view of Mr. Joe D. Average. Both Mr. Average and his wife work middle management professional jobs, 40 to 50 hours per week. Combined, they pull in pretty decent money, let's say $150,000 annually. Because they love their kids, and they want their kids to have a good education, they need a house in a good school district. So, after taxes, most of that money gets sucked into a nice house in a good part of town. But *The Averages* aren't flashy, so we'll assume they don't squander all of their money on fancy cars or big brand clothes. After expenses, and paying for their nice house in a nice neighborhood, let's say they have $20,000 annually left to invest.

Mr. Average is the assistant general manager at a factory, and Mrs. Average is a marketing manager at the local hospital. Between working two full time jobs and ferrying around their kids to all kinds of school and community events, they don't have a lot of time to study up on investing. Another way to look at it, frankly, is they don't make the time because they are secretly scared of money, and scared of losing the little that they are able to save.

So altogether, they may well choose real estate rather than stocks. Not an unreasonable choice; many people take comfort in being able to see and touch the place where their money is going. If they do choose stocks at all, they may very well take the common advice and just plunk the money into an S&P 500 exchange traded fund. Again, not a bad choice at all. In fact, the S&P 500 has consistently delivered returns in the 9-10% range over the last 60 years. If the Average Family owned any stock at all, they would still be better than 50% of Americans. Of the Americans that do own some kind of stock, 70% own stocks through an employer sponsored 401K or IRA plan. These employer sponsored 401K plans rarely offer individual stocks. So this means that, right off the bat, only a tiny minority of "regular Joe's" own individual stocks. Less and less Americans own stock at all, and of those that do, most just invest in a passive fund and prey to match the average long term returns of the market.

So, the statistics illustrate that, the day you chose to dedicate yourself to niche investing, you leave behind 90% of your potential competitors. We know that biotech offers explosive growth for the foreseeable future. Why do most people just settle for an S&P 500 index fund, if they have the guts to invest in stocks at all?

There are two main misperceptions that can work powerfully in your favor. The first misperception is that biotech investing is hopelessly complicated, and requires an advanced degree.

Starting and leading biotech is, in fact, very complicated, and may require an advanced degree. Investing in one is not! Simply put, an investable biotech with a strong management team HAS ALREADY DONE ALL OF THE HARD WORK, SO THAT YOU DON'T HAVE TO. The Joe Averages of the world have already psyched themselves out of the game. Before ever daring to open up E-Trade, or read the first few pages of an annual report, they have already decided that they need a PhD to make money in biotech. What a shame for Joe Average, what an advantage for you!

When you buy shares in a biotech company, you are an OWNER, not a worker! You're Not the one laboring for years or decades in a lab to push the envelope of known science. That professional is working for you, SO YOU DON"T HAVE TO. We will elaborate on this theme in much greater detail later, but the bottom line is: a good biotech company can summarize their work in simple, down to earth language in just one or two paragraphs. If you can't understand their work without a PhD, then you shouldn't invest. In fact, probably no one should. But your Joe Average investor got intimidated when he opened up the company's annual report and saw a picture of a molecule on the cover. Fear and description have pushed most of your investing competition out of the way before the game has even begun.

The second giant misconception is that biotech investing is too risky for Joe Average.

This misperception comes from three places. First, personal feelings related to the crash of 2009 that are misplaced. Second, the media. Third, a gross misunderstanding of the basic arithmetic involved.

The same studies that reveal that only about half of Americans own any kind of stock at all, also highlight that stock ownership has declined dramatically since 2008. A much-cited article in the Chicago Tribune states that as much as 62% of American households owned some kind of stock prior to 2008, while just about 50% do now. This may be due the much-documented decline of the American Middle Class, but is mostly related to residual fear from the 2009 crash. Everybody knows somebody who lived a horror story. That somebody might even be a family member, or yourself! Millions of Americans got burned by stocks so badly in 2009 that they could never get up the courage to try again.

Therefore, a lot of hard working, middle to upper middle-income families like Joe Average have already decided that stock, in general are too risky. Once again, Joe Average's mental errors are your advantage. We will discuss stock market crashes, and biotech crashes, much more in depth later.

Secondly, the media really, really wants middle class folks to invest in the S&P 500 and call it a day. When Vanguard funds John Bogle died, he was given a hero's send off. Bogle pioneered the low cost, passive ETF. You would think from his obituaries that he cured cancer. Oddly, one of the greatest stock pickers of all time, Warren Buffet, has famously stated that, when he dies, he has ordered his wife to put his estate 90% in a passive S&P 500 fund, and 10% in treasuries. This "Do as I say, not as I do" attitude broadcasted by the media has talked millions of average investors into the idea that specializing in a stock niche is just too complicated, and too dangerous. Of course, that has greatly reduced competition for investors who think the opposite…

Finally, a lot of people stay away from biotech because they just don't understand how the math works. If there is one thing you take away from this book, please understand the following: VOLATILITY DOES NOT EQUAL RISK. It is true that stock market valuations, even of large, established companies, can fluctuate almost at random. It is also true that, biotech stocks, and indexes composed of biotech stocks can fluctuate even more, and even more at random, because many of these companies are not well established. This can be very scary for Mr. and Mrs. Joe Average. But IF MANAGED PROPERLY, VOLATILITY IS AN OPPORTUNITY, NOT A RISK. I will present to you a tried and true volatility management system that will allow you to stay in the game when your weaker competitors are dropping left and right. But for now, let's just summarize as this: the numbers prove that, while more volatile in the short term, biotech investors benefit greatly from that extra volatility in the long run. The SUCCESSFUL BIOTECH INVESTOR FOCUSES RELENTLESSLY ON THE FUNDAMENTALS AND IGNORES RANDOM SHORT TERM FLUCTUATIONS.

The proof is in the pudding, as they say. According to the website Financialplanning.com, between 2008 and 2018, the TOP 4 out of the TOP 20 top returning exchange traded funds were biotech funds ($IBB, $XBI, $PJP, $FBT). The average 10-year return was 16% per year, vrs. 7.6% for the S&P 500. In other words, an investor who had ignored all the short term gyrations of the biotech market would have reaped DOUBLE the return of the S&P 500 over the last decade. All this didn't occur in spite of the fact that Joe Average was licking his wounds from the 2008 crash. It may well have happened BECAUSE Joe Average swore off "risky" stocks. The determined and astute biotech investor would have had little competition to snap up the best shares at the lowest prices......

DOING WELL, BY DOING GOOD

I am going to teach you how to make a fortune investing in biotech companies. But as we discussed earlier, this is not a "get rich quick scheme." This a plan to build real wealth. Which means that you will need to commit a significant amount of time, capital, and mental energy to the process. Leaving aside the pure financials for a moment, is this a worthy investment of your precious time on Planet Earth?

A quick examination of the facts would reveal that mastering biotech could actually be one of the most noble things you will ever do. When you are a purveyor of cutting edge 21st century medicines, you are not just generating profit by pleasing a client. You are keeping people alive, and keeping families whole.

In just the last decade, American healthcare companies have cured Hepatitis C, largely neutralized HIV, and, as cited before, made giant leaps against hopelessly incurable cancers. All of this progress is a direct product of the American Capitalistic method of invention and innovation. While you will never be wearing a white lab coat or playing with test tubes, every time you decide to risk your precious capital on a biotech venture, you are encouraging positive inventions that help humanity.

Let's think about it this way. Remember the list of critical ingredients to start a biotech company? Remember Forbes magazine estimating $650,000,000 as the very low-end figure to bring a new drug to market? Some of that large pool of risk money comes from pension funds, some from very wealthy venture capitalists, but the largest proportion comes from gutsy individual investors just like you. Remember Keytruda, the bold new immunotherapy that has quintupled survival rates in lung cancer? If you were a Merck shareholder, or you invested in one of the smaller companies that eventually became part of Merck along the way, it would not be absurd to say that you, personally, had helped save thousands of lives. Without people like you taking the risk, there would be no Keytruda, and newly diagnosed lung cancer patients would still have a 95% chance of being dead within five years.

Of course, the American system which has birthed so many medical advances is far from perfect. In fact, it's no secret that the System leaves much to be desired. As a shareholder in publicly traded companies, you will have an opportunity to advocate for changes if you so desire. Many of the market distortions and grotesque price hikes that cause so much controversy come into play after a medicine has been invented, and it's curative value has been proven. But if that medicine never comes into the world, if those very talented executives and scientists never bother to go through the stress and risk of discovering something new, then where would we be as a society? Fundamentally, as a biotech investor, you cannot earn outsized returns without helping your fellow human beings.

So there you have it. Why invest in biotech? Biotech is a business where demand will always outstrip supply, where your competition as an investor will be limited due to common misperceptions, and where you can always feel good about how you are spending your time.

Now that we have a solid understanding of why we are dedicating ourselves to biotech, we are ready to move forward with a concrete plan…

Chapter 2: The Numbers That Can Make You Rich

It might seem odd that a kid who was never better than average in math class grew up to become a biotech millionaire. Hollywood loves to cook up scenes filled with "super quant' PhD Wall Street Wizards making brilliant plays to become Masters of the Universe. But people go to the movies to escape reality for a while, and that is what Hollywood delivers…...gripping tales a million miles away from reality.

The reality is that I was never great in math, am still mediocre today, and you can be too. If you can do basic arithmetic and you have access to an internet browser in your home, you already have enough math skills to make a million dollars investing in biotech. The math is easy; some of the implications of the math may not be so easy. But understanding the basic calculations behind investment riches is an important towards step towards visualizing yourself actually achieving those riches. As Walt Disney once said, "If you can Dream it, you can Do it." Understanding the necessary numerical milestones gives you the temerity to dream, and the willpower to do….

Looking in your Crystal Ball….

In order to figure out just how fast, or slow, you could build wealth, we are going to use a financial calculator that we can find for free on the internet. It never ceases to amaze me how much money people feel that they must spend on formal education, when that very same education is now available for free all over the internet. I promise you on a stack of Bibles, the calculations that we are going to do over the next few minutes with a free internet program are really not that different from the spreadsheet calculations that some Harvard MBA paid $150,000 to learn.

There are every manner of financial calculators available for free on the internet. The selection itself can become overwhelming, and the offerings can became overly ornate, like a sushi bar with a chef who thinks he should be working in a five star restaurant. Even with every combination of seafood concoction imaginable at our fingertips, sometimes the most appealing thing on the buffet is just some simple, fresh fish. For this exercise, all we will need is the most simple investment calculator.

One such is the investment calculator available for free at Smartasset.com. In order to take a look into your financial future, you only need four simple pieces of information.

1) How much money are you starting with?
2) How much additional money are you able to save on a monthly or annual basis?
3) What is the rate of return on your investments?
4) How many years of investment growth are you taking into consideration?

Ten people could get ten radically different results based on what numbers they punch in for each of the four variables. So, it's important that we understand each variable. However, the internet does the math. Understanding the interplay between variables is critical for wealth building; actually being able to perform the math yourself is not.

I am not in the business of handing out specific advice, because I write for a broad audience. In order to illustrate the interplay between variables on this calculator, I am going to make up three case studies. Your reality might just happen to match one of these; most likely you will fall somewhere between the case studies, because we are all unique. I will however, bake in the following assumptions:

If you have purchased this book, and have made it to chapter 2, then you have already demonstrated more drive and resolve than 90% of Americans. You are probably somewhat more conscience than average when it comes to saving and striving. So I will create three simulations that assume that you are already tracking towards average, or better than average, financial results. For example, according to bankrate.com, the median American has a net worth of $100,000. So, you may be somewhat less than that, or even somewhat more, but I am going to assume that you already have some decent savings. People who don't bother to think of their financial future would probably not invest the time to read this book....

If you have purchased this book, then you already had some interest in the world of biotech investing, and the high returns that often come with it. So, I will mostly assume investment returns on the higher side of the spectrum. Achieving these kinds of returns is not without risk; we will talk about specific risk management tactics in subsequent chapters.

If you have purchased this book, you are probably not a 75-year-old retiree. I can show almost anyone how to amass significant wealth in biotech, but it's not an overnight process. You would need at least ten years to get anywhere. If you want to get rich quick, try late night TV or the darker corners of the internet....

Now let's get down to business. Here are three different ways that a person could make a million dollars investing in biotech stocks…...

Meet Sam: The world is his oyster, and he wants the pearl……

Sam is an ambitious young man. He majored in business at his university, and just months after graduation, he got an entry level job in banking. He has studied up on the FIRE movement (Financial Independence, Retire Early) and he understands that saving money is critical to building up his independence and financial freedom.

In order to become a Biotech Millionaire, he has made the following wise decisions.

-He makes $50,000 as a junior analyst at a bank, and he thinks he could make $70,000 within a few years. He doesn't yet have kids or a family, but he does have some student loans that he has to pay monthly. In order to keep his costs down and leave him some cash he can invest every month, he shares an apartment with two roommates. He drives a used car. He shops for his clothes at Marshalls. He tries to hunt for bars with good happy hour specials….

-Since Sam is young, he feels comfortable building a portfolio of the riskiest biotech stocks. He wants to own a piece of raw innovation for the long haul. If he crashes and burns a few times, he still has years to recover.

-He didn't inherit any great fortune, but when he graduated from college, his grandparents gave him $10,000 to get him started in life. He is holding $5,000 as an emergency fund, and going to use $5,000 to start building his biotech portfolio.

So, let's put the following assumptions into the calculator for Sam.

Starting Investment: $5,000
Monthly contribution: $500
Return on Investment: 14% per year

At this rate, how long will it take Sam to become a millionaire?

According to SmartAsset.com, Young Sam, who started life with just $5,000, will have an investment portfolio worth $1,132,99 in 23 years. Through dedication, hard work, and a little luck, Sam is a millionaire by age 45.

Meet Jim & Judy: One busy couple……

In a lot of ways, Jim and Judy are like most professional couples in major urban areas across the United States. They both have corporate careers. Their combined income is $160,000. They have two wonderful, but expensive, kids. They have a nice house in a good school district, but it's nothing fancy. The only way that they differ from most couples is that they have both the will and the way to become exponentially richer than most of their neighbors.

J&J drive used cars. Their house is nice enough, but the truth is they could afford something better if they stretched. They both have university degrees, but they both went to local state schools, and they know their kids will do the same. Jim is 39 and Judy is 35. They have already built up about six months' worth of cash, in case someone loses their job, and have already started building up an investment portfolio. So far, they have $75,000 invested. They started saving soon after they met in their mid-twenties.

Since they have six months of cash socked away for a rainy day, they know they can take some risk with their long-term investments. However, Judy tempers Jim's more aggressive investment instincts; they worked too long and hard to play with their savings as if it were a casino.

So let's put the following assumptions into the Smartasset calculator.

Starting Investment: $75,000
Monthly Contribution: $1,000 (includes employer matches on 401K)
Return on Investment: 12% per year

At this rate, how long does it take Jim and Judy to become biotech millionaires?

In 16 years, J&J will have an investment portfolio worth $1,082,338. This would be in addition to the equity they have built up in their home, and the six months emergency

250

fund they started with. As Jim approaches sixty years of age, he is looking at a secure and early retirement.

Meet Octavia: Putting some Gold in her Golden Years….

As she matures through her mid 50's, Octavia has a lot to look back upon with pleasure. Although her marriage didn't last, it did produce two great kids, and even a new grandbaby. The time she took off from work set back her career, but, in retrospect, her divorce settlement was fair. While it was tough to stand on her own two feet again, her career has been growing of late. She never wants to be dependent on someone else again, so after her kids moved out, she moved into a small studio and kept expenses low.

She currently makes $65,000 per year as a manager at a print shop, and she makes an extra $10,000 trading antiques on eBay. ten years ago she got $150,000 in her divorce settlement, which she has increased to $250,000 through diligent savings.

She thinks she can make her career last until at least age 65, and she knows that she just can't accumulate enough money to retire independently if she follows the conventional wisdom and chooses only conservative investments. Still, she's on her own in this world, so it makes her stomach turn in knots when she sees some of the fluctuations that can happen with biotech stocks. So, she will take as much risk as she can stand.

Let's put in the following variables for Octavia:

> Starting Investment: $250,000
> Monthly contribution: $650 (includes employer match)
> Return on Investment: 8%

If Octavia follows this plan, will she ever be a biotech millionaire?

You better believe it. Within 15 years, Octavia will have an investment portfolio worth $1,051,655. If Octavia can make her career last to age 70, she can still retire wealthy.

UNDERSTANDING THE COMMONALITIES

As you can see, there are a lot of paths to become wealthy through biotech stocks, even for regular, middle class folks. If they can do it, you certainly can too!

That being said, they all had a few elements in common. First, they make decent incomes. Not sky high! Not Wall Street Rader pay packages! But they earn professional level wages in corporate jobs. If you haven't at least gotten to that point, increasing your income should be your top priority. "How to increase your income?" is, of course, a whole other book. The struggles of the middle class in America today are well documented, so I know it can feel like a mountain to climb. But as you can see from the previous illustrations, you don't need a millionaire income to become well-to-do. Just get to "slightly better than average" and I will show you how to do the rest.

Second, you noticed that all three of my examples had a frugal streak. You may have had some contact already with the FIRE movement. This movement leverages an ever growing media presence; blogs, websites, and even mainstream media...all to let the world know that your quality of life is not necessarily linked to the quantity of money that you spend. FIRE believers believe that a person should live the most meager lifestyle possible, in order to accumulate money that can be invested into assets, as opposed to say, being squandered on a BMW lease. This book is not about FIRE, or frugality. However, the simple, cruel mathematical fact is that, unless your career and lifestyle combine to produce investable cash on a regular basis, you will never be able to accumulate your first stock market million. I can teach you how to maximize every penny that you invest; but first you have to find the pennies. Let's call us "50/50 partners."

Lastly, you will notice that nobody got rich overnight. I would probably sell a lot more books if I dared to promise you that I could wave a magical biotech wand and you would suddenly be living like a Kardashian. But I've never been a good liar. I can show you how to retire early, if you start early. I can show you how to catch up if you're behind. But it's going to take some work and dedication over a sustained period of time. Look at it this way; most people work hard year after year, decade after decade, but still wind up with nothing. You will need to work hard for a prolonged period of time, but you will wind up rich. Does that seem *more fair* than what happens to most people?

UNDERSTANDING THE VARIABLES

Just as important as the commonalities between our case studies, are the differences. Poor Sam started out in life with little cash, but much ambition. Jim and Judy made a pretty good income, but had two kids and a house to pay. Octavia had taken some pretty harsh blows in her divorce, but was still aiming for financial independence as she faced old age. Very different variables went into that calculator, yet somehow, all three wound up rich. How?

For the mathematically challenged, the simplest explanation is this: YOU NEED A LOT OF SOMETHING. Sam, had little money to start, but a lot of time. This allowed him to make riskier investments, and gave more time for those investments to grow. Jim and Judy had less time, and less tolerance for extreme risk, but they already had a nice savings base to build on. Octavia was running out of time; this meant that she needed somewhat more conservative investments than the other examples, and that she had less time for her investments to compound. However, she had a decent job of gathering assets, so her investments needed less risk or time to grow past that $1 million mark. You don't need a perfect life, where all the variables come up aces. But, YOU NEED A LOT OF SOMETHING.

There are a shocking number of people in America today that do have a lot of something, yet they don't wind up rich. Why? Don't tell anyone I said this, but the cold, hard, truth is: most people you meet will systematically turn a lot of something into absolutely nothing.

Most young people, who have the ability to live meagerly and build up assets, in fact just spend it all on night clubs and BMW leases. Then they wake up one day at 45 and realize they have nothing.

A lot of professional couples today are able to earn well into the six figures. But "deserve" the nicest house they can afford, and the kids "need" to go to private universities, so, they wind up saving nothing. They eventually get laid off from their high-powered professional job due to age discrimination, and they have to call their own kids looking for a loan.

A surprising number of people facing retirement have actually managed to hold onto a few dollars over the years, but they never really arm themselves with investing knowledge, and they wind up terrorized by sad stories from friends and the media. So, they plunk their savings into "safe" investments earning 3% per year, and they wind up having to scrimp and save their way into an old age cursed by poverty.

This last part is my specialty. We have seen from these examples that even regular people can make a fortune in the stock market if they receive the right coaching and training. Let's make a deal. You set up your life so that you have some amount of money to invest every month, and I'll provide the coaching and training to make you rich. Sound fair?

Chapter 3: Your Model Portfolio

Y ou may have noticed that I have used the word "build" a lot. "A plan to build wealth," "build a strong financial base," "build a biotech portfolio." That is because becoming wealthy through stock market investing, and biotech in particular, actually is a lot like constructing a building.

Consider the process. First, you must identify the opportunity to build something, and contemplate solid reasons for moving forward with the project. We did that in chapter 1. Then you must engage an engineer to do soil testing, and to make sure that the project is viable mathematically. We did that in chapter 2. Next, you must engage an architect to create a detailed blueprint that will leave you with a step by step plan on how to put the pieces of your dream together. This chapter is that blueprint.

If you buy one small pharmaceutical stock, then, technically, you have become a biotech investor. But there are big stocks, small stocks, dividend stocks, growth stocks, exchange traded funds, etc. There are literally thousands of ways a portfolio could be constructed. Just like an architect's blueprint, some combinations and formats will yield much better results than others.

In this case, how you should assemble your portfolio depends a lot on who YOU are. A ninety-year-old granny might want a very different portfolio than a kid coming out of college. A risk averse mother of three might need different kinds of stocks than a high-flying corporate exec who has been a risk taker his whole life.

As I said before, I don't give out personalized advice, and this format wouldn't be right for that anyhow. But I can give you some solid portfolio templates that will take you 90% of the way there. You will have to finish the last 10% of customization yourself. You are going to learn so much over time that, in a few short years, I doubt you'll need anybody's recommendations.

Below I am going to present three different biotech-oriented portfolios for three different types of investors; Beginner, Intermediate, and Advanced. Here I am not referring to age. A 70-year-old retired executive could be a beginner biotech investor, while a 35-year-old associate attorney could have fifteen years of experience under her belt. A lot also will have to do with your own personal comfort level with volatility and risk. The beginner portfolio will be organized to subject you to less volatility, and the advanced portfolio will expose you to more volatility. The assumption is that the advanced, or more experienced, investor will have already built up an emotional and financial toolkit that allows him to weather rougher storms. We will discuss the psychology of risk management much more in detail in a subsequent chapter.

You will note that each portfolio will be composed of a few different asset classes. The assets classes are "cash equivalents," "Big Pharma ETF" "Biotech ETF" and "Individual stocks." In this chapter, we will stick with those generic terms. Later on we will get much more specific about exactly how to select those assets, but for now, we are going to be focusing merely on the "how" and "why" of each category. Let's start out with the novice…

The Beginner Portfolio

As we mentioned above, a "beginner" could be anyone. She could be 17, or she could be 77. A beginner is anyone who has limited experience managing her own investments, and in particular, limited experience buying equities. The main goal of this portfolio is to allow the beginner to start her journey to financial knowledge by managing risk and volatility, while still providing access to the fabulous opportunities that healthcare has to offer. The percentages refer to what percent of the portfolio should be in each asset class.

<u>The Beginner Biotech Portfolio</u>

-30% cash, or cash equivalent
-30% Big Pharma ETF
-20% Biotech ETF
-20% Individual Biotech stocks

This portfolio has a very large allotment to cash. Why is that? One of the hallmarks of biotech investments is volatility. This means that, in the short run, your biotech stocks could fluctuate wildly, for no apparent reason. It's the nature of the beast. As I mentioned before, the data indicates that these short-term fluctuations are meaningless for the disciplined investor. Ultimately these companies are creating products that keep an ageing population alive; biotech has a bright future. But for the novice, the ups and downs of Mr. Market may take some time to get used to. A large cash component provides some stability to the overall value of your portfolio, which will help you stay cool during times of stress.

Let's discuss briefly the use of the words "cash" or "cash equivalent." Where, exactly, you stash your cash may depend a lot on the market conditions of the moment. As I write these words, simple bank accounts are paying decent interest rates, so it may make the most sense to just shop around for a competitive bank account or certificate of deposit, and put the cash in a bank.

But interest rates on cash deposits have varied wildly over the years; many pundits believe that very low interest rates will be the norm for the foreseeable future. If your current bank account rates fall to appalling lows, then you may need to shop around for cash equivalents, such as treasury bills, or short-term bond funds. These kinds of "bank account proxies" can easily be found at well-known low-cost providers such as Vanguard funds.

So, the large cash allotment will help the beginner stay cool when the chips are down. Another reason for a large cash allotment is that, over time, you will start to buy more and more individual stocks. This way you will have "dry powder" available when you see good buying opportunities.

The next item in the allotment is "Big Pharma ETFs." An exchange traded fund is a basket of stocks that trades as if it were one stock. So, for example, the iShares U.S. Pharmaceutical ETF (ticker symbol IHE) is comprised of the largest pharmaceutical companies in the United States; household names such as Pfizer, Merck, and J&J.

At 30%, the Big Pharma ETF is also a beefy allotment in the beginner's portfolio. There are two fundamental reasons for this.

First, you could envision Big Pharma as the older sibling of Biotech. Both types of companies sell medicines, but they are distinguished by size, speed, and culture. Big Pharma companies have often been around for one hundred years or more, and they move at the plodding pace you might expect from a $200,000,000,000 goliath. It's a poorly kept secret that the Pfizer's of the world aren't so great at innovating. Risk takers just aren't attracted to a company with thirty layers of management. So, they typically buy innovation. They let their smaller, younger, scrappier biotech siblings do a lot of the most grueling work, then they buy them out. A lot of the innovation that is born in small biotech labs eventually winds up in your bathroom cabinet courtesy of Merck or Eli Lilly. So, a generous allotment to Big Pharma makes sense, even if your real fascination is the more fast paced world of biotechs.

Secondly, and probably most importantly, these Big Pharma ETFs add ballast and safety to the novice portfolio. While even the mighty American Pharmaceutical Industry has good years and bad years, the sheer magnitude of these corporate behemoths adds safety to your portfolio. Care to guess how many major pharmaceutical concerns went bankrupt during the Great Recession of 2009? Zero. Pfizer, Eli Lilly, Johnson and Johnson, etc., are some of the most ancient organizations in Corporate America. They earned stellar returns for your grandfather, and they may well earn strong returns for your grandchildren. So, Big Pharma acts as a safety blanket for the budding investor.

The third allotment in the portfolio is 20% in a biotech ETF. This is the same concept as the Big Pharma ETF, but now the beginner is beginning to dip her toes in the deep end of the pool. Just like the Big Pharma ETF, this one stock will represent a wide variety of companies, but this time, you will be buying basket of smaller, newer, companies that are really chasing scientific breakthroughs. We would expect volatility from this part of the portfolio; it's not uncommon for this part to fluctuate up, or down by 20% in one year. However, for the beginner, the ETF still offers more safety than individual biotech stocks. These ETFs commonly represent between 30 and 60 biotech companies. Some will sky rocket, others will crash......but they won't all go bankrupt. As long as the general trajectory of scientific innovation is up, then your investment will eventually go the same way. The most well-known ticker symbols in this field are: IBB, XBI, and FBT. Remember, these three names all averaged more than 12% annual return between 2008 and 2018!

The last allotment in the starter portfolio is 20% in individual biotech stocks. This is the most turbulent part of the portfolio, but it is where most of the beginner's learning will come from. Here the beginner will choose between five and ten stocks. Some will do great. But someone with no experience may well get burned on a few. Any money lost here should be considered tuition paid at the University of Life. Even if a few of your initial picks flame out, you very likely will have invested far less in your education than if you had pursued an Ivy League MBA!

The whole point of this tranche is to learn from two critical angles. First, you will learn everything about biotech by doing. In a later chapter I will suggest specific exercises and techniques to grow your knowledge base slowly but steadily. But the key is to learn by doing, in a controlled, "safe enough" environment. The modest initial allocation to individual stocks is how you create this "safe enough" environment.

Most importantly, you will be learning about yourself! What is your true tolerance for market turmoil? If a stock gets hit by a bad media report, and drops 20% in one day, do you lose too much sleep? If your stock passes through a key trial, and goes up 50% in a month, do you go crazy and start throwing more money at it without doing your homework? You will start to learn your own tendencies. If you seem to handle temporary reverses with calm, then you know you can move to the next stage, "intermediate" or perhaps even straight to "advanced." If you find yourself trapped in a manic cycle of dread or ecstasy, then maybe you should just stick with the beginner profile. As we have explored previously, the market will eventually do all the work for you; the question is if your own personality will get in the way. The beginner portfolio is how you find out....

The Intermediate Portfolio

Once you have a few years under your belt, and you haven't lost too much sleep over the gyrations of the biotech market, you are ready to move to the intermediate portfolio. There aren't going to be any radical changes, just some adjustments that push you deeper into the world of biotech.

<u>The Intermediate Portfolio</u>

-20% Cash, or cash equivalent
-20% Big Pharma ETF
-10% Biotech ETF
-50% Individual Stocks

You may notice that the cash allocation is still significant. In this case, you would own cash and the Big Pharma for the same reasons you did as a beginner. Adding some heft is how we make your portfolio crash resistant. Even if we repeated 2009 again tomorrow, 20% of your portfolio would be unaffected, and the 20% of the portfolio in Big Pharma would be only slightly depressed. These two selections will give you endurance to stay in the game while competitors drop out.

As you move towards Intermediate level, we have reduced your investment in Biotech ETFs. Why? Because, as you gain more and more knowledge and experience on your own, you may well do better (and have more fun) selecting your own stocks. At this point, instead of owning just 5 to 10 stocks, you will probably own 10 to 15 stocks; you will have already created your own basket of stocks that span a wide range of disease states and company sizes…

So why keep the Biotech ETF at all? The ETF now serves as a landmark that you can measure your own stock picking against. Over long periods of time (1 year, 3 year, and 5 year) the return on investment from your individual stocks should match, or hopefully, exceed the ETF results. If not, then you might consider returning to the beginner portfolio. At this point in your journey, you should really take some pleasure out of the process of stock analysis and selection; if not, the beginner portfolio can be your permanent portfolio, because it doesn't require much work.

The Advanced Portfolio

A lot of people would find the Intermediate Portfolio to be nerve wracking. Even if you are the sharpest stock analyst in the world, your individual stocks will be a roller coaster ride. Some people get sick on roller coasters; others just can't stop going again and again. If, after a total of five or six years of experience, you find yourself loving that roller coaster, then the Advanced Portfolio is for you.

The Advanced Portfolio

15% Cash
15% Big Pharma ETF
5% Biotech ETF
65% Individual Biotech stocks

Even the investor who finds excitement as a "rider in the storm" should keep some cash and some more steady stocks. This would be your 15% and 15% allocation to cash and Big Pharma. Think of these as your insurance policy in case of a wide market meltdown, which just happens every great once in a while.

The Advanced Portfolio maintains just 5% in the Biotech ETF. So, the results flowing from this small portion of your portfolio will probably be irrelevant to your overall performance over time. I suggest you keep this 5% as a benchmark for your individual stock performance.

Over the years, the bulk of you portfolio, 65%, will have migrated to biotech stocks. We will explore the actual selection process for these stocks in depth in a later chapter, but the critical element here is passion and enjoyment. The Advanced Biotech investor loves to pour over financials and investment reports on weekends and nights. He follows the news surrounding his stocks, and is aware of the latest trends. This is more than a casual flirtation; this is a love affair.

"True love" is what will keep your biotech romance going even when you suffer a revolting year, or when the sector falls out of favor. We will discuss this more later, but it can't be emphasized enough: The journey to biotech riches is a game of endurance, not strength or speed!

You must stay in the game, even when the talking heads on CNBC say otherwise. To find outsized success with the Advanced Portfolio, you don't have to be smarter than anyone else; but you do have to be tougher and more determined. The good news is; you don't have to be born as one tough SOB. You develop these characteristics through some very specific methods. Methods you will learn in the next chapter.

Chapter 4: Your Emotional Toolkit

As I have insisted from the first chapter of this book, if you are reading this, you are very likely smart enough to make a fortune in biotech investing. This is partially a compliment to you, but partially just a simple fact. You will remember that most plain vanilla ETFs in the biotech field have averaged 14% or more annual returns since the Financial Crisis of 2008. Any biotech investor who just plunked her money into a plain vanilla ETF doubled her money every 5 years.

But what if I told you that even investors who invested in exchange traded funds often did much worse than the average of the fund itself? In other words, the average fund did just great, but the average investor did not. Was it lack of intelligence? No, all the investor had to do was buy the ETF and go to the beach for the next five years. It was lack of discipline.

What do I mean by discipline? Do I mean that the investor did not do enough pushups and sit ups while listening to "Eye of the Tiger?" No, mostly I mean he couldn't stomach the inevitable ups and downs that come with the outsize returns of the biotech industry. The fear generated by a sharp correction caused him to sell impulsively, and the euphoria caused by a market surge caused him to buy without demanding value. The result of these two emotional flaws is usually investment under performance on the part of the individual, even when the average has soared.

The good news is, you can build up your investing discipline through repetitions of specific exercises, just the way you would build up your body in the gym. Here are some mental exercises that will leave you with the mental toughness to excel in biotech.

THE UPSIDE DOWN

The single biggest trick is to rewire your brain to see opportunity where others see catastrophe. This doesn't mean we disagree with the conventional wisdom just for the sake of disagreeing; rather it means we are ready to exercise simple logic. If we want better results than average people, then we need to behave differently than average people.

Average people freak out when they see share prices dropping. They think of all the hard work and struggle that went into earning those investment dollars, and they simply can't bear to watch their investments shrivel, even if the facts indicate that the shrinkage is probably just temporary.

The rewired brain sees that share price drop, and jumps to a different visualization. The rewired brain doesn't focus on all the toil that went into earning the original investment capital; the rewired brain realizes that we can now scoop up discounted shares more cheaply, and thus work less for more ownership in something that has golden long-term prospects.

This reconfiguring of your mental process is easier to achieve with ETFs than with individual stocks; that is why the Beginner and Intermediate portfolio have more funds and less individual stocks. But you can begin to see volatility as your friend in both cases. Here is the trick.

In the case of Biotech Funds that track various forms of the Market, the logic is childishly simple. If you own a basket of 30 or 50 stocks, the fund price may gyrate, but you know that 30 companies aren't all going to go bankrupt at once. For your biotech ETF to cease to exist, Human Society would have to ground to a halt.

That said, ETF funds do bounce up and down a lot. They may overreact to political or scientific developments, or they may simply "get hot" or fall out of favor with the "smart money."   It's black magic really, and anyone who claims that they fully understand the fluctuations of a biotech fund is about as credible as a fortune teller with a crystal ball. We do know one thing for sure, though: people aren't getting any younger, and older bodies reliably fall apart. That means that, as long as we avoid a "Mad Max" future for Planet Earth, people are going to need to buy what biotech is selling. Therefore, any drop in share price is actually a buying opportunity.

While everyone else is running out the door because the wind is blowing the wrong way today, you will be visualizing the ever-growing need for biotech products and services down the road. That is how we take fear and turn it upside down.

With individual stocks, this "upside down" process can be more challenging; after all, individual companies can, and do, go broke. However, if you have properly selected your individual stocks, you will have confidence in the business case for each one and you will understand both the short and long-term trends. This will help you identify whether a sudden drop in share price is just a temporary setback, or a legitimate crisis. 90% of the time it is the former, thus representing a buying opportunity.

Have you noticed yet that I am a huge fan of buying stock, but not a big fan of selling? We will discuss this much more in depth in subsequent chapters, but for now, suffice to say, if you have done your research properly, you will feel more empowered while less educated shareholders cower in fear. This empowerment will allow you to enjoy endurance that other investors lack.

DON'T BUY WHILE FLYING HIGH

Would you believe that you can do TOO WELL in the stock market? What could I mean by that? This is America, after all, too much is never enough…...

What I mean by doing too well is that an investor can be lulled into a sense of over confidence, and throw all prudence to the wind, resulting in disaster. Remember your cousin who quit his job to be a day trader in 1999, only to lose everything by 2002? Now he hasn't invested properly in twenty years because he refuses to repeat "the same mistake" he made before. Yeah, that guy.

Doing too well means you start out with the Beginner Portfolio that I recommend early in the book, you do very well for one or two years, and then you decide to move all the way to Advanced without ever really having experienced a downturn. Then, when the downturn comes, you are over exposed to riskier stocks, you freak out, and you become that sad cousin who sits around dinner parties and waxes poetic about the fortune he lost in the stock market.

The other danger of believing in your own genius is that you may well buy at prices that are too high. This one of the most common pitfalls in biotech! When prices crash, people get discouraged and run away; when prices are flying high, everyone thinks they are a stock market genius who has figured out a new value paradigm, so they buy at higher and higher prices. Just as you must stay cool, calm, and collected when your stocks are having a bad month, or even a bad year, you must also stay level headed when your shares end the year 40% higher than they started.

Does this mean that you should NEVER buy shares that are rising in price? No. Sometimes, share prices are very well justified based on scientific or business events that pertain to a particular stock. Other times, frankly, stocks get hot for no real reason at all.

The difference between a gambler and an investor is that the investor does the research when he sees a stock going up. If the share price increase represents a sustainable trend, then he buys more. If it's just a happy blip on the radar, then he holds his capital for another day. Again, you don't have to be any smarter than the other players in the biotech game; you do have to exercise the discipline to research the situation carefully and deliberately. You wouldn't believe the quantity of people that buy merely based on euphoric feelings. People like to feel good; and stocks that skyrocket for no good reason make people feel good, right up until they don't.

PRACTICE MAKES PERFECT

You never know quite how you will react to a stock market crash until you have experienced one. That is why portfolio design is critical. The model portfolios presented earlier in this book are designed specifically to allow beginners to gain experience while also limiting risk. It's common for people to get scorched once, and then never invest again. What a shame that is. Rather than learning from experience, they are turning a learning experience into a wholly negative event in their lives.

I strongly suggest that you stick with the Beginner or Intermediate portfolio until you have experienced at least one stock market crash. Once you have seen those stocks flame out, and then seen those stocks slowly but surely rise from the ashes like a proud Phoenix, you will have passed your baptism of fire. Truth be told, there were just as many fortunes made in the Great Recession as lost. If you maintain your emotional discipline through practice and good portfolio design, you will come out a winner too.

Chapter 5: Learning How to Learn

If you are a finance geek, you have probably heard that most lottery winners are broke just a decade after a treasure lands in their lap. But have you ever thought about how this could be?

Most lottery winners go broke because they got money without the learning that was supposed to go with it. If, by some miracle, you wind up with a fortune but none of the struggle that usually goes with it, you really haven't gotten everything you needed. Simply put, "get rich quick" scenarios seem like fun, but she who gets rich quick, often gets poor quick, too.

Because this book is not a "get rich quick" scheme, but rather a "build wealth plan" I am going to make sure that when you make your money in biotech, you keep it. As Warren Buffet often says, "Risk comes from not knowing what you are doing."

So I am going to make sure that you know what you are doing. Actually, YOU are going to make sure that YOU know what you are doing. I am just going to help show you the right path, so that you can embark on your own journey of knowledge.

MBA? No, WSJ....

First, let's establish one bedrock principle. No one is born with superior knowledge of the stock market. It's not like mothers in Manhattan or The Hamptons, magically transfer some kind of genetic knowledge of price to earnings ratios and cash flow accounting to babies born in swank hospitals. Every single one of those confident talking heads that you see prognosticating on CNBC was once a blank slate with no knowledge of the world, much less the world of Wall Street. Just like you.

At some point, most of today's Masters of the Universe chose to be educated in the dark arts of Wall Street. Many went through a very time consuming, and very expensive education process, perhaps through some of the better-known Ivy League prestige factories.

After paying six figures for their fancy degree, they most likely served out some period of time with a large, well known financial institution. You can think of this as an apprenticeship of sorts, even though anyone who has worked as a junior employee on Wall Street will tell you that the experience is the closest thing to white slavery that is currently legal in the United States. At some point, they emerged with enough knowledge and enough prestige to become that serious looking man or woman on CNBC who just seems to know everything. Our bedrock principle is the following; the "experts" know a lot, but they don't know everything. And just as they learned by reading and doing, you can also learn by reading, and doing.

Did you ever hear an upper-class British person describe a college education at an institution such as Oxford? The phrase they use is "At Oxford I read history and maths…" Think about that phrase. "…. I read…." That is all a formal education really is. A whole lot of reading and discussion.

It used to be that the Oxfords of the world had a monopoly on education. Because they literally had the books, and they offered an environment for discussion that you just couldn't find at your local pub. But now we are living in the information age. In thirty minutes, you can find on the internet more resources than a thousand scholars could hoard at Oxford over a thousand years! And discussion? Reddit, Twitter, Facebook, the list goes on and on and on. While it's certainly true that most internet discussion threads lack the brainpower of say, an Oxford study session, with some effort you can sift through the junk and find quality.

The point is: if you want to read a lot, and enter into meaningful discussions with people who will give you knowledge for free, you are currently living in a golden age. There may still be good reasons why people pay Harvard huge amounts of money to get a piece of paper that says "MBA" on it, but raw knowledge is not one of the reasons. All of the business and scientific information you need to become a biotech ace is floating around out there, mostly for free, you just have to take the initiative to go get it.

That being said, there are three kinds of learning, and I am going to coach you up on all three. Think of it as a three-part tripod. Without a solid base in each leg of learning, your portfolio won't be able to stand. The three kinds of learning are: General Stock Market Knowledge, Specific Biotech Knowledge, and Practical Experience.

GENERAL STOCK MARKET KNOWLEDGE

Although I love biotech, and believe to my core that biotech is where the money will be for the next fifty years, I do own other kinds of stocks as well. You should too. And you should understand what makes biotech stocks different from regular stocks. So gaining a general understanding of the principles and practices of publicly traded companies will be critical to your success.

Think of it this way. Everybody knows that a Porsche is the sexiest, most badass car out there. But would your parents really have wanted you to learn how to drive with a Porsche? First, the most prudent move would have been to start learning how to drive with a plain, vanilla, Toyota Corolla. Once you have mastered the basics of driving, you would be ready to experience the true potential of automotive fury that is a Porsche. Same with regular stocks and biotech.

Start by reading the Wall Street Journal, every day. Whatever the monthly cost, it's about ½ of 1% the cost of a Harvard MBA. But you will be reading the same publication that all of the Harvard MBAs read, so guess what? You will start to pick up critical vocabulary and concepts at a rapid clip.

You really have to make a commitment to yourself. It might be hard at first. You may come across a lot of terms and concepts that seem like Chinese at first. Instead of putting down the publication in frustration, look at these new concepts as your homework. Look up terms on Wikipedia or Investopedia. Type in key phrases for concepts that you don't understand, and see what comes up on Google. If you are going to be somebody in the business world, you need to learn the language of business; as someone who speaks several languages, I can tell you that the fastest way to learn a language is through reading.

Once you have broken the ice with the Wall Street Journal, add other business publications to your list. In particular, I would recommend Barron's, the Financial Times, and Kiplinger's. These are more "hard core" business publications than the Journal. So first, get comfortable with the Journal, then "graduate" to these publications. While these publications are not free, they are super cheap next to the hundreds of thousands that many stock market analysts feel they must invest in an MBA.

I personally am a fan of "bootstrap" self-education. That being said, some people still yearn for some educational structure. No Problem! We are living in the era of the MOOC. (Massive Open Online Course). What if I told you that you could have access to the very same top business professors that grace the Ivy halls of Harvard, Yale, and Berkley? Twenty years ago, this would have been a pipe dream. Today you can sign up with any number of online education providers to take a structured online course in the business subject of your choosing.

Coursera, LinkedIn Learning, and MOOC.com are just a few of the many sites that offer a more formalized learning experience to accelerate your business learning. You won't finish the course with a fancy degree or certificate; but you will finish with knowledge, which is all you will need to get rich in the stock market.

I particularly recommend that you take online coursework in accounting. Remember, this is a tip coming from a guy WHO DOESN'T LIKE MATH. You don't need to be a CPA, CFA, or anything else to fend for yourself in the world of securities investment, but a basic understanding of accounting really separates "the men from the boys" in the world of investment.

Accounting is the basic language of business; you can't really understand the dry cleaner where you leave your clothes, or the Target where you do your shopping until you have a basic fluency in the accounting concepts that drive those businesses. In particular, I would urge you to learn just enough accounting to read the financial statements of the companies that you will be investing in. You can learn in just a month with Coursera or LinkedIn learning. If you plan on looking out for yourself financially, this investment in knowledge will pay dividends the rest of your life.

Once you start reading the business publications on a regular basis, and you've learned to confront words you don't understand, rather than run away from them, then you're ready to start acquiring expertise in the biotech niche. The same concepts you have learned about publicly traded companies in general apply to biotech investments, but there are several defining characteristics of healthcare stocks, and biotech in particular, which will demand your attention.

SPECIFIC BIOTECH KNOWLEDGE

Biotech stocks are located at the crossroads between business and science, so you'll need to learn a little about both. Emphasis on "a little!" You DO NOT need a PhD in biochemistry to make good biotech investments, and I'll tell you why.

When you buy stock, you are the owner of a company. Your ownership is split between many other shareholders, but, nonetheless, you own the company. The Ford motor company is still controlled by the Ford family….do you think that Bill Ford knows how to draw up engineering plans for a Ford Bronco? How good do you think Bill Ford is at welding?

Bill Ford, and the Ford family, understand the strategic direction of the company, and know about where the Ford company fits into the competitive landscape. But they don't have any special technical knowledge! They don't have to…they hire specialists to do all the heavy lifting. When you own a biotech, you need to understand the strategy of the company, and how the company plans to compete, but the science? You have teams of PhDs who work for you. As long as you can achieve a 9th grade understanding of the science, you can make a fortune off of the blood, sweat, and tears of those scientists.

That being said, you still need some understanding in order to make solid choices, so where would you begin?

The first thing is to figure out which disease states interest you, and to build up knowledge in those particular niches. For example, I think that Cancer and Neurology represent very large unmet needs currently, so I have really chosen to build my knowledge in those niches. No one could ever know everything about everything! Even an MD who has spent decades mastering the latest oncology technology might not be aware of the latest advances in orthopedics. Don't let yourself feel overwhelmed by the oceans of knowledge that are currently available to you. Just pick a few areas and start there.

If you feel like I do, and you think that Cancer and Neurology are still areas that are ripe for further innovation, you can start by going to Cancer.org and reading every post there. In just a few days, you will have begun to get a feel for the latest discoveries that are rocking the field. Of course, the American Cancer Society is just one of many well-established non-profits looking to push the scientific envelope. But what they all have in common is THEY ARE HEAVILY DEPENDENT ON DONORS, SO IT'S IN THEIR INTEREST TO EXPLAIN THE SCIENCE IN LAYMAN'S TERMS. A lot of Wall Street big shots make things as complicated as possible in order to increase their stranglehold over the dark arts of investing. For the American Cancer Society, or Susan G Komen, or any one of dozens of other non-profits, it's the exact opposite. They need the public to understand where we stand with the science. If you want a free tutorial in cancer, these websites are a great place to start.

Another amazing place for limitless learning is the blog-o-sphere. You can tap into this through Twitter, or directly, just by consulting Google. There are many hundreds, if not thousands, of finance nerds out there who spend countless hours writing about scientific advances, investing, or, (often) both. I hand out common sense analysis for free at www.sickeconomics.com   Why do I do this??

'Cause I like it, frankly. Making money in the stock market is fun. Teaching others how to do it is also fun. I am not the only person who gets a charge out of writing about biotech. Find them online, befriend them, learn from them.

Once again, these recommendations reflect my own personality, and my tendency to enjoy "mining for knowledge" on the internet. But if you want to learn from real PhD's, and MD's, I can't recommend Coursera, or LinkedIn learning, enough. There are a lot of science geeks out there who find biology to be fascinating. A quick scan of these websites will show you that many biology courses are available for a fraction of what you would pay to get a fancy piece of paper. Somehow, the knowledge, without the degree, is on sale at bargain basement prices. Take advantage.

Lastly, study the biotech websites themselves. We will go over this much more in detail later, but please keep this core principle in mind when it comes time to select your

Billion Dollar Biotech Babies. IF THEY CAN'T EXPLAIN IN SIMPLE TERMS WHAT THEY ARE TRYING TO DO AS COMPANY, STAY AWAY. Every successful biotech company should retain the top geeks and dorks in the scientific space, while employing at least a few executives who are fluent at translating science geek language to plain English. If the company has too many business people, and too few scientists, the innovation will be lacking. But if a company has too many scientists, and too few skilled communicators, then they won't go anywhere anyhow.

A stock must have a good "story" to really catch fire, and powerful stories are not told with language you would find in a biology textbook. Just try typing in "oncology" and "biotech." If you don't find some compelling stories that a ninth grader could understand, don't bother to invest.

PRACTICAL EXPERIENCE

Learning by doing is the last leg or our three-legged stool. It's probably the most important part! If you start investing diligently by age 30, by 50 you'll have just as much experience, if not more, than most of the highly paid analysts on Wall Street. At that point any gap in formal education will just be a memory.

The key thing to learning by doing is to do so in a "safe enough" environment. Let's be perfectly clear, right up front: at some point, you will get burned. You will probably buy at least one or two biotech stocks that go on to lose 90% of their value. But if you follow our model portfolio plan carefully, and you follow the self-learning regimen described above, on balance you will come out way, way ahead. That fear of a small initial loss stops millions of people from ever realizing the big gains that they deserve.

The key is to manage your risk early on. By sticking with the Beginner portfolio design while you are a beginner, you are automatically limiting your risk. The riskiest part of your portfolio, individual biotech stocks, will only equal 20% of your net worth. You will be risking 20% of your net worth knowing that, over time, returns of 200%, or even 2,000% are likely. If you can accept that risk/reward trade-off, then biotech investing is for you.

We will go into the actual selection process for individual stocks much more in depth in our last chapter. But suffice it to say, that our three-level portfolio model isn't static; rather it's designed as an evolution. You start out with a small allotment of individual stocks, very well aware that you really don't know what you're doing. As you slowly gain experience and confidence, your allotment to individual stocks grows over time. Only you can know when you are ready to move from Beginner to Intermediate, because it's really based more on emotional factors than any technical factors. How will you react to the inevitable swings in the market? Are you able to purchase a stock, and accept the natural gyrations as a learning opportunity, or does your stomach just tie itself in knots? If you lose a little money, do you count that as tuition paid to the University of Life, or do you toss and turn at night?

With that initial 20% allotment in your beginner portfolio, you will learn so very much about biotech investing. But most importantly, you will be learning more about yourself. If you can learn to enjoy the research process, and learn to take temporary setbacks in stride, then biotech investing is for you. Through this process of "learning how to learn" you will learn about business, science, and yourself. In today's "knowledge economy" she who learns the most, earns the most. Are you willing to become a learning machine so that you can build a cash machine?

Chapter 6: What Not To Do

If this book were only one chapter long, this one chapter would be well worth the purchase price of the entire book. That's because I'm about to share with you wisdom that took me years and thousands of dollars to learn. I got my business degree in the school of life; I paid my tuition in the school of hard knocks so that you won't have to.

Learning what NOT to do is just as important, if not more important, than learning what to do. Following these simple maxims from day 1 will automatically put you ahead of 90% of your competitors. To be perfectly clear: you will still make mistakes, which will cost you time and money. But if you follow these simple guidelines, your mistakes will be minimized, and will become valuable learning opportunities, as opposed to catastrophes. Avoid the following pitfalls, and you are already knocking on the door of biotech success…

DON'T BE A TRADER, BE AN INVESTOR

This is the single most important tip to be found in this book. Understand what the difference is between a "trader" and an "investor," learn why it's intrinsically smarter to be an investor, and embrace the maxim, "it's a marathon, not a sprint."

First, we need to understand why trading is not the same as investing. An investor treats shares of stock as ownership of a company, while a trader treats those same shares as simple commodities to be bought and sold based on market gyrations. This philosophical gap makes all the difference. The trader attempts to predict and outsmart the market, while the investor is much more concerned about the long-term fundamentals, thus the short-term whims of the market become secondary.

Investors look to make a large profit over years, or even decades, but traders hope to make a small profit, repetitively, again and again. One number you might hear is traders hope to make 2% per month on their money. Well, that doesn't sound like much, but if a trader really could hit that goal consistently, the numbers would compound to enormous profits.

It sounds a lot more fun to be a trader, doesn't it? Who wants to wait years for profits that may never come, when you could take an online day trading course and become a Wall Street sensation overnight? As I have stated emphatically, I truly believe that you have all the necessary tools to become a great biotech investor. I don't however, believe that you will find much long-term success with trading.

It's a lot easier to sell books and courses on trading; it would be a much better business model for me. But ultimately, amateur, and even "professional" traders rarely do well if the math is truly understood. Almost all long-term biotech investors do well as long as they stay invested. Remember, the XBI biotech index turned $10,000 in 2009 into $55,000 today. Any average joe who invested his money in that plain index, and left it there, reaped an 18% annual return. Almost no trader who is honest could tell you that.

So, if it's simple math that most traders lose out over the long run, while most patient investors prosper, why is everyone talking about trading? There are hundreds of blogs and websites maniacally focused on how to make the next hot trade of the day; all kinds of "training academies" have sprung up to teach you how to make millions from your computer overnight. All of this couldn't be sustained if people consistently lost money, right?

Wrong. I'll tell you a real-world story that happened to a friend of mine. Between 1994 and 2001, America experienced the greatest stock market boom of all time. Especially risky stocks such as tech and biotech soared in value. During this time, a friend of mine with a steady full-time job started "day trading" on the side. He did so well initially that he soon quit his job altogether so that he could "day trade" all day long. What exactly does "Day trading" consist of?

Day traders buy and sell stocks many times per day, sometimes many times per hour, hoping to capitalize on small jumps in price. For example, in the biotech world, a trader might hear a rumor about a possible drug approval. They might buy the stock the day before a big announcement. If the announcement is positive, the stock price jumps. Rather than holding on and reaping the long-term benefits of a company moving in the right direction, the day trader sells immediately, potentially booking a large profit in the moment. The goal would be to repeat this drill successfully on a regular basis. The most appealing part is that, in our modern world, day trading can be done anywhere, anytime, as long as you have access to a computer. Sounds a lot more fun than grinding 9-5 for the Man, doesn't it?

Well, it sounded fun to my friend, and on some level this career move made sense. He had an advanced degree in mathematics, he had low overhead (no kids to support), and he had some initial success day trading on the side. So, he quit his steady job, and jumped head first into the high-octane world of day trading.

It worked. For a while. He actually kept at this for several years, and made enough profits to live well, without ever having to go to an office, or answer to some creep of a boss. But eventually the great 90's dot-com bubble burst, and he lost everything. All at once. Hundreds of thousands of dollars vanished into thin air. Now he is back to working for the

Man 9-5, and further than ever from achieving his financial goals because he nuked it all in a blaze of glory.

What went wrong? How could a guy with a PhD in mathematics, and ample trading experience, just blow up after years of success? It turns out, the success actually emboldened him to take bigger and bigger risks, and a PhD in mathematics is no help when you're just gambling anyhow.

Most traders employ leverage. Leverage is just a fancy word for borrowed money. This is how they can potentially make enough money to live off of, even starting with modest capital, even if a stock moves up only modestly. We'll cover this more in depth in the next section, but let's just say that leverage is your best friend as long as the market is going up. If the market drops suddenly, which it often does in unpredictable ways, you can wind up burned to a crisp, much like my friend.

Have you ever heard the expression, "A rising tide lifts all boats?" My friend did have initial success trading, but that was really only because Mr. Market went on a manic bender between 1995 and 2001. Any fool can make money when the market only goes up. So my friend confused a great market with personal genius, as many people often do, and he became increasingly aggressive as the madness of the dot-com boom progressed. He took on more and more debt in order to amplify his trading profits. When the dot-com boom abruptly ended, his trading genius vanished with it, and his net worth went to $0 overnight.

This phenomena explains, to a large extent, the current buzz around traders. As of the writing of this book, we have experienced the longest bull market in American history. Starting at the depths of the 2009 Great Recession, the market has only gone up and up, year after year. This has emboldened everyone from baristas to postal workers to live out their wildest day trading fantasies, the way my friend did. I ask you, if it ended badly for an already well to do PhD in math, how will it probably end for your Uber driver?

But what if my friend the mathematician had used his skills in a different way? What if he had decided to commit to being an investor, rather than the "Fast Money" lifestyle?

An investor seeks to own a piece of tomorrow's brightest stars. She carefully analyzes each company for its current status, future potential, and long-term viability. Rather than buying and selling all the time, she purchases shares in companies that she believes in, so she buys 90% of the time, and sells only 10% of the time. The name of the game is accumulation. Selling a good stock would feel like an insult.

While my friend was day trading, I was investing. Despite not finding any joy in working a 9-5, I kept my job, and every month I put a little more money into the stock market. When it finally came tumbling down in the early 2000's, I had no debt, and I was able to maintain a steady income from my job. So, instead of disaster, I viewed the crash as opportunity. While my formerly high-flying friend was having his home foreclosed, I was buying Nasdaq and biotech stocks for pennies on the dollar. Of course I felt nervous, and queasy at times, but I had enough confidence in my research abilities that I felt capable of identifying companies with strong fundamentals that could weather the storm of the tech collapse. I repeated the same technique in the Great Recession of 2009. Today, I can retire at will, while my poor friend the PhD will work until he drops.

But don't take my word for it. Better to take advice from Warren Buffet, one of the richest investors in the world. When asked what his target holding period is for a stock, his reply was simple, "forever."

STAY AWAY FROM MARGIN

"Margin," "leverage" and "debt" are all fancy terms for borrowed money. "Margin" is usually the term used for debt when applied specifically to stock market investing. Everybody knows that you can use real estate as collateral to attain a loan; not everyone knows that you can also use stock as collateral for a loan. When you borrow money against stock specifically to invest, this is called "Margin Investing." In it's most fundamental core, margin acts as a magnifying glass in the investing world. It can make investing profits much larger, but it can also generate devastating, sudden losses as well. My best advice for most biotech investors is, STAY AWAY FROM MARGIN.

There are a few specific reasons for this. The first, and most important, boils down to the concept of "Staying Power."

Remember the example of my friend who lost everything? Was it because he had foolishly invested in all bad stocks and every stock went to $0 value? No, not at all. He lost everything because, when the market crashed, the heavy margin he was carrying suddenly worked against him, and he was forced to sell everything at depressed prices to pay off his debt. While he was forced to sell everything when the market swooned, I was buying. Low stock prices were an opportunity for me, but a disaster for him. Margin investing augmented his profits while Mr. Market was flying high, but robbed him of his ability to weather the storm when the hurricane arrived. The ability to outlast your competitors is what will eventually make you rich in biotech.

There may be some stocks out there that are better suited to act as collateral for a loan. Some stocks are very "low beta" meaning they do not fluctuate too much. Biotech stocks, however, are inherently "high beta" meaning that they soar and crash all the time, often temporarily. This volatility makes them bad collateral.

Let's say, you own $100,000 in biotech stocks, and you borrow $60,000 using the $100,000 in stock as collateral. If you owned stock in say, Walmart, and the market crashed, your $100,000 might only shrink to $80,000, and you would still have adequate equity to secure your $60,000 loan. However, if you have $100,000 in biotech stocks, and Mr. Market throws a temporary tantrum, your equity could crash to $65,000, which would cause your lenders to panic. They would then execute a "margin call", forcing you to sell some, or all, of your stock to pay off the loan. That's how you wind up burned.

Biotech stocks are inherently volatile. But with that volatility comes powerful long-term returns. Remember the XBI index that turned $10,000 into $56,000 over ten years? Those stellar returns were achieved with no debt, but there were a lot of big ups and downs along the way. Throughout this book we have talked about risk management strategies; investing with borrowed money is just piling on more risk that you don't need.

DON'T BET THE FARM

Along these lines of "risks you don't need" would be the "bet the farm" mentality. Some people fall in love with just one or two stocks, and put all of their assets into that one or two stocks. If your one biotech soars 300%, as biotechs sometimes do, you can get rich fast. If your biotech loses 80% of its value, as biotechs sometimes do, you are broke. Unless you have an extraordinary appetite for risk and more resilience than a trampoline, this is a bad way to go.

Our program will teach you how to research your stocks, and how to invest with confidence. Confidence is good. However, overconfidence is bad. Using the techniques in this book, you will learn to make educated guesses that will give you a true edge over time. But they're still just educated guesses. In the world of biotech, there are always calculated risks that no amount of research can wish away. If you take all your money and just bet on one big holding, this is the same as playing the roulette wheel in Vegas.

Let's say, for example, you are particularly interested in cancer therapy, and you encounter a company called "Cancertech." (This is a made-up example company). You find out that Cancertech is well funded, has a reputable board of directors, and a renowned executive team. They have had some promising stage 1 trial results, and even shown some amazing efficacy in phase II. Time to bet everything?

Even though you have done your homework, there are still too many things that can go wrong. Strong phase II results still sometimes lead to failure in phase III. Even if a product does hit the market with good clinical data, many drugs still sputter with disappointing sales. Even if the clinical data is strong, and sales take off, sometimes unknown side effects emerge, tanking a biotech stock overnight. If you do your homework, and you find a good opportunity, do invest with confidence. But not foolishness.

As you progress through your biotech journey, your end goal should be to curate a long-term portfolio of 10 to 15 stocks. If you have more than 15, then you will probably just wind up mimicking the results of the XBI index. If you have less than 10, then you are too vulnerable to the "unknown unknowns" that can scuttle the best laid plans.

The last, most important reason why you don't need a super-concentrated portfolio, is because that level of extreme risk is just not necessary to achieve astonishing returns. Many of the different exchange traded funds that we profiled earlier in this book produced long term returns above 14%. This means that your money doubles every five years. Do you really need better returns than that?

AVOID PENNY STOCKS AND SCAMS

There are a lot of genius scientists in the realm of biotech, but there are also more than a few carnival barkers and miracle-working scam artists. Your goal should be to take calculated risks, where projects may fail simply based on scientific disappointment. You don't need the added risk that comes with dealing with shady characters.

But you don't have a PhD in biology, and you don't attend enough scientific conferences to know what's real, and what's made up. How would you know who is working on something good in the lab, and who is just cooking up a scam?

Don't worry, almost everybody faces this dilemma. Remember, more than 90% of seasoned biotech investors are not MDs or PhDs… In fact, there are some very simple methods you can employ that will greatly reduce your risk of falling for a swindle.

The first question to ask yourself before investing in a biotech is, "Who would I be partnering with?" When you buy and hold stock in a company, you are partnering with management and the board of directors; typically you will be owning the same stock that they do. So you want to make sure that you are entrusting your funds to good people.

Any good biotech will have a board of directors composed of well-known scientists, MD's and venture capitalists. What would constitute, "well known?" Most MD's and PhD's should be affiliated with reputable, big name universities.

For example, many PhD's in the biotech world are also faculty members at Ivy League Universities, or large, well known state schools such as University of Michigan, University of California, or the University of Texas. While these affiliations do not offer full proof protection, it is important to remember that reputation is very important for legitimate scientists and business people. Being elected to the board of directors is a lucrative side gig, paying between $50,000 and $200,000 a year, and if they are seen to be part of a scandal, it can be very damaging to the career of an MD or PhD.

The board will probably have some non-scientists as voting members as well. They will often represent the venture capital companies that were early investors in the enterprise. What other scientific ventures have these executives been involved in? What kind of reputation does their firm have? You can find out almost anything on the internet these days. If you can't, it's a red flag. Most of these professionals have killed themselves to slowly build up a good name in the scientific and business community. People who are proud of their work don't hide in the shadows; if you can't easily research key players on the internet, stay away.

Another basic protection that usually works is published data. After about 100 years of pumping out new drugs and innovations, the Western World has well established norms and pathways for scientific data to be published.

Most credible data should be published in what are known as "Peer Reviewed" journals. A "Peer Reviewed" journal is a neutral third-party publication that is supervised by well-established scientists who have nothing to personally gain or lose while reviewing any particular scientific submission. A pharma company submits the data to the 3rd party journal, the data is reviewed for accuracy, completeness and transparency by a committee of scientists, and if the study passes muster, the data is published. The way the system has evolved, REPUTABLE SCIENTIFIC JOURNALS DO THE SCRUTINIZING SO THAT YOU DON'T HAVE TO. You don't need an advanced education to review the data; the journal's editors are already doing that for you.

So, a key question you should ask yourself when contemplating an investment in biotech is: "Where was this data published, and how much data was published?" Do they just have one study published in some 3rd tier journal out of Slovakia? Or do they have a dozen publications that were featured in marquis journals such as The New England Journal of Medicine? If it's one study in the Slovakian Journal of Podiatry, pass.

Additionally, you should make sure that the company's stock is traded on a respectable exchange such as NASDAQ or NYSE. While these exchanges are not investment nannies, and do not guarantee good results, they do enforce certain basic norms for their member companies. If the shares drop below a certain price, or if the share trading volume declines below a certain limit, companies are no longer deemed reliable, and are banished to "the Pink Sheets" or "Over the Counter."

You may have heard the term "Penny Stocks." Penny stocks are micro companies whose shares trade for less than $1, often on dodgy stock exchanges with little public scrutiny. These kinds of companies have gained notoriety as a haven for scammers, hucksters, and even gangsters. The reason why evil doers are attracted to these kinds of stocks is that they can be easy to manipulate, due to their small size and lack of transparency. Not all stocks traded "over the counter" are scams, but your risk climbs the farther you venture away from NASDAQ and NYSE. As a general rule, stay away.

Lastly, use your own common sense. If someone is making claims that seem too good to be true, they probably are. For example, great progress is being made in cancer research, but no one has found a "miracle cure" that instantly melts tumors using only chemicals derived from the spice curcumin. If cancer were that easy to miraculously cure, my great, great grandparents would still be alive, and I would be richer than Jeff Bezos.

As you gain experience, you will learn to easily spot scams, and avoid them.

DON'T GIVE UP!

If you want better results than most people, than you need better actions than most people. What 90% of investors do is: they go in both guns blazing, they make a bunch of mistakes, they lose too much money, and then they never invest in stocks again, because "it's too risky, and they won't repeat that mistake again." Sad.

You will make mistakes. You may lose some money. But if you follow the principals in this book, your losses will be limited, and the knowledge you gain through the process will eventually make you rich. Few people are only rich in money. Most self-made millionaires are rich in knowledge first, which leads to being rich in money.

People lose money all the time in the search for knowledge. Think about those Harvard MBA's you see on CNBC. The MBA alone cost $100,000. They may well also have a fancy undergraduate degree, another $100,000. If they financed any portion of that, which is common, their total outlay easily tops $250,000. But if you go to Harvard, no one calls that money, "lost." They call it "invested."

Even if you lose $25,000 while you are learning about biotech, you will have invested just 10% of what they invest, and wind up with ten times the practical knowledge. If that sounds like a good return on investment to you, then commit to yourself right now that you will power through whatever setbacks may occur. Remember your rich uncle Warren Buffett, and his saying, "we don't have to be smarter than the rest; we have to be more disciplined than the rest." Part of that discipline is the courage to keep going while others turn away in bitter frustration. We know for sure that biotech companies generate enormous wealth over time. What we don't know is if the average investor will keep going through thick and thin. If *you know* that you will keep going, then you are already on your way to becoming a stock market millionaire.

Now that we have laid out what NOT to do, let's move on to the fun part; learning how to pick winning stocks.

Chapter 7: How To Find Your Billionaire Biotech Babies

Here we are at last. The main course in our feast of stock market knowledge. The crescendo of our symphony of profit. The final act in our play about money.

No doubt I am about to disappoint some people. With the stellar results I have achieved in my personal investing life, and the winning techniques that I have described earlier in this book, a lot of people might be looking for a specific list of suggested stocks. "Just buy X, Y, and Z, and you'll be rich." I do sometimes make these kinds of picks for my readers. But I actually post specific stocks picks for free on my website, www.sickeconomics.com   What you are about to read is the good stuff that I charge for.

How can that approach make any sense? How can I give away profitable stock picks for free, but charge to teach my readers the methodologies that lead to profitable investments? Well, you know the saying, "Give a man a fish, and you feed him for a day. Teach him to fish, and you feed him for a lifetime." I will give the casual reader a juicy fish any time. Just go to my website, there are plenty. What is really worth the money is the knowledge that will allow you to pick your own biotech gems, time after time. Before you can increase your monetary wealth, you will need to increase your wealth of knowledge. If you have made it this far, then you have already invested a little money, and a lot of time, to work towards that goal. Now you are about to get the knowledge that you paid for. By the end of this chapter, you should be equipped to begin selecting your own biotechnology stocks, no PhD or MBA required.

START WITH THE END IN MIND

A lot of people never finish strong because they can't find the guts to start at all. I don't blame them; it can feel overwhelming. There are hundreds and hundreds of publicly traded biotechnology stocks, many dealing with obscure concepts such as proteins, messenger RNA, or glucose metabolism. Beginning can feel like the highest hurdle to cross. So, we are going to go over some good starting places, and discuss specific techniques that can help you take your first steps. If you have any children in your life, you know that the first few steps are a big deal; most kids are off to the races after they manage those first few tentative steps. You'll be the same as a biotech investor.

But before we talk about starting places, let's talk about our destination. Note, this is not plural. We are going to explore a number of places to start, but they should all lead you to more or less the same place; a well thought out, long term portfolio of 10 to 15 biotech stocks that will have minimal turn over as the years go by. If you choose well the first time, you won't need to buy and sell a lot. In fact, what you'll really need to do as your wealth grows and grows is: nothing. Go to the beach. Play with your kids. Go for a hike. Once your portfolio is set, you have essentially hired management teams to grow your money for you. As Cole Porter used to sing, "Nice work if you can get it, and you can get it, if you try."

Why 10 to 15 stocks? Why not less? Why not more? If you choose 10 individual biotech stocks, in addition to the other portfolio recommendations from earlier in this book, your individual "risk money" will break down to about 10% per stock. No matter how good you get at picking stocks, biotech is a field filled with surprises and unknowns. There are always certain things that can go wrong, just because they went wrong. If your money is spread across 10 different companies, then you can never be brought down by just a few unlucky choices.

If some diversification is good, then isn't more diversification better? Why not twenty or thirty stocks? Once you get above 15 stocks or so, you really have become a "closet indexer." A closet indexer is someone who has diversified across so many stocks, that, in reality, he just bought the average of the whole market. As we have discussed, there is nothing wrong with the passive, index approach offered by exchange traded funds such as XBI and IBB, but if you get more than 15 names in your portfolio, you have probably just copied the XBI, albeit in a less efficient way.

The last reason to aim for 10 to 15 biotech stock holdings is to maintain a sense of discipline. Let's say you begin to use the following techniques to choose 12 stocks. Then, over the following year, you hear about some other promising firms, and you up your holdings to 15 individual names. If you stick to my suggested guidelines, you will keep yourself from becoming a hoarder of random stocks. If you want to say "hello" to a new stock above the original 15, then say, "goodbye" to something else. While I strenuously advocate for the long term "buy and hold" philosophy, nothing is forever. Maintaining your biotech portfolio to between 10 and 15 holdings allows you to do some annual pruning of your money tree without denuding it. It also allows you to bring in fresh blood from time to time, without turning into a crazy day trader.

So, now we know that our goal is to choose between 10 and 15 biotech stocks that we will hold for a long time. Where to begin?

WHAT IS WRONG WITH YOU, ANYHOW?

If you're over 40, your health is probably less than perfect. If you're lucky, you may just have a chronic, low level malady like high blood pressure, cholesterol issues, or early diabetes. If you're a bit less lucky, you may have experienced something highly alarming such as cancer or an infectious disease. Even if you are young, or healthy as an ox, it's likely that someone in your family has a regular interaction with the medical community.

The great news is that, you no longer need to be just a passive victim! If you have cancer in your family, you probably should have used the internet to learn as much as you can about cancer......now you can actually make money this way. "Self Help for fun and profit," we could call it.

Every medical text book, every published study, every new breakthrough that your doctor has ever read is now also available to you online. The collective medical knowledge of the world is at your fingertips if you decide to dedicate yourself to study. Now there is nothing that is more of a drag than spending a lovely Sunday afternoon reading all about deadly diseases that have terrorized generations of human beings. But what if you felt that you were getting paid to learn?

Our biotech industry is currently churning out innovation at such an astounding rate, that you could never hope to keep up with all of the latest revelations. But you can master a niche. And you can leverage that mastery for profit. I'll give you an example.

In a prior life, I was a champion pharmaceutical salesman. I specialized in diabetes. In fact, it got to the point where a lot of my physician clients would go over patients' charts with me. There were even a few times when my MD clients pulled me into patient consults (Yes, that is a huge violation of all kinds of norms and laws, but it happened). The irony is that I just have a lowly bachelor's degree. I majored in History and Spanish, of all things. Why on earth would an MD, with so many years of study, preparation, and practical experience, be interested in my opinion?

The answer is that I had become an expert in a very narrow subject matter. I didn't know how to practice medicine. I didn't know how to discover or make new pharmaceuticals. But, through intensive independent study and practical experience, I had become an expert in the applications of my medicines in certain specific circumstances.

I would suggest that you learn about the certain, specific circumstances that effect your health, or the health of your loved ones, and make yourself an expert.

Let's say your mother died from lung cancer. (I hope that is not the case, but it does happen). Block off a Sunday afternoon; dedicate four hours to your own education.

Sit down at your computer and try typing in the following phrases:

"Lung Cancer/ New Research"
"Lung Cancer/Breakthroughs"
"Lung Cancer/ Clinical Trials"
"Lung Cancer/ Biotechs"
"Lung Cancer/Deals"
"Lung Cancer/Mergers and Acquisitions"
"Lung Cancer/New Drugs"

Let's say that you have $50,000 to invest. You know from the research that you have done, that a skillful biotech investor could triple this money in 10 years. So, the value of your research could be $100,000 over the long run. Let's say you spend 5 hours per week making yourself a mini-expert in lung cancer. You do this for twenty consecutive weeks, for a total of 100 hours. $100,000/100 equals a pay rate of $1,000 per hour. Wouldn't you agree that this is some lucrative work?

"Investment in Knowledge Pays the Best Interest."

-Benjamin Franklin

The Big Man Theory (or Big Person)
Another way to find great biotech companies is to focus on the great people who create them. Let's consider, for a moment, what it takes to found a publicly traded biotech corporation.

First, you need to have access to exciting, early stage technology. Even more than access, you really need control (in one form or another) of something that has been patented. Do you know a lot of people who have cooked up potentially revolutionary new molecules in their garage? These days, most patent-worthy innovations will come out of well established laboratories that are typically linked with major, big name universities, or private charitable foundations. In order for a scientist to have a significant ownership claim to that patent, they need to be already well established in this laboratory ecosystem. Then, on top of that, the early stage technology really needs to be dynamic.

How dynamic? Dynamic enough for someone to contribute somewhere in the range of twenty to fifty million dollars that they may well lose. Do you know anyone that has a cool thirty million laying around that they are willing to risk? Probably not.

So, the scientist in question needs to be well established in a prestigious lab, needs some form of control of a groundbreaking new technology, and needs deep connections to the venture capital world. (Venture Capitalists are business people who specialize in risking large amounts of money on risky, early stage businesses…).

One example of such a person is Dr. Jennifer Doudna. Dr. Doudna is one of the leading researchers in the burgeoning field of CRISPR gene editing. A few lines from her official bio at Wallmine.com, a website focused on biotech:

"Doudna is Principal Investigator at the Doudna Lab at UC Berkeley and has founded and serves on the scientific advisory boards of Caribou Biosciences, Inc. and Intellia Therapeutics, Inc., both leading CRISPR genome engineering companies."

Her list of scientific awards and credentials goes on and on, but above we have the few most relevant facts about her current status. She LEADS a lab at a major research university, and she has some CONTROL over the product of that lab. She has co-founded several publicly traded biotech companies, and she retains a role in shaping the science of those companies. In short, where Dr. Doudna goes, the money soon follows. It's pretty reasonable to assume that your money should go in her direction, as well.

How would one find such scientists? Well, if you were to look up Dr. Doudna's bio, you would quickly start to realize that she is a type of modern celebrity. In order to attract all of the clout, and funding, that she needs to bring her ambitious project to fruition, she has achieved a fairly high profile in the media. In short, celebrity attracts investment. Today's top scientists want to be found.

So find them. Repeat a similar learning process to what I described above, but this time, type in

"Cancer/Top Researchers"
"Cancer/Top Scientist"
"Biotech/Scientists"
"Biotech/Labs"
"Biotech/Entrepreneur"

Playing the game of "follow the leader" isn't absurd if we are talking about a good leader. Most of what you need to know is just a few keystrokes away….

The Local Yokel Theory (Or, not so Yokel).

One big complaint that a lot of people have about biotech investing is that it doesn't feel real. Even if you learn everything about the most prestigious researchers, and you teach yourself everything about RNA and proteins, for a lot of people it feels like investing in magic and fairy dust. They have to invest very real money, in hopes of getting a return over a long period of time that can feel tough to fathom. The necessary investment funds, however, feel very tangible. You can go to the ATM machine. You can feel the little green pieces of paper. You can use those green papers to buy something real, like groceries, or a gold watch.

This is one reason why more tangible investments, such as real estate, remain very popular. You can exchange your little green papers for something big, something solid, something you can drive to, and check out yourself. (By the way, that tangible quality also brings with it some very big downsides, but that is a topic for another book…).   If the idea of exchanging real money for theoretical gains just makes you feel a bit queasy, here is another tactic for you.

If you live on the Eastern seaboard, between Washington DC, and Boston, or almost anywhere in California, or even near a major university almost anywhere, you may very well be able to physically go and investigate biotech opportunities yourself.

This is because, even in our modern world of virtual everything, top scientists and venture capital investors have still shown a remarkable tendency to cluster together. When you are thinking about investing $30,000,000 on a wing and a prayer, you still want to meet face to face with the players involved. So, despite sky high taxes and cost of living, metro areas such as Boston, New York City, and Greater San Francisco are jam packed with young, publicly traded biotech stocks that want your money. Believe it or not, a fair amount of these young companies will answer the phone if you call, and many will actually agree to meet with you, face to face.

This face to face contact can come in a lot of forms. The simplest is to buy just a few shares in promising companies, and then be an active shareholder. These companies will often host scientific and financial events, and invite shareholders to physically attend. Almost no one will. When there is a room full of donuts, coffee, and poster presentations, and no one has shown up, whether you own 4 shares, or 4 million shares, you will seem like a valuable investor to whomever was tasked with setting up the event.

Alternatively, if you are very bold, and interested, you can literally pick up the phone and ask for a meeting. Of course, the larger and more well established the company, the less likely you will have success. But, in a biotech cluster such as Boston, there are probably several dozen young, publicly traded biotechs, that would welcome you into their conference rooms because they are trying to get noticed. Call this, "catch a rising star." It's like going to see Eddie Murphy when he was still playing small comedy clubs in 1979. Imagine if you could have bought stock in Eddie Murphy in 1979!

Another great way to interface with these smallish biotech companies is to travel to conferences and conventions. You might especially consider this tactic if you don't happen to live near a biotech cluster. These are events where dozens of biotech companies gather and create display booths, specifically to interact with the investing public. In addition to booths, these conferences will typically also feature big name speakers, who will educate you on a range of "hot topics" in the biotech field. Some of these conferences are "invite only" but, in reality, most will let you attend for a fee. The fees may seem expensive (typically between $500 and $1500 for a multi-day pass), but again, let's consider the math.

Let's say that you have $50,000 to invest. You pay $1000 to attend a biotech conference, and you spend another $1,000 on flight, room and board. So your investment is $2,000. At the conference you find three companies that you feel comfortable with, so you invest. The companies do well, and you proceed to triple your $50,000 over the next ten years, leaving you a return of $100,000. You just invested $2,000 to make $100,000. Seem like a fair deal?

There are a few other key advantages to this conference format. The fact that entry is not cheap immediately eliminates "tire kickers." The biotech companies that attend also pay big money to be there, and since everyone paid a fee to attend, they know they are dealing with serious investors. Also, should you attend these conferences, you will likely be surrounded by venture capitalists, investment bankers, and some of those very same analysts you see jibber jabbering on CNBC. The biotechs know you are there to invest, but they really don't know whether you have $500 in your pocket, or $5,000,000 in your pocket. Which treatment do you think that you are likely to get?

The general rule of thumb is: if you look like you belong there, then people will assume that you belong there. If you are the kind of person who prefers to shake someone's hand and look in their eyes before handing over your hard-earned capital, you can still become an ace biotech investor.

Don't Buy Gold; Buy Mining Equipment

Today we live in a blue jean world. Everybody from presidents to priests can be seen wearing different kinds of blue jeans. If you were to attend one of those biotech conferences that I recommend above, you would see an awful lot of Ivy League grads wearing fancy, expensive blue jeans.

But, believe it or not, there once was a time when blue jeans were new technology. They weren't just a new fashion trend; they actual texture and toughness of the cloth was invented to help workers accomplish specific tasks. In the case of Levi-Strauss & Co., that task was gold mining. Gold mining in the mid-1800's was tough, physical work, and miners needed clothing that wouldn't rip or tear easily. Enter: the blue jean.

Over the decades, many miners came to California with big dreams of finding gold. Some would go on to find a little gold; a few would go on to find "the motherload." Most, however, found nothing but disappointment and ruin. But everyone needed blue jeans. Thousands and thousands of miners bought blue jeans and other mining equipment; whether they ever found an ounce of gold or not, they couldn't even hope to get started without the proper tools. So guess who really wound up with a golden fortune? Mr. Levi Strauss, and his company.

I have found quite a bit of biotech gold myself employing basically the same tactic as Levi Strauss. In fact, today's California Biotech scene is really just a 21st century gold rush. A few biotech founders and investors will become fabulously wealthy when their discoveries hit the big time. Many will go nowhere. But they all need highly specialized diagnostic and scientific equipment.

You may have heard the term "personalized medicine." This has been a hot term for a long time, but just in the last few years we are finally starting to see the concept put into practice. Even though we are all 99.999% the same genetically, it turns out that last .001% really matters from a health perspective. Therefore, we are slowly, but surely moving away from "one size fits all" medicine to a new paradigm, where many treatment regimens are made to measure. If every single elderly cancer patient must be measured, and 10,000 people per day turn 65, someone is going to be selling a lot of measuring equipment.

Just as you can own patents on molecules, or production processes, you can also own patients on diagnostics devices and diagnostic methodologies. Just about everything in a modern biotech lab is patented by somebody. Successful labs needs the equipment, as well as middling and flat out unsuccessful labs. Doesn't that seem like a safer bet than praying that a molecule works out?

Try these phrases to begin your research:

"Personalized Medicine/Research"
"Personalized Medicine/Company"
"Diagnostics/Biotech"
"Cancer/Diagnostics"
"Biome/Diagnostics"
"Biotech equipment"
"Genetics/Analysis"

A wealth of opportunities to create wealth will tumble forth from Google. There is no reason why you can't be the Levi Strauss of the 21st century gold rush.

NEXT STEPS

If you follow the tactics above (as well as invent some of your own techniques, which I am sure will come with practice) you could easily find yourself with dozens of biotechs on your list, all of which seem appealing. The next step is to "separate the men from the boys," if you will. No one has a crystal ball to predict the future; there are certain unknowables with any company that you examine. But here are a few criteria that will help you increase your odds of success. Think of it like a casino. Casinos make millions upon millions of dollars every year, winning just 51% of the time. If you have made it this far in your studies, you already have a 49% chance of winning. The four simple factors below are that extra 2% that 99% of investors never consider. If you do your homework, you, too, can pile up millions.

1. INVESTIGATE THE PLAYERS

In its most simple form, when you buy stock in a company, you ARE the owner of that company. So why would I suggest that a regular Joe could somehow get rich owning a company that churns out cutting edge 21st century technology? Very simple. You OWN the company, but you are NOT running it. You have a CEO, COO, and CFO that, indirectly, work for you. You have dozens of PhD's, MD's, and VP's, all of whom work long, stressful hours so that you don't have to. So, if you are going to leave your very valuable company in the hands of a management team, wouldn't you want to investigate just who you are hiring to run the place? When you buy into a biotech company, you are employing executives to help grow YOUR company. Act like it.

This entire exercise has been made much, much easier by the internet. All of the personal info you would ever need is right out there, but you wouldn't believe the number of investors that never bother to do any research. The easiest place to start, of course, is the company's website.

Typically, the company will have short bios of the top few executives. They may also have bios of the Board of Directors. I'm not suggesting that you do a complete background check on everyone that has ever worked at your company. But I would focus on, at the least, the CEO, and the Chairman of the Board. These days, sometimes instead of the title "Chairman" or "Chairperson" they use the term "Lead Director." Sometimes the CEO and Chairman is the same person; in many of these cases there will be a "Lead Director" or "Lead Independent Director" who, theoretically, acts as a check on the power of the CEO, and represents the interests of independent shareholders (shareholders who are NOT also employees of the company). If these two executives are somewhat senior (60 years old, or older) I also add the COO to my investigation list; often there is a succession plan in place, either stated or implied, and today's Chief Operating Officer becomes tomorrow's Chief Executive Officer. Because we want to invest for the long term, we should feel comfortable with our next potential leader.

Of course, the bios on the website are rarely going to be objective, but even these polished, unblemished bios can give you a lot of quick information. What is the background of the company's leaders? Is it scientific, medical, or more Wall Street/Financial? A company led by an MD or PhD may well be more dedicated to long term scientific solutions, whereas Wall Street leadership could indicate a management team that would lean more towards "capitalism at any cost." Was the leadership brought in and "installed" by heavyweight investors, or are they the original MD's that found some radical molecules in a lab and decided to start a company? Management brought in from outside to provide "adult" supervision can sometimes mean a more orderly, formulaic growth plan, or it could mean that something went wrong with the original science and panicked investors sent in a rescue squad. A lot of these situations are open to interpretation, and what you find in these bios may require follow up research, but if you don't study with a critical eye, you're just rolling the dice.

Once you have the names of the leaders involved, you can troll the internet looking for information that comes from 3rd parties. This is how you get a more unbiased view of the leadership situation. You can check social media such as LinkedIn, and Facebook, you can just start Googling and see what comes up. If a leader is particularly well regarded, or has a history of trouble, it doesn't take a private eye to find the information. A lot of these high flyers are living their lives in the media spotlight.

One way of investigating the quality of the company's research is to investigate the quality of the researchers. Most smallish biotechs working on promising new stuff will have assembled a "scientific advisory board." This is a panel of neutral, third party experts, who may receive a token annual fee to examine the data that your biotech is producing. These are typically academics from well-known research universities and laboratories around the world.

Reputation is very important for these folks; in order to maintain and expand their reputation as scientific experts they must be associated with top scientific outfits. If your company has succeeded in assembling an advisory panel of well-known scientists from prestigious universities, it usually means that something exciting is going on in your lab, and that these researchers want their name associated with that exciting research. The opposite is also true. A lack of credentialed expert involvement is usually a red flag for a biotech investor.

Another exercise I like to go through is to investigate who else owns shares in the company. Remember, it's called a "public company" for a reason. Ownership of shares is a matter of public records; there should be full transparency as to who owns the company. You can literally type in the name of the biotech, and "ownership" and see what comes up. I personally just look up the company in E*TRADE; under the "Insider Activity" tab, there is a subtab "Ownership," where E*TRADE will break down for you exactly who owns how many shares. Most other online brokers also offer this information in a concise, easy to understand format.

You never quite know what you will find here. Sometimes the incumbent CEO and Lead Director owns a huge percentage of the company, meaning that they have effective control over your investment. Often, the incumbent CEO actually owns just a sliver of the company. For example, if your CEO owns 5% of a company valued at $500,000,000, it means he is quite rich, and very tied into the company's success. However, he doesn't have ironclad control of the company. He can be fired!

One reason why I tend to check out the ownership situation is to figure out who else thinks that this venture can be successful. Are other major venture capital companies invested? What about major investment firms such as Fidelity, Morgan Stanley, or Vanguard? Sometimes other, much larger, pharmaceutical companies are large shareholders. If your co-investors are large corporations, or even very wealthy tycoons, this may really open doors for your young biotech enterprise. In fact, it may even provide some much needed financial stability. Small companies with large shareholders are often thrown a lifeline if they get in trouble....

2. WHO HAS DEEP POCKETS?

Which brings me to point number 2. What kind of resources stand behind your biotech company? Many biotechs lose money for years before they reach the light at the end of the tunnel. Cash is the lifeblood that keeps the research alive until it can be commercialized, either through a sale of the company, a licensing of the rights to a molecule, or direct sales to patients/hospitals. Unprepared companies bleed to death all the time.

This is the part where I will beg you, beseech you, and implore you to learn just a little bit of accounting. Accounting is the language of business. You don't need to be a Chartered Financial Analyst, or MBA to learn how to pick good investments. But just a little bit of accounting knowledge goes a very long way. I would recommend online learning resources such as Coursera, LinkedIn Learning, or even affordable courses offered by your local community college. If the price that interests you is "free," then just go to your local library and dedicate a week to studying "Accounting for Dummies." Once you realize how easy it can be, you may feel like a dummy for not doing it sooner. I certainly did.

Even if you never make it to the library, understanding just a few key concepts, in the context of the biotech world, will immediately give you a clear picture as to the solvency of your target biotech. Once again, you could look at five different biotechs, and see five different situations. But here are the key concepts.

Many young biotechs burn cash. This means they are "Cash flow negative." Simply put, more money is going out than coming in. This could be because they are still in the research stage, and have no revenue at all. This could be because they have a young commercial product, and costs still exceed revenue. Or, very commonly during this last bull market, they have a profitable product, they could make money as a whole, but they keep reinvesting every penny that comes in the door because they want to grow at a breakneck pace. These three scenarios are all have slightly different implications, but the bottom line is, the company would need external funding. They make money disappear.

One of your very earliest steps in your due diligence process is simply to ascertain whether or not the company is cash flow negative, or cash flow positive. You do this by looking at the company's quarterly financial statements. Everyone out there has heard the phrase "bottom line…" Well, the bottom line of the statement is literally where you will find a number (often expressed in millions) that is either negative or positive. Sometimes negative numbers are connoted by a number in parentheses, or even in actual red ink. Often, it's just a negative number. If the number on the Income Statement is negative, then your company is currently losing money.

Next, you should check the Cash Flow statement. What is the difference between the Cash Flow Statement and the Income Statement? Believe it or not, you can actually have positive cash flow, but still lose money, due to intangible costs that are required to be accounted for under "accrual accounting," the most common form of accounting for public companies. One brief example would be the cost of compensating executives in stock. If my company has $10 million in the bank, and I pay out stock valued at $1 million, that does not mean that I currently have $9 million in the bank. There is a theoretical cost to using stock as payment, and that cost is recorded in the Income Statement. However, that stock payment won't make it harder for our company to pay it's monthly rent. So, for the biotech investor, the Cash Flow Statement is often more important than anything else. If I have $10 million in the bank, and I hand out $10 million in stock, I might be unwise, but I won't necessarily go out of business. If I have $10 million in the bank, and I spend $11 million setting up a stage three clinical trial, I may literally be having board meetings in the street next week.

So, make sure to determine whether your target company has negative or positive cash flow. Many promising early stage biotechs have negative cash flow. Some may have no money coming in the door at all! This is because they are very young companies still driving towards scientific breakthroughs, that they hope to sell for big bucks.

Once you have determined whether or not your biotech is cash flow negative, look at the bottom of the statement to see how much money they burned the last few years. Is it steady? Decreasing? Even, increasing? This last bull market has become infamous for a situation where companies actually BURN MORE as they grow. This could be bad, it sometimes can be good, but the most important thing for this exercise is simply to figure out how much cash the company is going to be burning moving forward. For the sake of example, let's say that you have gone to the bottom line of the Cash Flow Statement, and realized that your company burned $50 million in 2016, $70 million in 2017, and $72 million in 2018.

Your next step is for you go to the Balance Sheet. This is the part of the financial statement that reveals how many assets a company has, and how many liabilities. In a world of ideas and intellectual property valuing assets can become a tricky business indeed. But for this exercise, you don't need to worry about any of that. You simply need to figure out, how much cash does your biotech have on hand? This will often be labeled, simply "cash on hand." You would find it in the section labeled, "current assets." Current assets are real assets, either cash, or things that you could turn into cash quickly. This interests us the most, because we are just trying to make sure that the enterprise can pay its bills.

Let's say for the sake of example, that the business currently has $80 million in cash on hand. Well, last year, the business burned $72 million. Assuming that in 2019 they will burn a similar amount of cash in their operations, then this team is treading on very thin ice! They will need to raise more money within a year, or the next board meeting is on the steps of the bankruptcy court.

On the other hand, let's say that another company had the same burn rate. But you went to their "cash on hand" line on their balance sheet, and you saw the number $240 million. In this case, our research team is well funded. If they keep burning about the same amount of cash, they could go for more than 3 years without lining up a cash infusion.

As a general rule, the deeper the pockets, the lower risk for an investor. Of course there are many, many factors that can complicate investment decisions, but as a general rule, your scientific team has a better shot at pushing a product to commercialization stage if they don't have to worry about keeping the lights on. There may be times when you want to take a risky shot on a company that doesn't have much in the bank; but by mastering the exercise above, at least you can properly gauge your risk. A gambler puts a number on a roulette wheel and prays. An investor does enough research to weigh risk and reward, and based on that information, decides when to take a calculated risk.

3. VALUATION

Even in the new world of biotech investing, an old financial adage still holds true, "you don't make money when you sell…. you make money when you buy."   Every investor's goal, whether buying a dry-cleaning business, or buying a business that invents new proteins, is to buy $1 of value for $.75. There many fabulous businesses out there today that are priced like they are fabulous. Your goal needs to be: find a future fabulous business at a modest price today.

Just how much do you think the word, "maybe" could be worth?   Believe it or not, there is a price attached to the word "maybe" and fully understanding the pros and cons of that price will be key to your success in early stage biotech investment.

Traditional stock market valuation techniques rely on metrics related to either revenue or cash flow. Have you ever heard the phrase, "stock x is trading at 12x earnings?" This means that if you bought stock x at price y, you would be paying the equivalent of 12 times that company's annual earnings. This is called Price to Earnings ratio (PE ratio). It is a great starting point for the valuation of traditional, profitable, companies, because it allows for easy comparison between peer companies, or even different industries. For example, if the average PE ratio in the Big Pharma industry is 14, and your target company is trading at 17, then either your target company is offering something truly special, or it's just overpriced. Vice versa is also true. If the average PE ratio amongst a group of similar Big Pharma companies is 14, and your target company is 10, you are either going to be getting a great deal, or the company is cheap for a reason.

What about when a company is not yet making money? We have heard a lot about these kinds of scenarios of late, due to the "Unicorn" IPO phenomena. For example, UBER has billions and billions of revenue, but (sadly) no profit. So, the value of Uber, as opposed to a similar rival (LYFT) has been expressed as a multiple of revenue, instead of profit. Whether this is a good idea at all remains to be seen, but this kind of metric is common and well understood amongst companies that are thought to be generating innovative technology. For example, according to NYU Stern School of Business, the average biotech firm trades at 5.87 times sales. If you believe you are investing in a commercially viable start up that just hasn't quite hit profitability yet, this allows an investor to "shop around" and gauge whether or not a young company is properly valued.

But what if a company is so young, so raw, that it doesn't even have revenue yet?

What??? Why would a company with no profit, and not even revenue, be trading publicly to begin with? Why on earth would you want to invest in a company that hasn't even brought in a single dollar yet?

Before we go any further, let's be clear: investing in any pre-revenue company is risky business. If you choose to bet on this kind of company, you are hoping to buy into world-changing innovation early, while the price is still low, before the rest of the world discovers what is going on in the company's laboratories. You are taking a calculated risk, because any perceived value is theoretical, and based on things that you think will happen.

In this kind of scenario, biotech companies are much more like real estate development companies. Except, instead of developing communities or shopping malls, they are developing molecules. A real estate development company seeks to create physical projects that will eventually generate tangible, real revenue. But it may have to invest for years before any one project becomes obviously viable. It's the same scenario for a young biotech.

Try this mental exercise. You walk through a gentrifying part of town, and you notice a ramshackle building on a choice corner lot. The location is obviously great, but right now it's not worth much because the lot is occupied by a slum. The next month, you walk by the same lot, and you notice the slum has been razed, and there is a shiny new sign saying "coming soon, luxury rentals."

At that moment, the developer has already sunk huge amounts of money into purchasing the lot, razing the slum, and obtaining plans and permitting to move forward with a speculative new development. They haven't put one piece of rebar in the ground yet...revenue is far away. But does that mean the project has no financial value? Or, in fact, does it have a larger value than it did when it was just a slum, because substantial progress has already been made? This is just the same as a young biotech with novel agents in early clinical testing.

Now let's say, six months later, you walk by the same lot, and you notice that construction has begun, and a towering rental building is half built. Still, little tangible cash flow for the developer, and certainly no profit. Does that mean no real financial value? Is the lot worth more than it was six months ago, when it was a barren slum, or more now that it's halfway to being a brand-new venture? This would be the equivalent of a pre-revenue biotech with agents that have passed through some important trials, but are not yet ready for launch.

Finally, a year after you first laid eyes on the property, you see a tower has been mostly completed. At least the outside is all done, and the developer is planting trees and grass around the property...a new sign is up proudly pronouncing, "coming soon."

All this progress, but still no revenue, and certainly no profit! But would the value of the project be more than it was when it was only half built? This would be a biotech with an agent, or agents, that have just passed stage three testing, and about to file for FDA approval. Although the young company still hasn't made a dime in tangible profit, they obviously now possess assets that they have greatly increased in value.

The reason why these kinds of companies would want to be public would be to provide some liquidity to management and scientific teams that can toil for years to build up the company's scientific assets.

Let's say you are a chief medical officer, and you joined the young biotech when it's novel agent was still being tested in rats. Now you have an agent that has made it all the way through phase two testing. This means that your work has consistently increased the value of the company's assets for quite some time, even if this work has not yet resulted in revenue for the company. In fact, from "preclinical" to phase two could take years. But you have bills that need to be paid today. By earning shares in a young, pre-revenue company, you can keep paying your bills until your big breakthrough finally comes. Simply put, young companies that allow shares to trade publicly may well increase the patience and financial endurance of their high value executive teams. Revenue or not, value is being created as a drug marches along the development process, and share based compensation helps a young company make that value tangible for employees and early investors.

One such example would be Syros Pharmaceuticals, Inc. ($SYRS). Syros is a fledgling biotech, working to pioneer a method of modulating expression of genes. The theory would be that certain genes in your DNA can be turned on, turned off, turned up, or turned down, like the volume on a stereo. This would allow the company to treat all kinds of diseases that currently have a poor prognosis. Numbers used in the example came from publicly reported information as of August, 2019.

I was originally attracted to the company for a few reasons. First, I liked the company's focus on unmet medical needs and innovation. Second, the company boasts an experienced "who's who" team of executives with a strong track record in new drug innovation. Third, most importantly, I felt that I was getting a deal on the shares. In the last year, Syros's shares had fallen from over $12 to under $6. I bought hoping that I was getting viable innovation at half off.

Much like the promising real estate development that is only half done, there was value here. But value is in the eye of the beholder; in the absence of steady profit, or even steady revenue, traditional valuation techniques break down. I will share with you my value appraisal process; the goal was to find value that the stock market was missing.

The formula could be expressed as the following:

POTENTIAL REVENUE FROM ASSETS x NUMBER OF ASSETS X PROBABILITY OF SUCCESS

For the purpose of this analysis, we will exclude any "preclinical" assets. These are very young agents that are still being tested in mice, or in cell cultures. While these compounds also have value, the valuations are so murky that even I don't dare to assign a number.

As of August, 2019, Syros currently had two novel assets being tested in human beings. SY-1425, and SY-1365. The first number to contemplate was the financial potential for these two agents.

SY-1425 was being tested for AML, a kind of Leukemia that mostly strikes older adults. According to Cancer.org, there are about 20,000 new cases diagnosed each year in the United States, and about 10,000 deaths from AML. So, Syros was looking to treat a highly deadly disease whose prevalence will only grow with the ageing of the American population. If such a drug were successful at all, it could easily generate $1,000,000,000 in annual sales.

The second agent, SY1365 was being tested for relapsed ovarian and breast cancer. This would mean female cancer patients who have already failed other treatments, and are near death. Is there anyone who is not familiar with the Susan G. Koman foundation and the Pink Campaign? So a successful drug in this realm could generate $1 Billion without breaking a sweat....

So, that would mean that tiny Syros would easily be looking at $2,000,000,000 in revenue if it's two most advanced agents found success. However, that is a big "IF." According to a report from the *Biotechnology Innovation Organization*, between 2005 and 2015, drugs currently in phase one testing only had a 10% chance of making it all the way to FDA approval. Drugs currently in phase two testing had a 30% chance. So, before we start counting our biotech riches, let's handicap those profits. If SY1465 had a $1B potential, and it's currently in phase two testing, let's value it at 30%x $1B, or $300 Million. If SY1365 also had a $1 Billion potential, but it's only in phase one testing, let's value that one at $1 Billionx10%, or $100 Million.

As our last step, we ad up those potential assets to attempt to reach a realistic value for all of Syro's "work in progress." If SY-1425 were worth $300 Million, and SY1365 were only worth $100 Million, then the company's current R&D assets could have been worth $400 Million.

As of June 7th, 2019, Wall Street only valued the whole company at $243 Million. Twelve months ago, when Syros's assets were actually less advanced, Mr. Market valued the company at $500 Million. I saw value at a discount, and I bought. You can use this same process again and again to conduct your own biotech bargain buying spree. Everywhere is Costco if you know how to look...

4. WHAT WON'T CHANGE

I've done pretty well investing in biotech, so most of the advice of this book has been formulated by me, with occasional borrowings from well-known business luminaries. But here is a piece of advice from someone more successful than me. Much more successful than me. In fact, by some measures, he is more successful than any other business person on Planet Earth. When choosing to invest capital, Jeff Bezos has frequently been quoted as saying, "Focus on what WON'T change."

In no arena is this advice more important than in biotech. In the 1940's, finding a cure for Polio would have seemed like a lucrative business venture. Do you know anyone who has contracted Polio lately? With technology advancing so rapidly, if you're not careful, you could wind up buying stock in the next Sears or RadioShack.

But many things in the medical business just won't change. If you apply the critical thinking techniques from this book, you'll find plenty of opportunities on your own. My own way of thinking just keeps coming back to those 10,000 Baby Boomers per day and their Medicare cards.

The truth is, that a lot of our most feared diseases today are really diseases associated with the ageing process. You may not think of a 66-year-old cancer patient as very elderly, but just one hundred years ago, many people never made it to age 66. If you die from say...Polio, you never live long enough for your immune system to fall victim to cancer. Perhaps that 66-year-old cancer patient had a heart attack at age 54, but instead of dying like she would have thirty years ago, she lived long enough to contract cancer at age 66.

The more our medical interventions keep people alive, the more they will eventually fall victim to the underlying break down of their own body. We now have many political and business leaders performing well into theirs 70's or even 80's, but it's not a natural phenomenon. Look for medicines and treatments that address common ailments of an ageing population. Afterall, 79 is the new 49....

TURN THOUGHTS INTO ACTION

I will leave you with the exact same thought that I shared to start this book.

I am not any smarter than you. I am not much braver. I am not much tougher. But I did turn my hopes, desires, and thoughts into an action plan. An action plan that I wrote out in this book for you to follow.

Hopefully, by now, you are feeling a lot more comfortable with the idea that you CAN be a biotech millionaire. If I did my job at all, you should have some concrete ideas about where to start, and how to progress. You should certainly have clear goals in mind.

That being said, the first few steps are always the hardest. If you still struggle with some fear holding you back, try this one last mental exercise.

Snap on CNBC, or Fox Business right now. It's very likely that they will be interviewing some respected stock analyst who is supposed to be an "expert" in stock market investing, and has the Ivy League pedigree to prove it. It is true what you suspect: a lot of these people are very, very rich. Maybe as much as one hundred times richer than you.

Ask yourself the following simple question. Is this talking head on TV really one hundred times smarter than me? Is he really one hundred times tougher? Can anyone be one hundred times luckier than someone else?

If your answer to this question is, "NO," then you are ready to move forward with your career as a biotech investor. There are healthy profits to be made out there by someone......why shouldn't that someone be YOU?

Understanding Tech Valuations

An Essay

Inequality. It's all we read about these days. The rich are getting richer, and the poor are getting poorer. If you were to come to my hometown, I could show you a $30,000,000 mansion, and just a few miles away, ramshackle apartments that rent for $1,200 a month, with that monthly rent payment being a constant struggle for the unlucky families living there.

So the growing gap between the "haves" and the "have-nots" is common knowledge these days. But did you know that there is also a huge and growing chasm between the "haves" and "have-nots" in corporate America? What if I told you that, even amongst the S&P 500, the 500 largest American companies by market capitalization, just 5 companies have come to dominate everything? Five tech companies, to be precise. These five tech companies, which barely existed twenty years ago, have grown at such a prodigious rate, that they function like black holes...the bigger they get, the more strongly they pull revenue towards them, now approaching such massive sizes that barely a dollar escapes. That doesn't leave much left for anyone else.

Top 5 Components of the S&P 500 Dominate the Index

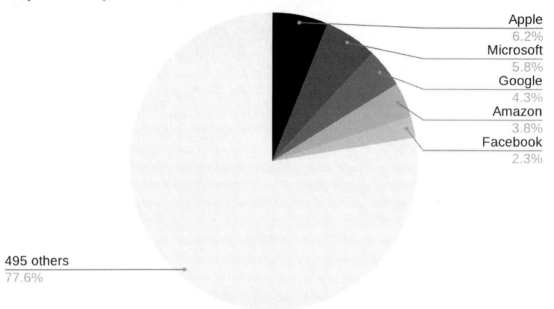

Apple
6.2%
Microsoft
5.8%
Google
4.3%
Amazon
3.8%
Facebook
2.3%

495 others
77.6%

Apple, Microsoft, Google, Amazon, and Facebook have grown so huge that their combined market capitalization equals 22.4% of the S&P 500 index…the remaining 77.6% is made up of 495 other companies. The "pipsqueak" companies that make up the remainder of the index are well-established household names like Disney, Home Depot, and Bank of America. Apple has almost *ten times* the market value of Coca-Cola!

Below, find another way to visualize the dominance of tech in America:

Top 5 S&P 500 Components Vrs. Average Market Capitalization

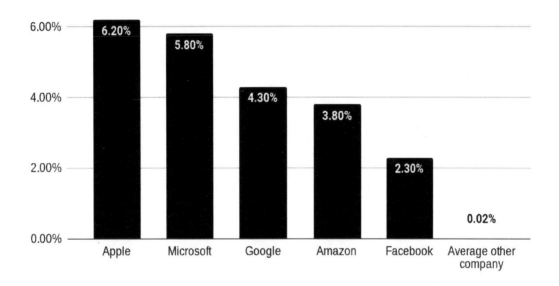

In other words, Apple's market capitalization *alone* currently makes up 6.2% of the entire index. But the average company in the index, well-established household names like Boeing, CVS, and Citigroup, make up just .02% of the index. The largest tech firms dominate so completely that it's like comparing Mount Everest to a pebble. How's that for inequality?

This domination didn't happen overnight. For most of these companies, it took two decades or more to grow to this size. Apple's comeback from near bankruptcy is the stuff of legend. Amazon didn't make money at all for many years. Microsoft was thought to be out of the game until a new CEO came in and refreshed the aging company's growth prospects. Tech shares are so sought after today, because many tech investors are feverishly trying to identify the next Google, the next Apple, etc. The hunt for the next Amazon has become more like the quest for the Holy Grail...with a mix of fact and legend leading to an "anything goes" type of investing environment.

Tech is not for the faint of heart. It is the highest "Beta" sector of the stock market, meaning that today's "wannabe Amazons" often feature highly volatile share prices that can soar or crash on as little as a whispered trading rumor. They often lose money. Sometimes, a *lot* of money for a *long time*. They're also prone to fraud and management scandals (look up the story of WeWork). However, for those intrepid crusaders hell bent on finding the next Apple, the potential reward is heavenly indeed. If you had invested in Apple in 2001, you would have enjoyed an astounding 51,000% return, somehow transforming $1,000 into $51,777. It's reasonable to speculate that some lucky tech investor today could enjoy the same returns if he manages to invest in the Apple of tomorrow.

Why is tech so damn lucrative? Is it just a coincidence? Great management? Fate? There are a few key, fundamental reasons why the tech sector has been one of the most lucrative bonanzas in all of financial history. All of the "Big Five" have certain characteristics in common that are inherent to true tech stocks. Below we will examine these common factors, so that you can look for these same factors in emerging technology companies. If you are going to hunt for gold, you will probably do better with a detailed topographic map of the area and some data, as opposed to just randomly swinging your pickaxe and praying.

MASTERS OF SCALE

The first concept to focus on is the concept of scale. If you delve into the venture capital or tech world, on social media or YouTube, you will hear this term thrown around a lot. In fact, it gets used so often that it's often abused or used in a misleading way. Scale simply means the ability for a business to get big fast with minimal additional costs. You could think of scale as the ability to press the gas pedal to the floor and accelerate. The faster you can scale, the faster your car can go from 0 to 60, using the least amount of resources.

It's not an exaggeration to say that Bill Gates and Microsoft almost single-handedly invented the concept of "mega scale" in the early 1980s. The old way of getting big involved massive, continuous investment, and huge quantities of low level employees. Think of Henry Ford and his Model T. In order for Henry Ford to put a Model T in every driveway in America, he had to build dozens of factories, source gargantum quantities of raw materials, and hire tens of thousands—or even hundreds of thousands—of low end labor. Growth cost time and money, and there were many risks to the bottom line along the way.

Not so for Microsoft. They only had to invest once. They only had to invest in the initial engineering and design of MS Windows and the MS Office suite. The creation of the product was a one time fixed cost. From there, whether they sold 10,000 software packages, or 10,000,000 software packages, their fixed costs were almost the same. The result? Oceans of pure profit, fast. Anyone past a certain age can remember groaning as you forked out $100 or more for the newest version of MS Office. That product cost Gates and company roughly $0.99 to make. No factories, no raw material, and relatively few employees. Pure profit at a sales volume that could grow exponentially without increasing costs very much. That is how Bill Gates became the richest man in the world. Scale.

The same pattern holds true for most of the tech giants. Google can provide services to millions upon millions of people while barely increasing costs and overhead; it's basically a software algorithm disguised as a company, and Google's fixed cost is roughly the same whether the algorithm serves 10,000 people or 10,000,000 people. Same thing with Facebook. Software and algorithms cost almost nothing to scale.

The one exception in the group is Amazon. Amazon's physical growth is a tale for the ages. As their business exploded upward during Covid, they hired 500,000 people in just one year! That is certainly not the same scalable model that made Bill Gates rich. But Amazon is a very misunderstood company. Almost all of the behemoth's profit comes from Amazon Web Services, which sells—you guessed it—software. Amazon Web Services allows companies around the world to store data and run operations on the cloud, a technique that Amazon pioneered between 2005 and 2010. This is by far the most profitable part of the business… all of the moving of boxes, overnight delivery, and warehousing is almost a side business. Lately, Amazon has been seeing huge growth in a new division that sells advertising. What is the primary benefit of online ad sales? Scale.

As I mentioned earlier, there are a lot of scale "fakers" out there. If you want to have success as a tech investor, you need to read everything you can get your hands on. You need to make sure you understand each business that you invest in. Because every aspiring entrepreneur who knows how to code will try to sell Wall Street on the idea that they are scalable the way Google and Facebook were. But there is a reason why only five companies rule the world. Massive, profitable scaling is easier said than done. Look for companies that can grow revenue without growing costs very much. Kick the tires, and remember, not all that glitters is gold.

Winner Takes All

The other thing you may notice when you examine "The Big Five" is that, in all practicality, they have no competition. Well, not zero competition. For example, if you really hated Google, you could use Bing, the almost forgotten search engine offered by Microsoft. There are also a few niche search engines out there. But almost nobody uses them. Just like you don't have to use Amazon. You could use Walmart.com, or even Macy's online. But few do. The Big Five have just enough competition on paper that they can't be sued for being monopolies, but so little competition that they divide a market of billions of clients with just one or two other major players. Good work if you can get it.

The reason why events unfolded this way is because of a phenomenon called the "network effect." No one really knows why or how the "network effect" came into existence, but it's a phenomenon that took shape between 2000 and 2010. The network effect is the tendency for one form of software or one website to eclipse all other competitors. In the network effect, the bigger a software or website gets, the more people flock to it. The more people "on the network," the more value people see in the network, and the more people are attracted.

One example of a "soft" network effect would be Google. Those of us who remember when the internet was young remember names like Lykos, Alta Vista, and even Yahoo. In the beginning, the market for online search was splintered. But somehow Google started to pull ahead of the pack. And as soon as they gained an early lead, all other competitors fell by the wayside. Even the mighty Microsoft, with the deepest corporate pockets of all time, never made much progress with their offering, Bing. The more people used Google, the more Google simply became ingrained in the mind of America as the place to go for information. Google became so entrenched that the word "Google" is not just a noun, but also a verb. When was the last time you heard anyone say, "I needed some info on the World Series, so I Binged it…" Google has very little meaningful competition because it pulled ahead early, and then just rode the momentum of a massively growing search and advertising market for the next two decades.

Of course the example par excellence of the network effect is the original social network, Facebook. The more people who used Facebook, the more value people attributed to the network, and the more people were drawn to the network. Everyone wants to be on Facebook, because that is the place where everybody is. Other well-funded competitors have tried to set up rival social networks, but failed miserably. There is only room for one real social network, and Facebook is so firmly lodged into that space that a monkey could run the company and still achieve massive profits. Once again, the phenomenon is that they pulled ahead early and achieved absolute domination of a small niche. As that niche grew exponentially over time, they grew with it. If you crush all competition early, unlimited growth and profit are yours.

Unusual Growth, Unusual Metrics

An obsession with the network effect is what drives some of the very unusual economics of the tech world. Pretenders to the Tech Throne typically operate under the core belief that they must get as big as possible, as quickly as possible, in order to harness the awe inspiring effect of the network effect. Remember that, once Google started to pull ahead, nobody could catch them. Even one of the biggest, most powerful software companies in the world (Microsoft) could not overcome the "first mover" aspect of the network effect. Therefore, emerging growth tech companies will do almost anything to get big fast, including losing money. Losing lots and lots of money.

Losing money in Silicon Valley is almost a badge of pride. Temporary losses, no matter how massive, seem to be irrelevant next to growth metrics. This world of bizarre "upside down" valuations can feel like a minefield for traditional investors.

Traditionally, the "gold standard" valuation metric to evaluate a stock is the price-to-earnings ratio. This ratio simply represents a multiple of the company's earnings. If a company has a price-to-earnings ratio of 10, then investors are willing to pay 10 times this year's earnings to own stock in the company. If a company has a price to earnings ratio of 22, then investors are willing to pay 22 times this year's earnings.

Typically, this ratio means very little in a vacuum. So, is a price-to-earnings ratio of 22 expensive or cheap? It depends on what other companies are trading for within the same sector. If you are looking at an oil company with a price-to-earnings ratio of 12, and all of the other similar oil companies trade at a price-to-earnings ratio of 8, then the company trading at 12 looks expensive. There may be a good reason for it to be expensive! Perhaps the company trading at 12 has better long-term prospects, or better management, or whatever. Or perhaps it's just over priced. That determination is the role of the investor.

The tech world takes this traditional metric and turns it on its head. If your company does $10 billion in sales, and is growing its sales at a 20% annual rate, but actually *loses* money, how would you value that? A price-to-earnings ratio would be useless, because there are no earnings.

By traditional valuation metrics, a company that does $10 billion in sales, but loses $2 billion, should be worth $0. Afterall, no one goes into business to lose money! However, in the new world of Silicon Valley, losses are often overlooked in favor of growth. Yes, the company is losing money now, but so did Amazon, for many years. And now look at them. Short-term losses are deemed unimportant next to the long-term opportunity to dominate a niche through the network effect.

So, if you are going to play the tech game, you need to accept the idea that large losses are actually good if they mean the company's revenues are growing like wildfire. Even if you can accept that idea, it still leaves a valuation problem. How do you compare a range of competing tech companies if the price-to-earnings ratio is irrelevant for all of them?

Enter the price-to-sales ratio. This functions very much like the price to earnings ratio, but it simply allows you to compare companies across a sector on an apples-to-apples basis. Price-to-sales values a company on a multiple of annual sales, leaving aside the question of profit. So, if two unprofitable companies in the tech sector trade at 10 times sales and 15 times sales respectively, the first company is trading at a lower valuation. Once again, there may be a good reason for this, or one company may simply be undervalued. That is for the tech investor to decide.

A word of caution here. Remember early in the chapter when I said that there are a lot of "fake" tech companies out there? The price-to-sales ratio is only useful in comparing truly apples-to-apples companies. But there are a lot of entrepreneurs, venture capitalists, and general flimflam men who are selling peaches and oranges disguised as apples. Why would that be?

Everyone is trying to grow a "tech" company because tech, as a sector, has sky-high valuations. According to data published by the NYU Stern School of Business on January 1, 2021, the average software company trades at a price-to-sales ratio of 14. The average household products company trades at a price-to-sales ratio of just 3.7. The average shipbuilding and marine company trades at just 1.12 times sales. Both the household products company and the marine company may well churn out more profit than the fledgling software company at the moment. But everyone remembers a 1980s supernerd collecting mega yachts like they were baseball cards. The tech sector is viewed as having vastly superior long-term growth prospects. How many household goods companies are in the top five of the S&P 500? Zero. How many tech companies? Five out of five. Thus, everyone wants to be a tech company. Your company's valuation can increase dramatically just because of the sector label that Wall Street assigns it. It's up to the individual investor to seek out emerging tech company diamonds amongst the wannabe tech coals.

Tips for Beginners

If you really have the instincts of an investor, I probably got your attention when I reported that Apple shareholders have reaped a 51,000% return over the last twenty years. Although the tech sector is risky as hell, volatile, and generally stomach churning, many people find the potential returns to be irresistible. If you feel this way, here are a few simple pointers to get you started.

First of all, remember that you really don't need to pick stocks. I was lucky enough to invest in the Nasdaq index in the early 2000s, and I have reaped a 1,400% return over the last two decades. I simply invested the money and sat tight. I rode out all of the various storms, and now I've turned a $10,000 investment into $140,000. Ok, it wasn't as good as if I had put all the money into Apple, but a 1,400% return in exchange for little work is hardly anything to laugh at.

You can do exactly the same if selecting individual stocks is too stressful or scary for you. A few great exchange traded funds that capture most of the upside of America's growing tech stocks are:

-QQQ (Nasdaq 100)
-VGT (Vanguard Information Technology)
-IYW (iShares US Technology)
-XLK (Technology Sector Select SPDR Fund)

These funds are very similar; they allow you broad exposure to the American tech sector at a very low annual cost. If you like tech, but you find the sector to be overwhelming, you can always "set it and forget it."

You can score some powerful long term returns with exchange traded funds; however, you will never find the next Apple that way. If you are determined to grab that 51,000% return for yourself, then you need to become an expert in something.

The word "tech" is just a broad catch-all term for an entire universe of software, AI, cloud, and other emerging technologies. Very few people would have the training, education, and time to master all of these niches. So one thing you can do is pick one sub sector that seems particularly interesting to you and study it closely. For example, maybe banking and money are interesting to you. Then you should read everything you can get your hands on about "fintech," a new emerging wave of technology companies that are disrupting traditional banking on a global scale. Maybe you watched a lot of movies like *2001: A Space Odyssey* and *Terminator* as a kid, and today you are interested in artificial intelligence. Then make a firm commitment to grow your own intelligence and spend your days scouring the internet for reading material regarding AI.

In this way, you can form what Warren Buffett calls a "circle of competence." A small but deep niche that you know inside and out. That will help you identify winning companies to invest in. Remember, it only takes one runaway hit to boost your entire portfolio.

The other exercise you should do when researching potential tech investments is to focus on the two aspects described above. Which companies are truly scalable candidates to benefit from the network effect? For every ten supposed tech companies that present themselves as the next Facebook, there are maybe two or three that really fit the criteria.

One example of a very controversial tech company is Tesla. Yes, obviously Tesla relies on innovation and commercialization of brand-new technology, and in many ways they have done an admirable job. But are they really worth 4 times as much as Toyota, which sells 20 times more cars than Tesla every year? Right now, Tesla enjoys a stratospheric valuation, trading at a price-to-sales ratio of 19. That might make sense if they fit the above criteria, but do they, really?

While Tesla aims to sell more software in the future, right now, they earn revenue by selling a variety of hardware, from cars to solar panels to batteries. Obviously, they can grow sales, but the more they grow, the more they must invest. Building factories around the world ain't cheap, and it ain't quick! (For example, the company has faced endless bureaucracy and protests regarding cutting down trees to build a factory in Germany.) Remember, for Bill Gates, it was just as easy to sell 100,000,000 copies of MS Windows as it was to sell 100. Does it seem that way for Tesla?

Secondly, whether or not Tesla really enjoys a network effect is up for debate. On one hand, Elon Musk's charismatic, rebellious brand has created a lot of loyalty from fanatical customers. But up until now, he has had very little competition. Within the next two years, he is about to face a tsunami of competition, both from reinvigorated traditional car makers and from new "cool kids" on the block, such as Lucid Motors. There is very little to stop Tesla clients from switching cars if they feel like it… which is not the definition of the network effect. We will have to see what happens.

While you are busy evaluating who truly fits the definition of a "tech" stock, you should also become proficient in the very specific metrics that are used to compare value in the sector. We already discussed price-to-sales above. Another metric that analysts in this sector focus on is growth rates. Which companies are growing the fastest, and why? In a culture where getting big is everything, stock prices can easily fluctuate based on the latest quarterly growth numbers and the trends they reflect. Is the growth accelerating or decelerating? Is the company growing faster than rivals or slower?

Lastly, you should consider a metric called "burn rate." Believe it or not, in the world of emerging growth stocks, it's so rare to make money that analysts tend to focus on how much the company is losing or "burning." Think of it as checking how much fuel is left in your rocket. It's great that each company is hell bent on blasting off into the stratosphere, but if their rocket runs out of fuel (cash), then investors are going to have problems. Over the last two decades, companies have rarely run out of money outright, due to one of the craziest fundraising atmospheres of all time. However, every time a company must issue new stock to raise cash, that can hurt existing shareholders. If new shares are sold, it can dilute the ownership of existing shareholders. By only investing in companies that are already well funded, you minimize this risk.

There just can be no doubt at all that one of the most lucrative investments of all time has been American Information Technology over the first decades of the 21st century. If you take a minute to think about all of the new technologies that have emerged during your lifetime, and the dizzying array of new technologies that are currently emerging, it seems likely that information technology will continue to be America's growth engine. But in order to grab your piece of the information technology pie, you need to *grow your own information about technology*. Ironically, booming technologies such as the internet and cell phones have made it easier than ever to gain information about technology. Today, studying technology is like studying gold mining in previous centuries. Tech is 21st century gold. Self education is the only tool you need to be a successful miner for glittering returns in the stock market.

Recommended Resources

Magazines
Kiplinger's Magazine
Wall Street Journal
Barron's Magazine

Websites:
WhiteTopInvestor.com
HumbleDollar.com
FourPillarFreedom.com
DealForma.com
WolfStreet.com
WallStreetZen.com
SeekingAlpha.com
Investopedia.com
Dividend.com
CEFConnect.com
SureDividend.com
DividendDetective.com
Reit.com
Reitnotes.com
LeonbergCapital.com

Books:
Accounting for Dummies
Reading Financial Reports for Dummies
The Millionaire Next Store, Thomas J. Stanley, PhD
Rich Dad, Poor Dad, Robert Kiyosaki
Fed Up: An Insider's Take on why the Federal Reserve is Bad for America, Danielle DiMartino Booth